Korean Made Easy • **Grammar** Ⅰ Beginner

Korean Made Easy • Grammar ❶ Beginner

Written by	Seung-eun Oh
Proofreader	Isabel Kim Dzitac
First Published	March, 2025
First Printing	March, 2025
Publisher	Kyu-do Chung
Editors	Suk-hee Lee, Jihee Han
Designers	Na-kyoung Kim, Hyun-joo Yoon
Illustrated by	Seok-hyun Choi

DARAKWON Published by Darakwon, Inc.

Darakwon Bldg., 211, Munbal-ro, Paju-si, Gyeonggi-do, Republic of Korea 10881
Tel: 82-2-736-2031 (Sales Dept. ext.: 250~252; Book Publishing Dept. ext. 420~426)
Fax: 82-2-732-2037

ISBN: 978-89-277-3347-8 14710
　　　978-89-277-3246-1 (set)

http://www.darakwon.co.kr
http://koreanbooks.darakwon.co.kr

※ Visit the Darakwon homepage to learn about our other publications and promotions and to download the contents of the book in MP3 format.

Korean made easy

easy

Seung-eun Oh

Grammar I

Beginner

DARAKWON

서문

*Korean Made Easy - Grammar I (Beginner)*는 한국어를 배우는 독자들에게 오랫동안 사랑받아 온 *Korean Made Easy* 시리즈의 문법 교재이다. 이 책은 외국인 학습자와 해외 동포 학습자가 초급 한국어 문법을 체계적이고 포괄적으로 학습할 수 있도록 설계되었다. 이를 통해 학습자들이 문법의 기초를 탄탄히 다지는 것은 물론, 실제 생활에서 문법이 어떻게 활용되는지를 이해할 수 있도록 하는 것을 목표로 하였다.

이 책은 복잡한 문법 용어를 지양하고 쉬운 언어로 작성되어, 언어학을 전공하지 않은 일반 독자도 부담 없이 이해할 수 있다. 특히 영어권 학습자를 위해 친숙한 문법 용어를 사용하고자 하였다. 또한 한국어와 영어 간의 차이점, 유사한 문법적 의미 차이, 문법 용법의 뉘앙스를 강조하여, 학습자가 실제 대화와 일상적인 상황에서 문법을 효과적으로 적용할 수 있도록 구성하였다.

초급 문법을 보다 체계적이고 포괄적으로 학습할 수 있도록 이 책은 네 부분으로 구성되어 있다. **Part 1**에서는 조사, 어미, 시제, 부정, 활용 등 한국어의 기초적인 문법 개념을 소개한다. **Part 2**에서는 종결어미와 문법 표현을 통해 의도, 추측, 능력, 가능 등 다양한 의미와 기능을 익힌다. **Part 3**에서는 연결어미와 문법 표현을 통해 나열, 대조, 인과, 조건 관계 등의 문장 간 의미 관계를 배우며 문장을 효과적으로 연결하는 방법을 학습한다. **Part 4**에서는 전성어미, 반말, 격식체, 존댓말을 통해 한국어 문법이 한국 문화와 어떻게 연관되는지를 살펴본다. Part 1을 제외한 문법 순서는 문법 난이도가 아닌 문법적 범주와 의미 관계를 기준으로 구성되었으므로, 학습자는 자신의 목표와 필요에 따라 자유롭게 순서를 조정하여 학습할 수 있다.

각 단원은 **Grammar Essentials**와 **Grammar in Action**으로 나뉘어 있다. **Grammar Essentials**에서는 문법의 의미와 구조, 기능, 예문을 제시하고, **Grammar in Action**에서는 실제 문법적 활용과 문화적 통찰을 보여줌으로써 한국어 문법을 심도 있게 학습할 수 있도록 하였다. 각 단원의 끝에는 **QR 코드**로 제공되는 연습 문제를 통해 학습한 내용을 점검하고 문법적 이해를 강화할 수 있다.

이 책이 완성되기까지 많은 분들의 도움이 있었다. 먼저, 한국어 교사로서 학습자들이 더 명확하고 쉽게 이해할 수 있도록 조언해 주신 오승민 선생님께 감사드린다. 또한, 한국어 학습자 경험을 바탕으로 영어권 학습자들이 복잡한 한국어 문법 개념에 더 쉽게 접근할 수 있도록 영어 교정을 맡아 주신 Isabel Kim Dzitac 님께 깊은 감사를 전하고 싶다. 이 책의 기획부터 완성까지 지원해 주신 다락원의 정규도 대표님과, 책의 완성도를 높이기 위해 헌신적으로 노력해 주신 다락원의 한국어출판부 편집진께 진심으로 감사드린다.

마지막으로, 언제나 저를 자랑스럽게 여기며 기도와 지지를 아끼지 않으신 어머니와 하늘에 계신 아버지께 감사드린다. 그리고 *Korean Made Easy* 시리즈를 사랑해 주시고 한국어 학습에 열정적인 모든 독자분께도 진심으로 감사드린다. 이 책이 한국어 학습의 여정을 시작하는 여러분께 즐거움과 성취감을 선사할 수 있기를 바란다.

오승은

Korean Made Easy - Grammar I (Beginner) is part of the beloved *Korean Made Easy* series, well-known for its practical and accessible content among Korean language learners. This grammar book is specifically designed for foreign learners and overseas Koreans to systematically and comprehensively study beginner-level Korean grammar as a second or foreign language. It aims to help learners build a strong grammatical foundation while understanding how grammar is used in real-life situations.

Written in simple and accessible language, the book avoids complex grammatical terminology making it easy to understand even for those without a background in linguistics. Special care has been taken to use grammatical terms familiar to English-speaking learners. By highlighting key differences and similarities between Korean and English, along with nuances in grammatical usage, the book equips learners to apply grammar effectively in daily conversations and real-life situations.

The book is divided into four parts to provide a comprehensive learning experience. **Part 1** introduces fundamental grammatical concepts, including particles, endings, tense, negation, and conjugation. **Part 2** explores final endings and related grammatical expressions, covering concepts such as intention, possibility, ability, and speculation. **Part 3** focuses on conjunctive endings and grammatical expressions, examining relationships such as enumeration, contrast, cause and effect, and conditional connections. **Part 4** delves into derivational endings, informal and formal speech, and honorific expressions, offering insights into how grammar reflects Korean cultural contexts. Except for Part 1, grammar points are organized by grammatical categories and semantic relationships rather than by difficulty level, allowing learners to study in any order based on their goals and needs.

Each lesson consists of two sections: **Grammar Essentials** and **Grammar in Action**. The **Grammar Essentials** section presents the meaning, structure, and key examples of essential grammar points, while the **Grammar in Action** section offers cultural insights and practical applications to deepen understanding. Each lesson concludes with practice exercises accessible via **QR codes**, enabling learners to review and reinforce their understanding.

This book would not have been possible without the support of many people. First, I would like to extend my sincere gratitude to Seung-min Oh, a Korean language teacher, for offering valuable advice to make the content clearer and more accessible for learners. I am also deeply grateful to Isabel Kim Dzitac, who, drawing from her experience as a Korean language learner, edited the English text to make complex Korean grammar concepts more understandable for English-speaking learners. My heartfelt thanks go to Kyu-do Chung, CEO of Darakwon, and the dedicated Korean Book Publishing team at Darakwon, who worked tirelessly to enhance the quality of this book.

Lastly, I express my deepest gratitude to my mother, who has always supported me with pride and prayers, and to my late father in heaven. To the passionate readers who love the *Korean Made Easy* series and are committed to learning Korean, I extend my sincere thanks. I hope this book brings you joy and a sense of accomplishment on your journey to mastering the Korean language.

Seungeun Oh

How to Use This Book

✦ Overview

This book covers all beginner-level grammar points from the Test of Proficiency in Korean (TOPIK) and the Standard Curriculum for Korean Language (SCK). It focuses on the meanings, functions, key characteristics, and usage contexts of essential grammar points, ensuring learners understand how grammar works in various real-life situations.

Additionally, the book emphasizes cultural understanding, enabling learners to apply Korean grammar effectively, accurately, and appropriately through a comprehensive yet practical approach designed for real-world communication.

Part 1 **Basic Expressions**

Focuses on fundamental grammatical concepts essential for constructing Korean sentences, including particles, endings, numbers, time expressions, negation, and conjugation.

Part 2 **Meaning-Focused Endings and Expressions**

Covers sentence-final endings and patterns that express various meanings and functions, such as intention, possibility, ability, and speculation.

Part 3 **Clause-Connecting Endings and Expressions**

Explores conjunctive endings and patterns that connect clauses, showing how different clauses are linked by enumeration, contrast, cause and effect, chronological sequence, and conditional relationships.

Part 4 **Derivational Endings and Speech Styles**

Discusses derivational endings and speech styles that reflect the cultural aspects of the Korean language, including adnominal, adverbial, and nominalizing endings, speech, formal speech, and honorific speech.

Index

Provides a Korean alphabetical index that lists headwords as well as all grammar expressions mentioned throughout the book, each accompanied by page numbers for easy reference, allowing learners to quickly locate specific grammar points.

✦ Structure of Each Lesson

Introduction ▮ ▮ ▮ ▮

Provides Korean grammar headwords with English translations. Each grammar point's difficulty level is indicated based on TOPIK (Test of Proficiency in Korean) levels and the International Standard Korean Language Curriculum.

• **Grammar Difficulty Level**

Shows the difficulty level based on TOPIK (Test of Proficiency in Korean) and SCK (Standard Curriculum for Korean Language).

• **Target Grammar**

Presents the target grammar point for each lesson in both Korean and English.

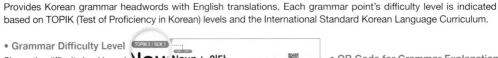

TOPIK I | SCK 1

You Noun + -이다 I am, You are, He/She/It is...

안녕하세요. Hello.
저는 김민수예요. I am Minsu Kim.
한국 사람이에요. I am Korean.
나이가 27살이에요. I am 27 years old.
직업이 회사원이에요. I am an office worker.
취미가 축구예요. My hobby is playing soccer.

14

• **QR Code for Grammar Explanation in Korean**

Provides a QR code linking to additional grammar explanations in Korean.

• **Illustration**

Provides visual context to help learners intuitively understand how the grammar is used.

• **Representative Sentences**

Presents key example sentences featuring the target grammar, shown in both Korean and English to illustrate contextual usage.

Grammar Essentials

This section explains the core meaning, structure, and function of the grammar point using clear explanations and practical examples.

- **Core Meaning of the Grammar Point**

  Introduces the fundamental meaning with relevant examples.

- **Grammatical Features**

  Highlights important aspects such as tense, negation, and grammatical rules and exceptions.

- **Conjugation Table**

  Shows conjugation patterns for verbs and adjectives.

Grammar in Action

This section demonstrates how grammar is applied in real-life situations and cultural contexts, enabling learners to develop practical communication skills.

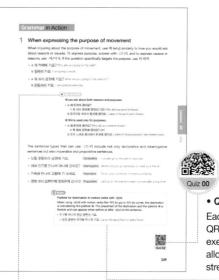

- **Quiz Yourself**

  Each unit concludes with QR-code-accessible practice exercises for self-assessment, allowing learners to review and strengthen their understanding.

Tip

Provides comparisons between similar grammar points in Korean, explaining subtle differences in meaning and usage distinctions, including Korean-English comparisons for deeper understanding.

✳ Be careful!

Lists common mistakes and gives practical tips to avoid errors.

🛈 Note

Offers additional information or cultural context relevant to the grammar point.

Table of Contents

Part 4   Derivational Endings and Speech Styles

PART

1

Basic Expressions

TOPIK I | SCK 1

Noun + -이다 I am, You are, He/She/It is...

Kor. 01

안녕하세요. Hello.

저는 김민수예요. I am Minsu Kim.

한국 사람이에요. I am Korean.

나이가 27살이에요. I am 27 years old.

직업이 회사원이에요. I am an office worker.

취미가 축구예요. My hobby is playing soccer.

Grammar Essentials

1 Noun + 이다

The ending 예요/이에요 is used to conjugate the informal polite present tense of 이다 (to be) after a noun, describing the identity or characteristics of a subject. 예요 is added when the preceding noun ends in a vowel, while 이에요 is added when the preceding noun ends in a consonant. However, when spoken, both 예요 and 이에요 are pronounced similarly in everyday speech, despite their different spellings.

When ending in a vowel	When ending in a consonant
이름이 민수예요.	취미가 등산이에요.
(My) name is Minsu.	(My) hobby is hiking.

Be careful!

There is no space between the noun and 예요/이에요!
- 저는 김민수 예요. (✗) → 저는 김민수예요. (O)

2 Subject particle 이/가

The subject particle 이/가 is attached after a noun that indicates the subject. It signifies that the preceding noun in the subject of the sentence. Depending on whether the preceding noun ends in a vowel or a consonant, it is used as follows.

When ending in a vowel	When ending in a consonant
취미가 요리예요.	이분 이름이 레이첼이에요.
My hobby is cooking.	This person's name is Racheal. (= She is Racheal.)

In informal speech, the subject can be omitted when the speaker and listener can recognize the subject of a sentence based on the context.

- 저는 이수민이에요. (저는) 대학생이에요.
  I am Lee Su-min. (I) am a college student.

- (당신이) 호주 사람이에요?
  Are (you) Australian? [looking at the listener]

- 마크 씨가 미국 사람이에요. (마크 씨가) 25살이에요.
  Mark is American. (Mark is) 25 years old.

3 Negation

The negative form of 예요/이에요 is 아니에요, which is the informal polite present tense of 아니다.

- 진수가 축구 선수가 <u>아니에요</u>. Jinsu is not a soccer player.

While 이/가 before 아니에요 may appear to function as a subject particle, it is not actually a subject particle. When expressing the negation of the identity or characteristics of a subject, both the subject particle 이/가 and 이/가 아니에요 can coexist in a single sentence. However, for clarity and to avoid confusion, it is recommended to use the particle 은/는 instead of the subject particle 이/가 when indicating the subject of a sentence.

- <u>진수가</u> 축구 선수가 아니에요. Jinsu is not a soccer player.
  = <u>진수는</u> 축구 선수가 아니에요.

- <u>서울이</u> 제 고향이 아니에요. Seoul is not my hometown.
  = <u>서울은</u> 제 고향이 아니에요.

이/가 before 아니에요 is used depending on whether the preceding noun ends in a vowel or a consonant.

When ending in a vowel	When ending in a consonant
저는 가수가 아니에요.	이것은 제 가방이 아니에요.
I am not a singer.	This is not my bag.

4 Tenses

였어요/이었어요 represents the past tense of 이다 with -았/었- in informal polite speech. When the preceding noun ends in a vowel, you can add 였어요, and when the preceding noun ends in a consonant, you can add 이었어요. The past tense of 아니에요 is 아니었어요.

- 아버지가 변호사였어요. 그런데 지금은 퇴직했어요. My father was a lawyer. However, he retired now.

- 작년에 저는 학생이었어요. 그런데 지금은 회사원이에요.
  I was a student last year. However, I am now an office worker.

- 어머니는 간호사가 아니었어요. 의사였어요. My mother was not a nurse. She was a doctor.

When expressing the speculative meaning of 예요/이에요, you can use 일 거예요 whether the preceding noun ends in a vowel or a consonant.

- 진수가 아마 마크 씨 친구일 거예요. Jinsu will probably be Mark's friend.

- 아마 에이미 씨가 미국 사람일 거예요. Amy will probably be American.

When expressing the speculative meaning of 아니에요, you can use 아닐 거예요.

- 저 사람이 우리 선생님이 아닐 거예요. That person will probably not be our teacher.

Grammar in Action

1 When asking Yes/No questions in Korean

Unlike in English, the sentence order of both questions and answers is the same in Korean. Look at the following Yes/No questions, the sentence order of the question and the answer is the same, but the intonation at the end of the sentence goes up for the question and the intonation at the end of the sentence goes down for the answer. 네 is used for affirmative answers while 아니요 is used for negative answers.

- A 학생이에요? Are you a student?

  B 네, 대학생이에요. Yes, I am a university student.

- A 미국 사람이에요? Are you American?

  B 아니요, 미국 사람이 아니에요. 캐나다 사람이에요. No, I am not American. I am Canadian.

However, in Korean, instead of using "you" to the person you are talking to, you usually add 씨 (Mr./Ms.), after the name or refer to it by its title. If you don't know the other person's name, you can point to them with your hand or look at them instead.

 Be careful!

Although they may have similar forms, they actually have different meanings!

- 아니요. No.
- 아니에요. (somebody/something) is not.

2 When asking WH-questions in Korean

As for WH-questions, you can ask questions about people, objects, time, and places by adding question words 누구, 뭐, 언제, and 어디 to -예요/이에요 as shown below.

People	이 사람이 누구예요? Who is this?	(이 사람이) 제 친구예요. He/she is my friend.
Objects	직업이 뭐예요? What is your job?	(직업이) 요리사예요. I am a cook.
Time	파티가 언제예요? When is the party?	(파티가) 금요일이에요. It is on Friday.
Locations	식당이 어디예요? Where is the restaurant?	(식당이) 강남이에요. It is in Gangnam.

Quiz 01

17

있다/없다 Possession and relationship
have/don't have

언니 ✕

제 가족이에요. This is my family.

저는 아버지하고 어머니, 오빠가 있어요.
I have a father, a mother, and an older brother.

여동생도 있어요. I also have a younger sister.

그런데 언니가 없어요. But I don't have an older sister.

Grammar Essentials

1 있다 and 없다

있어요 is the informal polite present tense conjugation of the verb 있다 (to have). It is used to indicate that the subject of the sentence possesses something or has a relationship with someone/somthing. Conversely, 없어요, the opposite of 있어요, indicates that the subject of the sentence does not own something or is not in a relationship with someone/something.

	Affirmative	Negative
Relationship	저는 이모가 있어요. I have an aunt.	제가 삼촌이 없어요. I don't have an uncle.
Object of possession	친구가 여권이 있어요. My friend has a passport.	동생이 카드가 없어요. My younger brother doesn't have a card.

2 Particles used with 있다/없다

When using 있다/없다, it is important to note that the particle 이/가 is used instead of the object particle 을/를 for the object of the sentence that the subject possesses or is in a relationship with.

- 저는 자전거를 있어요. (✕) → 저는 자전거가 있어요. (〇) I have a bicycle.

- 동생이 여권을 없어요. (✕) → 동생이 여권이 없어요. (〇) My sister doesn't have a passport.

- 저는 한국 친구를 있어요. (✕) → 저는 한국 친구가 있어요. (〇) I have a Korean friend.

- 제 친구가 형을 없어요. (✕) → 제 친구가 형이 없어요. (〇) My friend doesn't have a brother.

In sentences like the following where 있다/없다 is used, the particle 이/가 can appear twice in one sentence, but there is only one subject. It is recommended to use the particle 은/는 instead of the particle 이/가 after the subject to avoid confusion by repeating 이/가.

- 제가 한국 친구가 있어요. → 저는 한국 친구가 있어요. I have a Korean friend.
    Subject   Object   Having a relationship

- 동생이 돈이 없어요. → 동생은 돈이 없어요. My younger brother has no money.
    Subject Object Not owned

> **Note**
>
> When expressing possession, 가지고 있다 can be replaced with 있다. However, when using 가지고 있다, the object of ownership is expressed by using the object particle 을/를. 가지고 있지 않다 can be changed to 없다.
>
> - 친구가 자전거가 있어요. → 친구가 자전거를 가지고 있어요. My friend has a bicycle.
> - 친구가 자동차가 없어요. → 친구가 자동차를 가지고 있지 않아요. My friend doesn't have a car.

19

3   Omission of the subject in context

The subject of 있다/없다 can be omitted if the speaker and listener share context.

- 저는 오빠가 있어요. 그리고 (저는) 동생이 있어요.
  I have an older brother. And (I) have a younger brother.

- 폴이 한국 친구가 있어요. 그런데 (폴이) 일본 친구가 없어요.
  Paul has a Korean friend. But (Paul) doesn't have any Japanese friends.

- 진수가 자동차가 있어요. 그런데 (진수가) 집이 없어요.
  Jinsu has a car. But (Jinsu) doesn't have a house.

- 여권이 있어요? 그리고 사진이 있어요?
  Do (you) have a passport? And do (you) have a picture?

4   Tenses

있었어요/없었어요 is the informal polite past tense conjugation that is formed by adding -았/었- to 있다/없다, indicating ownership or a relationship in the past.

- 전에는 돈이 많이 있었어요. 그런데 지금은 돈이 없어요.
  I had a lot of money before. But now I have no money.

- 작년에 한국에 친구가 없었어요. 그런데 지금 친구가 있어요.
  I had no friends in Korea last year. But now I have a friend.

있을 거예요/없을 거예요 is a speculative form created by adding -(으)ㄹ 거예요 to 있다/없다, suggesting a guess about possession or a relationship.

- 내일 레이첼이 회의가 있을 거예요.
  Rachel will have a meeting tomorrow.

- 아마 제 친구가 시간이 없을 거예요.
  My friend will probably not have time.

Grammar in Action

1 When indicating whether the subject is owned or not

있다 indicates possession of a certain object and 없다 indicates no possession of an object. Remember the particle 이/가 is added to the object of ownership.

- A 민수 씨, 신분증이 있어요? Minsu, do you have ID?

  B 아니요, 신분증이 없어요. No, I don't have an ID.

뭐가 is used when asking about the object of possession.

- A 지금 뭐가 있어요? What do you have?

  B 핸드폰이 있어요. I have a cell phone.

When asking about the owner, you can use 누가 if the owner is a person, and 뭐가 if the owner is an object.

- A 누가 고양이가 있어요? Who has a cat?

  B 친구가 고양이가 있어요. My friend has a cat.

- A 뭐가 스피커가 있어요? What has a speaker?

  B 이 핸드폰이 스피커가 있어요. This cell phone has a speaker.

2 When indicating a relationship with the subject

있다 indicates that there is a relationship with the subject, and 없다 indicates that there is no relationship with the subject. The particle 이/가 is added to the object that has a relationship with the subject.

- A 유나 씨, 오빠가 있어요? Yuna, do you have an older brother?

  B 아니요, 오빠가 없어요. No, I don't have an older brother.

When asking about someone you are in a relationship with, you use 누가.

- A 진수 씨, 형제 있어요? 누가 있어요?
  Jinsu, do you have siblings? Who do you have? (Who is in your family?)

  B 저는 남동생이 있어요. I have a younger brother.

누가 is also used when asking about the subject in a relationship.

- A 누가 여동생이 있어요? Who has a younger sister?

  B 민수 씨가 여동생이 있어요. Minsu has a younger sister.

Quiz 02

TOPIK I | SCK 1

있다/없다 Existence and location

There is / There is not

Kor. 03

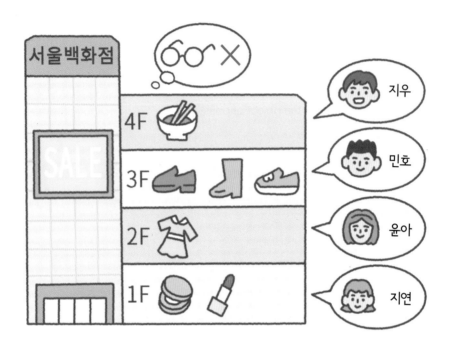

여기는 서울 백화점이에요.

This is Seoul Department Store.

1층에 화장품 가게가 있어요. 화장품 가게에 지연 씨가 있어요.

There is a cosmetics store on the first floor. There is Jiyeon at the cosmetics store.

2층에 옷 가게가 있어요. 옷 가게에 윤아 씨가 있어요.

There is a clothing store on the second floor. There is Yuna at the clothing store.

3층에 신발 가게가 있어요. 신발 가게에 민호 씨가 있어요.

There is a shoe store on the 3rd floor. Minho is at the shoe store.

4층에 식당이 있어요. 식당에 지우 씨가 있어요.

There is a restaurant on the 4th floor. Jiwoo is in the restaurant.

그런데 서울 백화점에 안경 가게가 없어요.

However, there are no glasses stores in Seoul department stores.

Grammar Essentials

1 있다 and 없다

있어요 is the informal polite present tense conjugation of the verb 있다 (to be). It is used to indicate the existence of the subject within a specific space. Conversely, 없어요 is the opposite of 있어요, indicating the absence of the subject in a specific space. To express 있어요/없어요, add the subject particle 이/가 to the subject of the sentence.

Affirmative	Negative
사람들이 많이 있어요. There are a lot of people.	지금 선생님이 없어요. There is no teacher now.
자판기가 있어요. There is a vending machine.	화장실이 없어요. There is no bathroom.

2 Place particle 에

Place particle 에 is used to indicate the presence or absence of the subject in a specific space, combined with the verbs 있어요/없어요. In Korean, as long as the verb 있어요/없어요 is at the end of the sentence, the meaning remains the same even if you switch the positions of the subject and the adverb (the noun and the place particle 에).

- 가족이 상하이에 있어요. = 상하이에 가족이 있어요. My family is in Shanghai.

- 가방에 여권이 없어요. = 여권이 가방에 없어요. There is no passport in the bag.

> (✱ Be careful!)
>
> 예요/이에요 and 있어요 are both interpreted as the English "be" verb, but their meanings are different. 예요/이에요 is akin to "A=B", indicating the identity or characteristic of subject A as B, whereas 있어요 indicates that the subject exists or is located in a specific space. Additionally, 예요/이에요 is attached to the preceding noun, but 있어요 is used with the preceding noun and the subject particle 이/가, with a space between 있어요 and the subject.
> - 마크 씨가 미국 사람이에요. Mark is American.
> - 집에 마크 씨가 있어요. Mark is at home.

3 Tenses

있었어요/없었어요 is the informal polite past tense conjugation of 있다/없다, formed by adding -았/었-. It indicates the presence or absence of the subject in a specific space in the past.

- 어렸을 때 우리 집이 부산에 있었어요. When I was young, my house was in Busan.

- 어제 버스에 사람이 없었어요. There was no one on the bus yesterday.

있을 거예요/없을 거예요 is a speculative form created by adding -(으)ㄹ 거예요 to 있다/없다. It conveys a guess about the presence or absence of the subject.

- 나중에 공지가 있을 거예요. There will be an announcement later.

- 아마 지금 제 동생이 집에 없을 거예요. My younger brother will probably not be at home right now.

Grammar in Action

1 When asking about a specific location

When asking about a specific location where the subject of a sentence exists, ask the question using 어디에 (the question word 어디 and the particle 에 indicating location).

- A 어디에 학교가 있어요? Where is the school?

  B <u>부산에</u> 학교가 있어요. There is a school in Busan.

When focusing on a specific location in the discourse, the subject may be omitted.

- A 친구가 어디에 있어요? Where is your friend?

  B (친구가) <u>홍콩에</u> 있어요. (My friend) is in Hong Kong.

2 When expressing a specific location of the subject

To express the specific location of a person or object, use the following location expressions along with the particle 에 for indicating the location.

자동차가 집 앞에 있어요.
The car is in front of the house.

여자가 자동차 안에 있어요.
There is a woman in the car.

개가 자동차 밖에 있어요.
The dog is outside the car.

계단이 집하고 공원 사이에 있어요.
The stairs are between the house and the park.

공원이 집 옆에 있어요.
The park is next to the house.

나무 아래에 벤치가 있어요.
There is a bench under the tree.

고양이가 벤치 위에 있어요.
The cat is on the bench.

자전거가 나무 뒤에 있어요.
The bicycle is behind the tree.

24

3 When asking about a subject in a specific location

When asking about a subject that exists in a specific location, you can use 누가 or 뭐가 (= 무엇이). If the subject is a person, use 누가. If the subject is an object, use 뭐가 (= 무엇이). The informal form 뭐가 is mainly used in casual conversations, whereas in formal speech, 무엇이 is used.

- A 누가 집에 있어요? Who is in your house?

  B ① 동생이 집에 있어요. My younger brother is in my house.

  ② 집에 아무도 없어요. There is no one in my house.

- A 뭐가 (= 무엇이) 집에 있어요? What is in your house?

  B ① 냉장고가 집에 있어요. There is a refrigerator in my house.

  ② 집에 아무것도 없어요. There is nothing in my house.

4 When expressing directions

To express the directions 동 (east), 서 (west), 남 (south), and 북 (north), use the directional words combined with 쪽 and the particle 에 to indicate location. When pointing with your fingers, add 이 or 저 (e.g., 이쪽 (this way), 저쪽 (that way)), and use the particle 에 to indicate the direction you are pointing to.

- 김포공항이 서울의 서쪽에 있어요. Gimpo Airport is to the west of Seoul.

- 창문이 남쪽에 있어요. The window is to the south.

- 화장실이 저쪽에 있어요. The restroom is over there.

When asking about directions, you can use 어디에 or 어느 쪽에.

- A 식당이 어느 쪽에 있어요? Which direction is the restaurant?

  B (식당이) 동쪽에 있어요. (The restaurant) is to the east.

Quiz 03

Sino-Korean numbers

Kor. 04

전화번호가 010-3923-6847
(공일공에 삼구이삼에 육팔사칠)이에요.

The phone number is 010-3923-6847.

강남아파트 103(백삼) 동 908(구백팔) 호예요.

This is Unit 908, Building 103, Gangnam Apartment.

노트북이
1,950,000(백구십오만) 원이에요.

The laptop is 1,950,000 won.

저는 2006(이천육) 년에 태어났어요.

I was born in 2006.

제 생일이 7(칠) 월 24(이십사) 일이에요.

My birthday is July 24th.

Grammar Essentials

1 Sino-Korean numbers

There are two number systems in Korean: Sino-Korean numbers and Native Korean numbers. The Sino-Korean numbers system is used to read numbers.

1	2	3	4	5	6	7	8	9	10
일	이	삼	사	오	육	칠	팔	구	십

11	12	13	14	15	16	17	18	19	20
십일	십이	십삼	십사	십오	십육	십칠	십팔	십구	이십

• 교실이 8(팔) 층에 있어요. The classroom is on the 8th floor.

• 식당이 15(십오) 층에 있어요. The restaurant is on the 15th floor.

This section explains how to read Sino-Korean numbers from 10 to 100. Let's practice with the numbers below:

10	20	30	40	50	60	70	80	90	100
십	이십	삼십	사십	오십	육십	칠십	팔십	구십	백

• 사무실이 901(구백일) 호예요. The office is room 901.

When reading numbers, commas are typically placed every three digits, but in Korean units, numbers are read based on 만 (four digits).

100 백	1,000 천	10,000 만	100,000 십만	1,000,000 백만
200 이백	2,000 이천	20,000 이만	200,000 이십만	2,000,000 이백만
300 삼백	3,000 삼천	30,000 삼만	300,000 삼십만	3,000,000 삼백만
400 사백	4,000 사천	40,000 사만	400,000 사십만	4,000,000 사백만

• 우리집이 214(이백십사) 동 1403(천사백삼) 호예요. My house is unit 1403, building 214.

• 냉장고가 3,650,000(삼백육십오만) 원이에요. The refrigerator costs 3,650,000 won.

 Be careful!

The final consonants ㅂ, ㄱ are pronounced as [ㅁ, ㅇ] due to the influence of the initial sound ㅁ of the following syllable.

• 100,000 십만 [심만], 60,000 육만 [융만]

As for compound words, when the final consonant of the preceding syllable is followed by the vowel ㅣ, ㅑ, ㅕ, ㅛ, ㅠ, it is pronounced with ㄴ added between the consonant and the vowel.

• 16 십육 [심뉵], 106 백육 [뱅뉵]

1 When reading a number

1 Reading Sino-Korean numbers

When reading numbers such as phone numbers, car numbers, page numbers, or other numbers, Sino-Korean numbers are used. For phone numbers, each digit is read individually, and "0" is pronounced as [gong].

• 사무실 전화번호가 02-3665-6871(공이에 삼육육오에 육팔칠일)이에요.
The office phone number is 02-3665-6871.

• 한국의 긴급 전화번호가 119(일일구)예요. The emergency phone number in Korea is 119.

> **Note**
> When reading a phone number digit by digit, the hyphen "–"
> in the middle of the number is pronounced as [에] in Korean.

2 Asking about numbers

To ask for a number, use 몇 followed by a noun that indicates the unit, such as 쪽 (page), 층 (floor), or 번 (number).

• A 사무실이 몇 층이에요? On what floor is the office?

  B 12(십이) 층이에요. It's on the 12th floor.

• A 정답이 몇 쪽에 있어요? On what page is the answer?

  B 267(이백육십칠) 쪽에 있어요. It's on page 267.

• 선생님, 4(사) 번 문제를 다시 말해 주세요. Teacher, could you please repeat question number 4?

The pronunciation of 몇 changes depending on the initial sound of the syllable that follows it.

1. When the syllable after 몇 starts with a vowel, the final consonant [ㄷ] of 몇 connects to the initial sound of the following syllable.
   • 몇 월 [며 뒬], 몇 원 [며 뒨]

2. When the syllable after 몇 starts with one of the consonants ㅂ, ㄷ, ㄱ, ㅈ, the final consonant [ㄷ] of 몇 is pronounced as a tense sound [ㅃ, ㄸ, ㄲ, ㅉ].
   • 몇 번 [면 뻔], 몇 점 [면 쩜]

3. When the syllable after 몇 starts with the consonant ㅎ, the final consonant [ㄷ] of 몇 is pronounced as the aspirated sound [ㅌ].
   • 몇 호 [면 토]

4. When the syllable after 몇 starts with the consonants ㅁ, ㄴ, the final consonant [ㄷ] of 몇 is pronounced as [ㄴ].
   • 몇 년 [면 년]

Tip

Reading numbers in daily life

The following are methods for reading commonly encountered numbers in daily life. "0" is read as [공] when read digit by digit, but as [영] when part of other numbers.

2:0(이 대 영)으로 이겼어요.
I won 2:0.

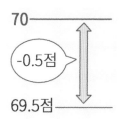

0.5(영 점 오) 점 부족해요.
It's short by 0.5 points.

시험 점수를 94.2(구십사 점 이) 점 받았어요.
I received a test score of 94.2 points.

체온이 36.7(삼십육 점 칠) 도예요.
The body temperature is 36.7 degrees.

오늘 날씨가 −10(영하 십) 도예요.
Today's temperature is -10 degrees.

2 When expressing dates

1 Reading dates

In Korean, dates are read using Sino-Korean numbers. Unlike English, the order of reading or writing dates in Korean is from the largest unit to the smallest: year, month, and day. When reading the year, it is read as a four-digit number followed by 년 (year). Unlike in English, years are not read in two-digit pairs in Korean.

2025년   **9월**   **24일**   September 24, 2025

이천이십오   구   이십사

> For numbers ending with the final consonant sound [ㄹ] like 1(일), 7(칠), and 8(팔), when followed by 년 ([ㄴ] as the initial sound), the [ㄴ] of 년 is pronounced as [ㄹ].
> • 1(일) 년 [일련], 7(칠) 년 [칠련], 8(팔) 년 [팔련]

When reading 월 (month) in Korean, Sino-Korean numbers are used. However, there are exceptions for June and October:
* June is written and read as 유월.
* October is written and read as 시월.
These changes occur for ease of pronunciation.

In contrast, for 일 (day), there are no exceptions, and it is always read as Sino-Korean numbers. When expressing events or actions on specific dates, the time particle 에 is used to indicate when something happens.

1월 일월	2월 이월	3월 삼월	4월 사월

M	T	W	T	F	S	S
1	2	3	4	5	6	7
8	9	10	11	12	13	14
15	16	17	18	19	20	21
22	23	24	25	26	27	28
29	30	31				

M	T	W	T	F	S	S
				1	2	3	4
5	6	7	8	9	10	11
12	13	14	15	16	17	18
19	20	21	22	23	24	25
26	27	28	29			

M	T	W	T	F	S	S
				1	2	3
4	5	6	7	8	9	10
11	12	13	14	15	16	17
18	19	20	21	22	23	24
25	26	27	28	29	30	31

M	T	W	T	F	S	S
1	2	3	4	5	6	7
8	9	10	11	12	13	14
15	16	17	18	19	20	21
22	23	24	25	26	27	28
29	30					

5월 오월	*6월 유월	7월 칠월	8월 팔월

M	T	W	T	F	S	S
		1	2	3	4	5
6	7	8	9	10	11	12
13	14	15	16	17	18	19
20	21	22	23	24	25	26
27	28	29	30	31		

M	T	W	T	F	S	S
					1	2
3	4	5	6	7	8	9
10	11	12	13	14	15	16
17	18	19	20	21	22	23
24	25	26	27	28	29	30

M	T	W	T	F	S	S
1	2	3	4	5	6	7
8	9	10	11	12	13	14
15	16	17	18	19	20	21
22	23	24	25	26	27	28
29	30	31				

M	T	W	T	F	S	S
				1	2	3	4
5	6	7	8	9	10	11
12	13	14	15	16	17	18
19	20	21	22	23	24	25
26	27	28	29	30	31	

9월 구월	*10월 시월	11월 십일월	12월 십이월

M	T	W	T	F	S	S
						1
2	3	4	5	6	7	8
9	10	11	12	13	14	15
16	17	18	19	20	21	22
23	24	25	26	27	28	29
30						

M	T	W	T	F	S	S
	1	2	3	4	5	6
7	8	9	10	11	12	13
14	15	16	17	18	19	20
21	22	23	24	25	26	27
28	29	30	31			

M	T	W	T	F	S	S
				1	2	3
4	5	6	7	8	9	10
11	12	13	14	15	16	17
18	19	20	21	22	23	24
25	26	27	28	29	30	

M	T	W	T	F	S	S
1	2	3	4	5	6	7	8
9	10	11	12	13	14	15
16	17	18	19	20	21	22
23	24	25	26	27	28	29
30	31					

- 졸업식이 2(이) 월 23(이십삼) 일에 있어요. The graduation ceremony is on February 23.
- 제 생일이 10(시) 월 10(십) 일이에요. My birthday is on October 10.
- 현충일이 6(유) 월 6(육) 일이에요. Memorial Day is on June 6.

② Reading the day of the week

The day of the week is written after the year, month, and day.

- 2025년 12월 31일 수요일
  December 31, 2025, Wednesday

When indicating the day of the week on a specific date, use 이다 with the day of the week. For events or actions occurring on a specific day of the week, use the time particle 에.

- 오늘이 금요일이에요.
  Today is Friday.

- 이번 주 목요일에 가족을 만나요.
  I meet my family this Thursday.

③ Asking about dates

When asking about dates, 언제 (when) is used. For specific dates, 몇 년 (what year) and 몇 월 (what month) are used by adding 몇 before 년 and 월. Note that when asking about the day, 며칠 (what day) is used instead of 몇 일. For the day of the week, ask 무슨 요일 (what day of the week).

- A 몇 년에 학교가 시작했어요? = 언제 학교가 시작했어요?
  What year did school start? = When did school start?

  B 1960년에 학교가 시작했어요. School started in 1960.

- A 몇 월에 졸업해요? = 언제 졸업해요?
  What month do you graduate? = When do you graduate?

  B 2월에 졸업해요. I graduate in February.

- A 며칠에 여행에서 돌아와요? = 언제 여행에서 돌아와요?
  What day do you return from the trip? = When do you return from the trip?

  B 15일에 돌아와요. I return on the 15th.

- A 무슨 요일에 파티가 있어요? = 언제 파티가 있어요?
  What day of the week is the party? = When is the party?

  B 토요일에 파티가 있어요. The party is on Saturday.

3 When expressing prices

① Reading prices

When expressing prices, the units 일 (one), 십 (ten), 백 (hundred), 천 (thousand), 만 (ten thousand), 억 (hundred million) are used, and numbers are read in Sino-Korean. It is important to remember that while commas are placed every three digits (thousand units, e.g., 1,000) when writing numbers, in Sino-Korean, the grouping changes to every four digits (ten thousand units, e.g., 10,000).

130원	백삼십 원 one hundred thirty won
2, 450원	이천사백오십 원 two thousand four hundred fifty won
35, 980원	삼만 오천구백팔십 원 thirty-five thousand nine hundred eighty won
781, 260원	칠십팔만 천이백육십 원 seven hundred eighty-one thousand two hundred sixty won
5, 340, 870원	오백삼십사만 팔백칠십 원 five million three hundred forty thousand eight hundred seventy won
63, 152, 340원	육천삼백십오만 이천삼백사십 원 sixty-three million one hundred fifty-two thousand three hundred forty won
875, 294, 120원	팔억 칠천오백이십구만 사천백이십 원 eight hundred seventy-five million two hundred ninety-four thousand one hundred twenty won

TIP

Key Points on Reading Prices with Sino-Korean Numbers

▶ **No "일" before 십, 백, 천, 만:**
Do not add "일" (one) before 십 (10), 백 (100), 천 (1,000), or 만 (10,000) when the first digit is 1.

100원: 백 원 (O), 일백 원 (×) 110원: 백십 원 (O), 일백일십 원 (×)
1,000원: 천 원 (O), 일천 원 (×) 1,100원: 천 백 원 (O), 일천일백 원 (×)
10,000원: 만 원 (O), 일만 원 (×) 11,000원: 만 천 원 (O), 일만 일천 원 (×)

▶ **Grouping numbers by units:**
Large numbers are grouped by 만 (10,000) and 억 (100,000,000).

20,300원: 이만 삼백 원 (2만 + 3백) 250,000,000원: 이억 오천만 원 (2억 + 오천만)
51,000원: 오만 천 원 (5만 + 1천) 2220,000,000원: 이십이억 이천만 원 (22억 + 2천만)

▶ **When to Use "일":**
만 (10,000) is read as 일만 (ten thousand) when it is part of a larger number.
억 (100,000,000) is always read as 일억 (one hundred million) when it starts with 1.

10,000원: 만 원 100,000,000원: 일억 원
111,000원 → 십일만 천 원 (11만 + 1,000) 1,100,000,000원: 십일억 원
1111,000원 → 백십일만 천 원 (111만 + 1,000) 11,110,000,000원: 백십일억 천만 원

- 전기 요금이 21,000원(이만 천 원)이에요. The electricity bill is 21,000 won.
- 옷이 130,000원(십삼만 원)이에요. The clothes cost 130,000 won.
- 냉장고가 3,110,000원(삼백십일만 원)이에요. The refrigerator costs 3,110,000 won.
- 집의 보증금이 110,000,000원(일억 천만 원)이에요. The deposit for the house is 110,000,000 won.

2 Asking about prices

To ask about prices, use "얼마예요?".

- A 이 시계가 얼마예요? How much is this watch?

  B <u>207,000(이십만 칠천)</u> 원이에요. It's 207,000 won.

- A A 옷이 얼마예요? How much are the clothes?

  B <u>63,000(육만 삼천)</u> 원이에요. They are 63,000 won.

> **✱ Be careful!**
>
> The final sounds ㅂ, ㄱ in 십, 육 change to [ㅁ, ㅇ] when followed by a consonant ㅁ (as in 만).
>
> • 100,000원: 십만 원 [심마눤]   • 1,000,000원: 백만 원 [뱅마눤]

3 Expressing approximate numbers

When expressing approximate numbers, the term 쯤 ("about" or "approximately") is added after the number. To ask about approximate prices, phrases such as "얼마나 해요?" or "얼마쯤 들어요?" are used. This format helps convey a sense of estimation rather than exact figures.

- A 택시비가 얼마나 해요? How much is the taxi fare?

  B 30,000원쯤 해요. It's about 30,000 won.

- A 여행비가 얼마쯤 들어요? How much will the trip cost?

  B 150,000원쯤 들어요. It's about 150,000 won.

> **Tip**
>
> **How to indicate an approximate price**
>
> - 21,000원–22,000원: 이만 원 넘어요.
>   21,000 won to 22,000 won: It's over twenty thousand won.
>
> - 20,050원쯤: 이만 원쯤 해요.
>   Around 20,050 won: It's about twenty thousand won.
>
> - 18,000원–19,000원: 이만 원이 안 돼요.
>   18,000 won to 19,000 won: It's less than twenty thousand won.

Quiz 04

저는 한국 친구가 두 명 있어요.

I have two Korean friends.

한 친구 이름이 준수예요.

One friend's name is Junsu.

준수가 열 아홉 살이에요.

Junsu is 19 years old.

다른 친구 이름이 민기예요.

The other friend's name is Mingi.

민기가 스물 한 살이에요.

Mingi is 21 years old.

그런데 한국 여자 친구가 한 명도 없어요.

But, I don't have a single female Korean friend.

Grammar Essentials

1 Native Korean numbers

When counting numbers in Korean, they are read using Native Korean numbers.

1	2	3	4	5	6	7	8	9	10
하나	둘	셋	넷	다섯	여섯	일곱	여덟	아홉	열

하나 둘 셋…

✱ Be careful!

The final consonant ㄼ in 여덟 is pronounced as [ㄹ].

• 여덟 [여덜]

Let's read the following Native Korean numbers for 11, up to 30:

11	12	13	14	15	16	17	18	19	20
열하나	열둘	열셋	열넷	열다섯	열여섯	열일곱	열여덟	열아홉	스물

21	22	23	24	25	26	27	28	29	30
스물하나	스물둘	스물셋	스물넷	스물다섯	스물여섯	스물일곱	스물여덟	스물아홉	서른

Let's read the following native Korean numbers for 10, 20, 30, up to 100:

10	20	30	40	50	60	70	80	90	100
열	스물	서른	마흔	쉰	예순	일흔	여든	아흔	백

 Note

Units over 100 (백), such as 1,000 (천) or 10,000 (만), are expressed using Sino-Korean numbers. Native Korean numbers are typically used from 1 to 99. In everyday life, 101 can be read as 백하나 in Native Korean numbers or 백일 in Sino-Korean numbers.

Grammar in Action

1 When counting the number of objects

1 Counting objects

When expressing the number of objects in Korean, a counter word corresponding to the object is used along with the number. For objects, the counter word 개 (counter for things) is used, and for people, the counter word 명 (counter for person) is used. Remember that the counter word follows the native Korean number.

- 방에 의자가 5(다섯) 개 있어요. There are 5 chairs in the room.

- 한국 친구가 10(열) 명 있어요. I have 10 Korean friends.

Exceptionally, the Native Korean numbers 1 (하나), 2 (둘), 3 (셋), 4 (넷) and 20 (스물) are used as 한, 두, 세, 네 and 스무 respectively, in front of the counter word.

- 가방 1(한) 개 주세요. Please give me one bag.

- 저는 동생이 2(두) 명 있어요. I have two siblings.

- 집에 우산이 3(세) 개 있어요. I have three umbrellas at home.

- 우리 반에 여자가 4(네) 명 있어요. There are four girls in our class.

- 사과가 한 박스에 20(스무) 개 있어요. There are twenty apples in a box.

* Be careful!

In Korean, when expressing the number of objects, it is not necessary to use the plural suffix 들 to indicate plurality.
- 두 의자들 (X), 의자 두 개 (O)
- 세 모자들 (X), 모자 세 개 (O)

The counter word used when counting varies depending on the object.

개		Objects (e.g., hats, glasses, pens)	한 개	두 개	세 개	여러 개
명		People (e.g., men, women, students)	한 명	두 명	세 명	여러 명
분		Respected people (e.g., grandparents, parents)	한 분	두 분	세 분	여러 분
마리		Animals (e.g., dogs, cats, birds, fish)	한 마리	두 마리	세 마리	여러 마리
잔		Beverages & alcoholic drinks (e.g., coffee, juice, beer, soju)	한 잔	두 잔	세 잔	여러 잔
장		Flat & thin items (e.g., paper, photos, cards, glass)	한 장	두 장	세 장	여러 장
병		Bottles (e.g., beer, soju, water, cola)	한 병	두 병	세 병	여러 병
권		Books (e.g., books, notebooks)	한 권	두 권	세 권	여러 권

The number of objects in a sentence is expressed as follows.

- 친구가 책이 네 권 있어요. My friend has four books.

- 생선이 두 마리 있어요. There are two fish.

- 보통 하루에 커피 세 잔 마셔요. I usually drink three cups of coffee a day.

2 Asking about the number of objects

In Korean, when asking about the quantity of an object, 몇 is placed before the counter word. The choice of the counter word varies according to the object in question.

- A 가방이 몇 개 있어요?
  How many bags do you have?

  B (가방이) 세 개 있어요. (I have) three bags.

- A 한국 친구가 몇 명 있어요?
  How many Korean friends do you have?

  B (한국 친구가) 네 명 있어요. (I have) four friends.

- A 한국어 책이 몇 권 있어요?
  How many Korean books do you have?

  B (한국어 책이) 열 권 있어요. (I have) ten books.

 Be careful!

Pay attention to the pronunciation!
- 몇 명 [면 명]
- 몇 마리 [면 마리]

몇 with the same form but different meanings

몇 looks the same but has different meanings depending on the context. When used in an interrogative sentence, it asks about a number. When used in a declarative sentence, it indicates a small number.

- A 한국 친구가 몇 명 있어요? How many friends do you have?
  B 몇 명 있어요. A few friends.
- A 우산이 몇 개 있어요? How many umbrellas are there?
  B 몇 개 있어요. A few umbrellas.

3 Emphasizing negation

To emphasize the absence of objects, the particle 도 is used with "한 [counter word]도 + negation" to indicate that there is not even one of the objects.

- 사람이 한 명도 없어요. There isn't even one person.

- 표가 한 장도 없어요. There isn't even one ticket.

- 책을 한 권도 안 읽었어요. I haven't read even one book.

2 When expressing age

제 가족이에요.
This is my family.

아버지가 62(예순 두) 살이에요.
My father is 62 years old.

어머지가 54(쉰 네) 살이에요.
My mother is 54 years old.

저는 31(서른 한) 살이에요.
I am 31 years old.

아내가 29(스물 아홉) 살이에요.
My wife is 29 years old.

남동생이 19(열 아홉) 살이에요.
My younger brother is 19 years old.

딸이 8(여덟) 살이에요.
My daughter is 8 years old.

아들이 3(세) 살이에요.
My son is 3 years old.

1 Expressing age

When expressing age in Korean, Native Korean numbers are used followed by the counter word 살.

- 저는 25(스물다섯) 살이에요. I am 25 years old.

- 제 어머니가 56(쉰여섯) 살이에요. My mother is 56 years old.

When expressing age, the Native Korean numbers for 1, 2, 3, 4 and 20 change to 한, 두, 세, 네, and 스무 respectively before 살:

- 동생이 20(스무) 살이에요. My younger sibling is 20 years old.

- 고양이가 13(세) 살이에요. The cat is 13 years old.

> **Note**
>
> In Korean, there are two counter words for expressing age: 살 and 세. 살 is used with Native Korean numbers and is mainly used informally in spoken language, while 세 is used with Sino-Korean numbers and is mainly used formally in written language. Native Korean numbers precede 살, and Sino-Korean numbers precede 세.
>
> - 31 years old → 31살: 서른 한 살   Spoken
>
>   → 31세: 삼십일 세   Written

2 Asking age

When asking someone's age, 몇 precedes 살 to form the question 몇 살.

- A 친구가 몇 살이에요? How old is your friend?

  B (친구가) <u>스물 여덟</u> 살이에요. My friend is twenty-eight years old.

- A 동생하고 몇 살 차이가 나요? What is the age difference between you and your sibling?

  B <u>세 살</u> 차이가 나요. There is a three-year difference between us.

- A 언니가 몇 살 나이가 많아요? How much older is your sister?

  B 언니가 저보다 <u>두 살</u> 나이가 많아요. My sister is two years older than me.

The way to ask about age varies depending on whom you're asking:

▶ "나이가 몇 살이에요?": Used when asking peers or those younger.

- A 남동생이 몇 살이에요? How old is your younger brother?

  B <u>15(열 다섯)</u> 살이에요. My brother is fifteen years old.

▶ "나이가 어떻게 되세요?": Politely used when meeting someone for the first time.

- A 선생님 나이가 어떻게 되세요? How old is the teacher?

  B <u>32(서른 두)</u> 살이에요. The teacher is thirty-two years old.

▶ "연세가 어떻게 되세요?" Honorific form used for elders or those of higher status.

- A 아버지 연세가 어떻게 되세요? How old is your father?

  B <u>59(쉰 아홉)</u> 살이세요. My father is fifty-nine years old.

살 vs 년

Korean differentiates between the age of animate objects (people, animals) and the years of inanimate objects using different unit nouns. 살 is used with Native Korean numbers for the ages of people and animals, while 년 is used with Sino-Korean numbers for the years of objects. Questions about age or years thus differ, asking "몇 살이에요?" for animate and 몇 년 됐어요? for inanimate.

- A 아이가 몇 살이에요? How old is your kid?
  B 아이가 10(열) 살이에요. My kid is ten years old.
- A 개가 몇 살이에요? How old is your dog?
  B 개가 2(두) 살이에요. My dog is two years old.
- A 이 건물이 몇 년 됐어요? How old is this building?
  B 이 건물은 10(십) 년 됐어요. This building is ten years old.

Quiz 05

Kor. 06

AM 9:00 ~11:00	회의
PM 4:00 ~4:30	회의
PM 7:00 ~10:00	친구·약속
PM 11:00	집

아침 9시에 회의가 있어요.
There's a meeting at 9 AM.

회의가 11시에 끝나요.
The meeting ends at 11 AM.

두 시간 동안 회의해요.
The meeting lasts for two hours.

오늘 다른 회의가 오후 4시에 있어요.
There's another meeting today at 4 PM.

오후 회의가 30분 동안 해요.
The afternoon meeting lasts for 30 minutes.

저녁 7시에 친구하고 약속이 있어요.
I have plans with a friend at 7 PM.

저녁 7시부터 10시까지 3시간 동안 친구를 만나요.
I meet my friend from 7 PM to 10 PM for three hours.

밤 11시에 집에 가요.
I go home at 11 PM.

Grammar Essentials

1 Time

In Korean, when expressing time, 시 (hour) is read with Native Korean numbers, while 분 (minutes) and 초 (seconds) are read with Sino-Korean numbers. The Native Korean numbers before 시 are changed to 한 시, 두 시, 세 시, 네 시 for 1 o'clock to 4 o'clock respectively.

	시 (hour) Native Korean numbers	분 (minute) Sino-Korean numbers	초 (second) Sino-Korean numbers
오전 (AM)	5(다섯) 시	5(오) 분	10(십) 초
오후 (PM)	10(열) 시	10(십) 분	20(이십) 초

> **Note**
> 30 minutes can be referred to as 반 (half).
> • 1시 30분 (1:30) = 1시 반 (half past one)

2 Time particle 에

The particle 에 is used after a noun indicating time to express when a specific event or action occurs.

- 오후 1시에 회의가 있어요. 그런데 오후 2시에 회의가 없어요.
  There is a meeting at 1 PM, but there is no meeting at 2 PM.

- 금요일에 약속이 있어요. 그런데 토요일에 약속이 없어요.
  I have an appointment on Friday, but I don't have an appointment on Saturday.

- 식당이 아침 10시에 문을 열어요. 그리고 저녁 8시에 문을 닫아요.
  The restaurant opens at 10 AM and closes at 8 PM.

The particle 에 should be used only once in a sentence, so it is placed at the end of the time expression.

- <u>7월 28일에 토요일에 저녁 6시</u>에 약속이 있어요. I have an appointment at 6 PM on Saturday, July 28th.

  (time)

3 Expressions for time of the day

In formal situations, 오전 (AM) and 오후 (PM) are used to express the precise time, while in informal situations, words like 아침 (morning), 오후 (afternoon), 저녁 (evening), 밤 (night), and 새벽 (dawn) are used. In Korean, the time of day is mentioned before the time.

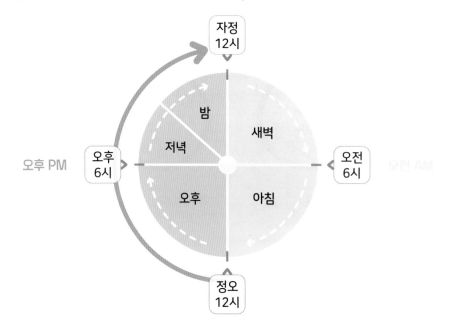

- 기차가 오전 8(여덟) 시 10(십) 분에 서울에서 출발합니다. The train departs from Seoul at 8:10 AM.

- 기차가 아침 10(열) 시 20(이십) 분에 부산에 도착해요. The train arrives in Busan at 10:20 AM.

- 오후 1(한) 시 30(삼십) 분에 점심을 먹어요. I eat lunch at 1:30 PM.

- 저녁 8(여덟) 시 20(이십) 분에 친구를 만나요. I meet my friend at 8:20 PM.

- 보통 새벽 1(한) 시에 자요. I usually go to sleep at 1 AM.

Tip

Common mistakes with time-of-day expressions

In Korean, expressions like 지난 (last), 이번 (this), 다음 (next) are not used with time of the day nouns like 아침, 오후, 저녁, and 밤.

- 어젯밤에 잠을 못 잤어요. I couldn't sleep last night.
- 오늘 오후에 만나요! Let's meet this afternoon!
- 내일 저녁에 출발해요. We leave tomorrow evening.

Grammar in Action

1 When expressing time

When expressing the time at which an event or action occurs in Korean, the time particle 에 is attached to nouns, functioning like an adverb. However, for adverbs such as 오늘 (today), 어제 (yesterday), and 내일 (tomorrow), the time particle 에 is not needed. Below are the distinctions between time expressions that require the time particle 에 and those that do not.

Requiring 에 (Noun + 에)	Not requiring 에 (Adverbs)
3시에 at 3 o'clock	어제 yesterday
지난주에 last week	오늘 today
이번 주에 this week	내일 tomorrow
다음 주에 next week	지금 now
주말에 on the weekend	아까 a little ago
주중에 on a working day	이따가 later

- 이번 주에 약속이 없어요. I don't have any plans this week.
- 오늘 데이트가 있어요. I have a date today.

When asking about time, 몇 시 (what time) is used. To inquire about the current time, ask "몇 시예요" and to ask when a specific event or action occurs, use 몇 시에.

- A 지금 몇 시예요? What time is it now?

  B 오후 2시예요. It's 2 PM.

- A 몇 시에 약속이 있어요? What time is the appointment?

  B 오후 2시에 약속이 있어요. The appointment is at 2 PM.

To inquire about a specific moment in terms of hours, minutes, or seconds, place 몇 (what) before 시 (hours), 분 (minutes), or 초 (seconds) to form questions like 몇 시, 몇 분, or 몇 초.

- A 결혼식이 몇 시에 시작해요? What time does the wedding start?

  B 2시에 시작해요. It starts at 2 o'clock.

- A 시험이 몇 분에 끝나요? When does the exam finish?

  B 시험이 20분에 끝나요. The exam finishes 20 minutes past the hour.

Instead of 몇 시 (what time), 언제 (when) can be used to ask about time. While 몇 시 combines with the time particle 에 to form 몇 시에, 언제 does not combine with the particle 에.

- A 발표 시간이 언제예요? When is the presentation?

  B 오후 5시예요. It's at 5 PM.

- A 회의가 언제 있어요? When is the meeting?

  B 금요일 아침 9시 30분에 있어요. The meeting is at 9:30 AM on Friday.

2 When expressing the duration of time

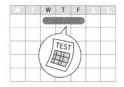

이번 주 수요일부터 금요일까지 시험이 3(삼) 일 동안 있어요.
There are exams from Wednesday to Friday this week,
lasting for three days.

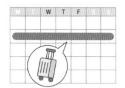

다음 주 월요일부터 일요일까지 일주일 동안 휴가예요.
I'm on vacation for a week from Monday to Sunday next week.

5월부터 한 달 동안 재택근무해요.
I'm working at home for a month starting from May.

일 년 동안 한국에 있어요.
I'll be in Korea for a year.

In Korean, the following units of time are used to express the duration of time. Pay attention to whether Sino-Korean (SK) or Native Korean (NK) numbers are used.

SK + 년 (years)	1(일) 년	2(이) 년	3(삼) 년	4(사) 년
NK + 달 (months)	1(한) 달	2(두) 달	3(세) 달	4(네) 달
SK + 개월 (months)	1(일) 개월	2(이) 개월	3(삼) 개월	4(사) 개월
SK + 주 (weeks)	1(일) 주	2(이) 주	3(삼) 주	4(사) 주
NK + 일 (days)	*하루	*이틀	3(삼) 일	4(사) 일
NK + 시간 (times)	1(한) 시간	2(두) 시간	3(세) 시간	4(네) 시간
SK + 분 (minutes)	1(일) 분	2(이) 분	3(삼) 분	4(사) 분
SK + 초 (seconds)	1(일) 초	2(이) 초	3(삼) 초	4(사) 초

- 2(두) 시간 동안 수업이 있어요. There is a class for two hours.

- 4(사) 일 동안 여행 가요. I'm going on a trip for four days.

- 5(오) 개월 전에 한국에 왔어요. I came to Korea five months ago.

- 2(이) 년 동안 한국에서 살았어요. I lived in Korea for two years.

When expressing the starting point of the duration, the particle 부터 is attached after the time noun, and for the end point, the particle 까지 is used.

- 다음 주부터 시간이 있어요. I am free starting next week.

- 금요일까지 시간이 없어요. I am busy until Friday.

- 9시부터 6시까지 회사에서 일해요. I work at the company from 9 to 6.

 Be careful!

> 1. …부터 …까지: Used to indicate the start and end points of time.
>   - 월요일부터 금요일까지 일해요. I work from Monday to Friday.
>
> 2. …에서 …까지: Used to indicate the start and end points of space or distance.
>   - 집에서 회사까지 30분 걸려요. It takes 30 minutes from home to the office.

The length of a duration is expressed by adding 동안 after the duration.

- 2시부터 5시까지 3시간 동안 공부했어요. I studied for 3 hours from 2 to 5.

- 30분 동안 친구를 기다렸어요. I waited for a friend for 30 minutes.

- 1년 동안 핸드폰을 무료로 수리 받을 수 있어요. I can get the phone repaired for free for a year.

To ask about the duration, use 얼마 동안. For specific durations, use 몇 before the noun indicating the duration, followed by 동안.

- A 몇 시간 동안 회의해요? = 얼마 동안 회의해요?
  How long is the meeting? = How much time does the meeting take?

  B 1시간 30분 동안 회의해요. The meeting is for 1 hour and 30 minutes.

- A 몇 년 동안 한국어를 공부했어요? = 얼마 동안 한국어를 공부했어요?
  How long have you studied Korean? = For how much time have you studied Korean?

  B 3년 동안 한국어를 공부했어요. I have studied Korean for 3 years.

- A 며칠 동안 여행해요? = 얼마 동안 여행해요?
  How many days are you traveling? = For how long are you traveling?

  B 일주일 동안 여행해요. I'm traveling for a week.

When asking about the time it takes, you can say "시간이 얼마나 걸려요 (How long does it take)." To inquire about the duration of other actions or activities, use 얼마 동안.

- A 집에서 회사까지 시간이 얼마나 걸려요? How long does it take from home to the office?

  B 1시간 걸려요. It takes an hour.

- A 얼마 동안 지하철을 타요? How long do you ride the subway?

  B 20분 동안 지하철을 타요. I ride the subway for 20 minutes.

Quiz 06

Informal polite present tense –아/어요

Kor. 07

월요일에 한국어를 공부해요. I study Korean on Mondays.

한국어 공부가 재미있어요. Studying Korean is fun.

수요일에 일해요. I work on Wednesdays.

정말 바빠요. I'm really busy.

금요일에 친구하고 한국 음식을 먹어요.
I eat Korean food with my friends on Fridays.

한국 음식이 맛있어요. Korean food is delicious.

일요일에 쉬어요. I rest on Sundays.

집이 편해요. I feel relaxed at home.

Grammar Essentials

1 Infinitive form -다 vs. Conjugated form -아/어요

In Korean, the infinitive forms of verbs and adjectives are composed of the stem followed by -다 (stem + -다). This form is the base form found in dictionaries and is not used in everyday speech or writing. To speak or write, the -다 is removed, and various endings are attached to the stem for conjugation. Honorifics and tenses can be inserted between the stem and the final endings to express a variety of meanings.

먹다

| 사전 [먹다] Q |
| 먹다 |
| 1. eat, have |
| 2. take, get |
| 3. get older |

먹 + -어요 = 먹어요.
stem   ending   conjugation

먹어요

2 Informal polite present tense -아/어요

The ending -아/어요 attaches to the stem of verbs and adjectives to indicate the informal polite present tense. Verbs express an action performed by the subject; while adjectives, describe the subject's state. The specific form of the ending -아요, -어요, or -여요 depends on the final syllable of the stem:

- If the stem is 하다, 하 combines with -여요 to form 해요.
- If the last syllable of the stem contains the vowel ㅏ or ㅗ, it combines with -아요.
- If the last syllable does not contain ㅏ or ㅗ, and the verb is not 하다, it combines with -어요.

	해요 (하 + -여요)	-아요	-어요
Verbs	공부하다 → 공부해요	가다 → 가아요 → 가요	먹다 → 먹어요
	식사하다 → 식사해요	일어나다 → 일어나요	읽다 → 읽어요
	운동하다 → 운동해요	살다 → 살아요	만들다 → 만들어요
	노래하다 → 노래해요	찾다 → 찾아요	쉬다 → 쉬어요
	연습하다 → 연습해요	오다 → 오아요 → 와요	마시다 → 마시어요 → 마셔요
	일하다 → 일해요	보다 → 보아요 → 봐요	주다 → 주어요 → 줘요
Adjectives	유명하다 → 유명해요	싸다 → 싸아요 → 싸요	길다 → 길어요
	피곤하다 → 피곤해요	작다 → 작아요	맛있다 → 맛있어요
	필요하다 → 필요해요	좋다 → 좋아요	재미없다 → 재미없어요

✳ Be careful!

When the same vowels are repeated, one of the vowels is omitted.

- 가다: 가 + 아요 → 가요
- 자다: 자 + 아요 → 자요

When two vowels are combined, they are contracted.

- 배우다: 배우 + 어요 → 배워요
- 마시다: 마시 + 어요 → 마셔요

1   When expressing habitual actions or facts

The -아/어요 form is used to express current facts, truths, and habitual actions. It is often combined with adverbs such as 보통 (usually) and 매일 (every day).

- 사람은 보통 7시간을 자요. People usually sleep for 7 hours.

- 배가 고플 때 아기가 울어요. Babies cry when they are hungry.

To ask about habitual actions, you can use "뭐 해요 (What do you do)." Use 누가 (who) when asking about the subject acting, and 누구를 (whom) when asking about the object of the action.

- A 보통 주말에 뭐 해요? What do you usually do on weekends?

  B 보통 주말에 친구하고 놀아요. I usually hang out with friends.

- A 누가 음식을 만들어요? Who makes the food?

  B 윤아가 음식을 만들어요. Yuna makes the food.

- A 진수가 누구를 좋아해요? Who does Jinsu like?

  B 진수가 수지를 좋아해요. Jinsu likes Suji.

- A 보통 누구한테 이메일을 써요? Who do you usually email?

  B 보통 가족한테 이메일을 써요. I usually send emails to my family.

2   When expressing current actions or behaviors in action

The -아/어요 form is used with adverbs like 지금 (now) to express actions that are currently ongoing. In this context, -아/어요 carries a similar meaning to -고 있다 (be doing).

- On the phone

  A 지금 뭐 해요? What are you doing now?

  B 음식을 만들어요. I'm making food.

- A 여기에서 뭐 해요? What are you doing here?

  B 친구를 기다려요. I'm waiting for my friend.

- A 지금 어디에 가요? Where are you going now?

  B 지금 공원에 가요. I'm going to the park now.

3 When expressing states or features

The -아/어요 form is used to describe the state or feature of the subject. Adjectives in this context always require a subject and are used with the subject particle 이/가.

- 음식이 맛있어요. The food is delicious.

- 음악이 아름다워요. The music is beautiful.

In Korean, adjectives serve to modify nouns or describe the state of the subject. Unlike in English, when describing the subject's state with an adjective, the verb 이다 (to be) is not required.

- 날씨가 좋아요. (O) The weather is nice.

  날씨가 좋은이에요. (✕) → 좋은 날씨예요. (O) It is nice weather.

When asking about the state or feature of the subject, use 어때요 along with the subject particle 이/가.

- A 한국어 공부가 어때요? How is studying Korean?

  B 재미있어요. It's fun.

When inquiring about the state or feature of the subject, use 누가 (who) for people and 뭐가 (what) (= 무엇이) in formal speech for objects.

- A 누가 아파요? Who is sick?

  B 동생이 아파요. My younger sibling is sick.

- A 뭐가 비싸요? What is expensive?

  B 가방이 비싸요. The bag is expensive.

Adjectives made from a phrase

In Korean, there are not only single-word adjectives but also adjectives made from phrases (e.g., 관심이 있다 (to be interested), 키가 크다 (to be tall)). These adjectives require a subject, so the subject particle 이/가 is used. To avoid repetitive use of the particle 이/가, the particle 은/는 can be used instead.

- 라이언 씨가 키가 커요. 그런데 캐리 씨가 키가 작아요.

  = 라이언 씨는 키가 커요. 그런데 캐리 씨는 키가 작아요.
  Ryan is tall, but Carrie is short.

- 동생이 이 노래에 관심이 많아요. 그런데 제가 이 노래에 관심이 없어요.

  = 동생은 이 노래에 관심이 많아요. 그런데 저는 이 노래에 관심이 없어요.
  My sister is very interested in this song, but I am not interested in it.

Quiz 07

Lesson 07

Informal polite present tense -아/어요

TOPIK I | SCK 1

Informal polite past tense -았/었어요

Kor. 08

username
Address

#친구하고식사 #커피

어제 날씨가 정말 좋았어요.
The weather was really nice yesterday.

친구를 만났어요.
I met a friend.

친구하고 점심을 먹었어요.
커피도 마셨어요.
We had lunch together and also drank coffee.

username
Address

#공원

그다음에 공원에 갔어요.
Then we went to the park.

친구하고 많이 얘기했어요.
Talked a lot with my friend.

정말 재미있었어요.
It was really fun.

245 likes
username Lorem ipsum dolor sit amet

rem ipsum dolor sit amet

Grammar Essentials

1 Informal polite past tense -았/었어요

-았/었어요 is the informal polite past tense ending for verbs and adjectives in Korean, formed by adding -았/었- to the verb or adjective stem. The specific form, -았어요, -었어요, or -했어요, is determined by the last syllable of the stem:

- If the stem is 하다, 하 combines with -였어요 to form 했어요.
- If the last syllable of the stem contains the vowel ㅏ or ㅗ, the stem combines with -았어요.
- If the stem does not contain 하다 and the last syllable does not contain ㅏ or ㅗ, the stem combines with -었어요.

	-했어요 (하 + -였어요)	-았어요	-었어요
Verbs	공부하다 → 공부했어요	가다 → 가았어요 → 갔어요	먹다 → 먹었어요
	식사하다 → 식사했어요	보다 → 봤어요	마시다 → 마시었어요 → 마셨어요
	운동하다 → 운동했어요	만나다 → 만났어요	주다 → 줬어요
	일하다 → 일했어요	놀다 → 놀았어요	만들다 → 만들었어요
	시작하다 → 시작했어요	찾다 → 찾았어요	쓰다 → 썼어요
Adjectives	유명하다 → 유명했어요	싸다 → 쌌어요	멀다 → 멀었어요
	피곤하다 → 피곤했어요	낮다 → 낮았어요.	느리다 → 느렸어요
	필요하다 → 필요했어요	좋다 → 좋았어요	젊다 → 젊었어요
	깨끗하다 → 깨끗했어요	높다 → 높았어요	쉽다 → 쉬웠어요
	따뜻하다 → 따뜻했어요	아프다 → 아팠어요	예쁘다 → 예뻤어요

- 지난 주말에 친구를 만났어요. I met a friend last weekend.
- 제 친구가 방금 도착했어요. My friend has just arrived.
- 어제 시험이 쉬웠어요. Yesterday's test was easy.
- 저는 어렸을 때부터 키가 컸어요. I have been tall since I was young.

2 Informal polite past tense of "Noun + 이다"

The informal polite past tense of "noun + 이다 (to be)" in Korean is formed by adding -였어요 when the noun ends in a vowel and -이었어요 when it ends in a consonant.

	Vowel-ending nouns	Consonant-ending nouns
Present	제 친구가 지금 변호사예요. My friend is a lawyer now.	저는 지금 대학생이에요. I am a college student now.
Past	제 친구가 1년 전에 변호사였어요. My friend was a lawyer a year ago.	저는 10년 전에 대학생이었어요. I was a college student ten years ago.

1 When expressing past actions or events

-았/었어요 is used in combination with the verb stem to express actions or events that occurred in the past.

- 어제 친구가 30분 동안 저를 기다렸어요. My friend waited for me for 30 minutes yesterday.

- 지난번 회의가 너무 늦게 끝났어요. The last meeting ended too late.

To ask about past actions or events, use "뭐 했어요 (What did you do)."

- A 제주도에서 뭐 했어요? What did you do in Jeju Island?

  B 바다를 봤어요. I saw the sea.

  A 또 뭐 했어요? What else did you do?

  B 해산물도 먹었어요. I also ate seafood.

2 When expressing past states or features

-았/었어요 is used in combination with the adjective stem to express states or features in the past.

- 어제 날씨가 좋았어요. The weather was nice yesterday.

- 옛날 영화가 정말 무서웠어요. Old movies were really scary.

To ask about past states or features, use "어땠어요 (How was it)."

- A 여행이 어땠어요? How was the trip?

  B 여행이 진짜 재미있었어요. The trip was really fun.

- A 어제 축제가 어땠어요? How was the festival yesterday?

  B 불꽃놀이가 멋있었어요. The fireworks were amazing.

When asking about the subject of past states or features, use 누가 (who) for people and 뭐가 (what) for objects.

- A 어제 누가 멋었어요? Who was cool yesterday?

  B 어제 윤아가 진짜 멋있었어요. Yuna was really cool yesterday.

- A 시험에서 뭐가 어려웠어요? What was difficult on the exam?

  B 한국어 발음이 어려웠어요. The Korean pronunciation was difficult.

3 When expressing a completed action or state

-았/었- indicates that an action or state has been completed in the past.

- 조금 전에 교통사고가 났어요. A traffic accident just happened.

- 갑자기 전화가 와서 깜짝 놀랐어요. I was surprised when I suddenly received a phone call.

Compare the usage of -아/어요 and -았/었어요.

- 보통 친구가 약속에 늦으면 화가 나요. I usually get angry when a friend is late for an appointment.

- 지금 부장님이 화가 났어요. 왜 이렇게 늦었어요? The manager is angry now. Why are you so late?

4 When expressing actions or states continuing from the past

-았/었어요 is used in combination with the adjective stem to express states or feature in the past.

- 저는 3년 전에 결혼했어요. I got married 3 years ago.

- 2년 동안 한국어를 배웠어요. I have been learning Korean for 2 years.

- 3일 전부터 아팠어요. I have been sick since 3 days ago.

To describe the current clothing someone is wearing, -았/었어요 is used to show that the action of putting on the clothes was completed in the past and the state of being dressed continues.

- 지금 윤아 씨가 운동화를 신었어요. Yuna is now wearing sneakers.

- 민수 씨가 오늘 청바지를 입었어요. Minsu is wearing jeans today.

5 When expressing discontinuation from a past state

Using -았/었- repetitively to form -었었- indicates a discontinuation from a past state.

- 10년 전에 결혼했어요. The state of being married continues
  I got married 10 years ago.

- 10년 전에 결혼했었어요. Divorced as a discontinuation from the state of being married
  I had been married 10 years ago.

When verbs 가다/오다 (to go/come) are combined with -었었-, it signifies that the completed action or state is disconnected, having no impact on the present.

- 동생한테서 전화 왔어. Currently waiting for a call from the sibling
  I received a call from my younger sibling.

- 동생한테서 전화 왔었어. Received a call earlier but have already hung up
  I had received a call from my younger sibling.

- 누가 찾아왔어. Someone has come and is currently waiting
  Someone came to visit.

- 누가 찾아왔었어. Someone had visited but has already left
  Someone had come to visit.

Quiz 08

Informal polite
future tense -(으)ㄹ 거예요

Kor. 09

내일부터 이번 주 일요일까지 제주도를 여행할 거예요.
I will be traveling to Jeju Island from tomorrow until this Sunday.

내일 바다에 갈 거예요. 바다가 정말 예쁠 거예요.
I will go to the sea tomorrow. The sea will be really beautiful.

그다음 날에 한라산을 등산할 거예요.
The next day, I will climb Mount Halla.

등산이 재미있을 거예요.
The climb will be enjoyable.

Grammar Essentials

1 Informal polite future tense -(으)ㄹ 거예요

-(으)ㄹ 거예요 is commonly used in informal polite speech to indicate future intentions, plans, assumptions, or speculations based on the speaker's belief or certainty.

- 내년에 대학교를 졸업할 거예요. I will graduate from university next year.
- 다음 주에 한복을 입을 거예요? Will you wear a hanbok next week?
- 내일 축구 경기를 할 거예요. I am going to play a soccer game tomorrow.
- 그 사람은 꼭 돌아올 거예요. He will definitely come back.
- 아마 내일 날씨가 좋을 거예요. The weather will probably be nice tomorrow.

The informal polite future tense -(으)ㄹ 거예요 can be combined with the stems of verbs, adjectives, or "noun + 이다". For verbs and adjectives, -ㄹ 거예요 is added if the stem ends in a vowel, while -을 거예요 is added if the stem ends in a consonant.

- 다음 주에 고향에 돌아갈 거예요. I'm going back to my hometown next week.
- 내일 책을 읽을 거예요. I will read a book tomorrow.
- 아마 저 가게가 더 비쌀 거예요. That store will probably be more expensive.
- 저 가수가 한국에서 인기가 많을 거예요. That singer will be popular in Korea.

For "noun + 이다", add 일 거예요 regardless of whether the noun ends in a vowel or consonant. This grammatical pattern is used to express predictions or assumptions about the identity or state of the subject.

- 저 사람이 아마 진수 씨 친구일 거예요. That person is probably Jinsu's friend.
- 저분이 아마 사장님일 거예요. That person will probably be the boss.

2 Conjugation

-(으)ㄹ 거예요					
보다	볼 거예요	부르다	부를 거예요	돕다	*도울 거예요
읽다	읽을 거예요	듣다	*들을 거예요	낫다	*나을 거예요
쓰다	쓸 거예요	살다	*살 거예요	그렇다	*그럴 거예요

1 When expressing future plans or scheduled events

-(으)ㄹ 거예요 is used with future time expressions, such as 내일 (tomorrow), 이따가 (later), and 나중에 (afterward), to express plans or scheduled events.

- 내일 부동산에서 집을 구할 거예요. I am going to find a house at the real estate agency tomorrow.

- 3년 후에 고향에 돌아갈 거예요. I will return to my hometown in 3 years.

To ask about plans or schedules, use "뭐 할 거예요" or "어떻게 할 거예요." "뭐 할 거예요" is for asking about plans, while "어떻게 할 거예요" is for asking about solutions in a given situation.

- A 수업 후에 뭐 할 거예요?   Asking about plans
    What are you going to do after class?

  B 점심을 먹을 거예요. I'm going to have lunch.

- A 회사를 그만뒀어요. 앞으로 어떻게 할 거예요?   Asking about solutions
    I quit my job. What are you going to do now?

  B 다른 일자리를 찾을 거예요. I will look for another job.

In Korean, the near future can sometimes be expressed using the present tense.

- 내일 여행 갈 거예요. = 내일 여행 가요.   Near future
  I'm going on a trip tomorrow.

- 10년 후에 회사를 그만둘 거예요.   Distant future
  I will quit my job in 10 years.

2 When expressing the speaker's will

-(으)ㄹ 거예요 can also express the speaker's will or strong belief. It can be emphasized with adverbs like 꼭 (definitely) or 반드시 (certainly).

- 요즘 몸이 안 좋아요. 내일부터 꼭 운동할 거예요.
  I've been feeling unwell lately. I will definitely start exercising from tomorrow.

- 친구가 약속을 지킬 거예요. My friend will keep his promise.

- 저는 신을 믿어요. 신이 반드시 있을 거예요. I believe in God. God will definitely exist.

3 When expressing vague speculation about present events or states

-(으)ㄹ 거예요 is used to indicate the speaker's vague speculation about present events or states. It can be emphasized with the adverb 아마 (probably). This form can be used with verbs, adjectives, and "noun + 이다".

- 아마 제 친구가 저를 찾을 거예요. My friend will probably look for me.
- 아마 다음 주에 일이 바쁠 거예요. Work will probably be busy next week.
- 이 가방이 아마 진수 씨 가방일 거예요. This bag is probably Jinsu's.

To ask about someone's vague speculation, use 혹시 with -(으)ㄹ까. For responses, use 아마 with -(으)ㄹ 거예요.

- A 혹시 내일 비가 올까요? Might it rain tomorrow?

  B 네, 아마 내일 비가 올 거예요. Yes, it probably will rain tomorrow.

- A 혹시 지금 공원에 사람이 많을까요? Are there many people in the park now?

  B 아니요, 아마 지금 사람이 없을 거예요. No, there probably won't be any people now.

4 When expressing vague speculation about past events or states

The structure -았/었을 거예요 indicates the speaker's vague speculation about a completed past event or state. This usage is often accompanied by time expressions such as 어제 (yesterday), 지난주 (last week), or 벌써 (already) to emphasize that the event or state has already happened.

- 진수 씨가 지난주에 혼자 일했어요. 아마 힘들었을 거예요.
  Jinsu worked alone last week. It must have been hard.

You can observe the difference between current speculation and past speculation as follows:

- 제주도는 지금 아마 비가 많이 올 거예요.   Current speculation
  Jeju Island is probably getting a lot of rain now.

- 제주도는 지난주에 아마 비가 많이 왔을 거예요.   Past speculation
  Jeju Island probably got a lot of rain last week.

When forming questions to express vague speculation about a completed past event or state, the structure -았/었을까 is used.

- A 택시를 못 탔어요. 만약 택시를 타도 늦었을까요?
  I couldn't catch a taxi. Would I have been late even if I had caught one?

  B 네, 택시를 타도 이미 늦었을 거예요.
  Yes, you would have been late even if you had caught a taxi.

Quiz 09

57

Kor. 10

토요일에 on Saturday

집에서 at home

진수 씨가 Jinsu

음식을 food

만들어요. makes

토요일에 집에서 진수 씨가 음식을 만들어요.
Jinsu makes food at home on Saturday.

Grammar Essentials

1 Meaning and function of particles

In Korean, particles (also known as markers) are attached after nouns to indicate their function (such as subject, object, etc.) in relation to the predicate (e.g., a verb). Unlike in English, the order of words in Korean sentences is flexible due to the role of particles, as long as the predicate is at the end of the sentence. These particles clearly denote the function within the sentence (subject, object, adverb, etc.).

- 진수가 책만 읽어요. = 책만 진수가 읽어요. Jinsu reads only books.

- 동생은 금요일에 식당에서 친구를 만났어요. = 식당에서 금요일에 동생은 친구를 만났어요.
  The younger sibling met a friend at the restaurant on Friday.

In Korean, since particles indicate the function of the words in the sentence, the word order in interrogative sentences is the same as that in declarative sentences.

- A 금요일에 수업이 있어요? Is there a class on Friday?

  B 네, 금요일에 수업이 있어요. Yes, there is a class on Friday.

- A 어제 무엇을 먹었어요? What did you eat yesterday?

  B 어제 비빔밥을 먹었어요. I ate bibimbap yesterday.

- A 민수 씨가 어디에 있어요? Where is Minsu?

  B 민수 씨가 헬스장에 있어요. Minsu is at the gym.

2 Case particles: indicating essential functions in a sentence

Case particles (also known as case markers) follow nouns to indicate their crucial roles within a sentence, such as subject, object, complement, or adverb.

1 Subject particle 이/가

The particle 이/가 indicates the subject of a sentence. 가 is used if the preceding noun ends in a vowel, and 이 is used if it ends in a consonant.

- 친구가 미국 사람이에요. The friend is American.

- 한국 음식이 매워요. Korean food is spicy.

2 Object particle 을/를

The particle 을/를 indicates the object of a sentence. 를 is used if the preceding noun ends in a vowel, and 을 is used if it ends in a consonant. In spoken language, 을/를 can be omitted.

- 제가 영화를 좋아해요. I like movies.

- 남동생이 음악(을) 들어요. The younger brother listens to music.

3 Complement particle 이/가

The particle 이/가 is used before 되다, 아니다 to indicate the complement of a sentence. You can use both the subject particle 이/가 and the complement particle 이/가 in one sentence. To avoid repetition of 이/가, the particle 은/는 can be used after the subject instead of the subject particle 이/가.

- 이 시계가 제 시계가 아니에요. = 이 시계는 제 시계가 아니에요. This watch is not mine.

- 여동생이 대학생이 되었어요. = 동생은 대학생이 되었어요.
  The younger sister has become a university student.

4 Possessive particle 의

The particle 의 is used to show possession or a relationship between two nouns. It connects the possessor to the object being possessed. 의 can be used regardless of whether the preceding noun ends in a consonant or vowel. It is pronounced as [에] in speech and can often be omitted in casual conversation.

- 친구(의) 딸이 5살이에요. The friend's daughter is 5 years old.

- 저 사람이 동생의 친구예요. = 저 사람이 동생 친구예요. That person is the younger sibling's friend.

▶ **When 의 must not be omitted**

The particle 의 cannot be omitted when it is needed to clarify the relationship between the owner and the possessed object/relationship, especially when modifiers are involved. Omitting 의 in these cases makes the sentence unclear or incorrect.

- 친절한 직원 이름이 뭐예요? (✕) → 친절한 직원의 이름이 뭐예요? (〇)
  What is the name of the kind employee?

- 친구 빨간색 자동차가 멋있어요. (✕) → 친구의 빨간색 자동차가 멋있어요. (〇)
  My friend's red car is cool.

- 친절한 직원 새로운 역할이 뭐예요? (✕) → 친절한 직원의 새로운 역할이 뭐예요? (〇)
  What is the new role of the kind employee?

▶ **When 의 should be omitted**

In Korean, when the possessive particle 의 appears multiple times in the same sentence, you can omit the middle 의 to make the sentence simpler and more natural. However, the last 의 must always be kept to clearly show the ownership or relationship.

- [유나 씨의 가방]의 주머니에 핸드폰이 있어요. There is a cell phone in the pocket of Yuna's bag.

- 저는 [동생의 친구]의 이름을 몰라요. I do not know the name of my younger sibling's friend.

- 저는 아시아에서 [한국의 대중문화]의 [영향의 결과]에 대해 공부하고 있어요.
  I am studying the results of the influence of Korean pop culture.

3 Adverbial particles

Particle 하고

The particle 하고 is used regardless of whether the preceding noun ends in a vowel or a consonant.

1 Particle indicating "doing together"

The particle 하고 is used after a noun to signify that the preceding noun is involved in an activity or action together with someone or something.

- 진수는 친구하고 같이 여행 가요. Jinsu is going on a trip with my friend.

- 저는 항상 음악하고 함께 공부해요. I always study together with music.

2 Particle indicating "comparisons or counterparts in actions"

The particle 하고 is also used after a noun to indicate comparisons or the counterpart involved in an action.

- 제가 어머니하고 닮았어요. I resemble my mother.

- 한국 문화가 미국 문화하고 너무 달라요. Korean culture is very different from American culture.

- 어제 친구하고 싸웠어요. I fought with a friend yesterday.

Particles 한테 and 한테서

1 Particle 한테

The particle 한테 is used to indicate giving an object to or performing an action towards a particular target. It is attached after a noun regardless of whether the preceding noun ends in a vowel or a consonant.

- 저는 친구한테 이메일을 썼어요. I wrote an email to my friend.

- 어머니가 딸한테 선물을 줬어요. The mother gave a gift to her daughter.

2 Particle 한테서

The particle 한테서 indicates receiving an object from or being the recipient of an action from a particular source. In spoken language, 서 can be omitted, making it 한테. Therefore, 한테 must be interpreted based on the context of the sentence.

- 제가 친구한테서 책을 받았어요. I received a book from my friend.

  = 제가 친구한테 책을 받았어요.

- 친구가 가족한테서 전화를 받았어요. The friend received a call from their family.

  = 친구가 가족한테 전화를 받았어요.

Particle 에

1 Particle indicating time

The particle 에 is used after expressions of time, to indicate the time.

• 저는 2007년 3월 29일에 태어났어요. I was born on March 29, 2007.

The time particle 에 can only be used once in a sentence.

• 이번 주에 금요일에 7시에 만나요! Let's meet on Friday this week at 7 o'clock!

2 Particle for the destination of motion verbs

The particle 에 is used with motion verbs such as 가다 (to go), 오다 (to come), and 다니다 (to attend) to indicate the destination of the action. It specifies where the subject is heading.

• 오늘 늦게 학교에 가요. I am going to school late today.

• 올해 한국에 왔어요. I came to Korea this year.

3 Particle for place

The particle 에 is used after nouns indicating place to specify where the subject of verbs like 있다 (to be) or 없다 (to not be), or where a state is with a verb or adjective.

• 식당이 2층에 있어요. The restaurant is on the second floor.

• 교실에 선생님이 없어요. There is no teacher in the classroom.

4 Particle indicating unit or range

The particle 에 is used after nouns indicating time or quantity to express a unit or range.

• 일주일에 한 번 영화를 봐요. I watch a movie once a week.

• 사과가 10개에 만 원이에요. It is 10,000 won for 10 apples.

Particle 에서

1 Particle for location

The particle 에서 is used after nouns indicating a place that specifies where an action takes place. It is used with action verbs.

• 저는 집에서 음식을 만들어요. I cook food at home.

• 친구가 학교에서 한국어를 공부해요. My friend studies Korean at school.

2 Particle for point of departure or starting point

The particle 에서 is used after nouns indicating a place to denote the point of departure or starting point.

• 서울에서 부산까지 5시간 걸려요. It takes 5 hours from Seoul to Busan.

• 저는 미국에서 왔어요. I came from the United States.

3 Particle for source

The particle 에서 is used after a noun to indicate the source.

- 이 정보를 인터넷에서 찾았어요. I found this information on the internet.

- 그 얘기를 뉴스에서 들었어요. I heard that story from the news.

4 Particle for range or limitation

The particle 에서 is used after a noun to express range or limitation.

- 제 친구들 중에서 진수가 제일 바빠요. Among my friends, Jinsu is the busiest.

- 세계에서 러시아가 땅이 제일 커요. Russia has the largest land area in the world.

Particle (으)로

The particle (으)로 is used after preceding nouns ending in a vowel or the consonant ㄹ as 로, and with preceding nouns ending in a consonant (other than ㄹ) as 으로.

1 Particle for the direction of movement

The particle (으)로 is used after nouns with motion verbs to indicate place, direction, or direction of movement.

- 위로 올라오세요. Come up.

- 편의점에서 오른쪽으로 가세요. Go right from the convenience store.

2 Particle for direction of change

The particle (으)로 is used after nouns to indicate the direction of change, specifying the result or state that the subject transitions into.

- 파란색 모자를 빨간색 모자로 바꿔 주세요. Change the blue hat to a red hat.

- 어제 달러를 원으로 환전했어요. I exchanged dollars for won yesterday.

3 Particle for the path of movement

The particle (으)로 is used after nouns to indicate a path or route of movement.

- 바다에 갈 때 이 터널로 가세요. Go through this tunnel when going to the sea.

- 고양이가 이 구멍으로 나갔어요. The cat went out through this hole.

4 Particle for means or methods

The particle (으)로 is used after nouns to denote means or methods used to perform an action.

- 지하철로 회사에 가요. I go to work by subway.

- 한국 사람들은 빨간색으로 이름을 쓰지 않아요. Koreans do not write names in red.

5 Particle for reasons

The particle (으)로 is used after nouns to indicate reasons or causes.

- 동료가 교통사고로 다리를 다쳤어요. A coworker injured his leg in a car accident.

- 아직도 사람들이 암으로 고생해요. People still suffer from cancer.

6 Particle for materials or ingredients

The particle (으)로 is used after nouns to indicate the material or ingredient from which something is made.

- 이 의자가 나무로 만들었어요. This chair is made of wood.

- 이 음식이 간장으로 만들었어요. This dish is made with soy sauce.

7 Particle for status or qualification

The particle (으)로 is used after nouns to indicate a person's qualification, role, or status in a specific context.

- 저는 발표자로 회의에 참석해요. I attend the meeting as a presenter.

- 아버지가 이 대학에서 선생님으로 일해요. My father works at this university as a teacher.

Other particles

1 Particle for comparison 보다

The particle 보다 is used after the object of comparison when comparing two or more subjects.

- 오늘이 어제보다 더 더워요. Today is hotter than yesterday.

- 불고기가 비빔밥보다 더 맛있어요. Bulgogi is tastier than bibimbap.

2 Particle for comparison or as a metaphor 처럼

The particle 처럼 is used when the preceding noun is compared to or metaphorically related to the subject based on similarity.

- 제 친구가 천사처럼 착해요. My friend is as kind as an angel.

- 저는 요리 프로그램처럼 만들 수 없어요. I can't cook like they do on cooking shows.

3 Particle for degree 만큼

The particle 만큼 indicates that the subject is of a similar degree to the preceding noun.

- 제 친구는 가수만큼 노래를 잘해요. My friend sings as well as a singer.

- 빵이 얼굴만큼 커요. The bread is as big as a face.

4 Special particles: markers that add special meaning

Some particles do not specify the function such as subject, object, or adverb within a sentence, but they add special meanings. These particles can be combined with subjects, objects, and adverbs in various ways within a sentence.

Particle 은/는

The particle 은/는 attached to a noun; using 는 after a vowel-ending noun and 은 after a consonant-ending noun.

1 Topic particle

The particle 은/는 is used after a noun to highlight the topic of discussion, acting similarly to pointing out a specific subject within the conversation.

- 안녕하세요. 저는 김진수입니다.   When introducing oneself
  Hello, I am Jinsu Kim.

- 좋아하는 색은 흰색이에요.   When talking about favorite colors
  My favorite color is white.

- 윤아   주말을 어떻게 보냈어? How did you spend your weekend?

  진수   나는 주말에 친구하고 놀았어.   Jinsu talking about himself
  I played with my friend over the weekend.

  너는 주말을 어떻게 보냈어?   Asking the other person
  How did you spend your weekend?

  윤아   나는 집에서 쉬었어.   Yuna talking about herself
  I rested at home.

2 Particle for comparison or contrast

The particle 은/는 can be used to set apart or to emphasize the object of comparison or contrast.

- 동생은 매운 음식을 좋아해요. 그런데 저는 매운 음식을 안 좋아해요.
  My younger sibling likes spicy food, but I don't like it.

- 회사에서는 말을 많이 해요. 그런데 집에서는 말을 안 해요. I talk a lot at work, but not at home.

3 Particle for emphasis

The particle 은/는 is used after a noun to emphasize something.

- 제가 과자를 많이 먹어요. 그런데 과일은 많이 안 먹어요. I eat a lot of snacks, but not much fruit.

- 어제 일이 많았어요. 그래서 숙제는 못 했어요.
  I had a lot of work yesterday, so I couldn't do my homework.

Other special particles

1 Particle for addition or inclusion 도

The particle 도 signifies addition or inclusiveness. It is attached after a noun regardless of whether the preceding noun ends in a vowel or a consonant.

- 제가 음악을 좋아해요. 친구도 음악을 좋아해요. I like music, and my friend likes music too.

- 한국에서 젓가락을 사용해요. 일본에서도 젓가락을 사용해요.
  Chopsticks are used in Korea, and also in Japan.

2 Particle for exclusivity or uniqueness 만

The particle 만 emphasizes exclusivity or uniqueness, indicating that the preceding noun applies uniquely to the subject or object mentioned, without including others.

- 저는 소고기하고 닭고기를 좋아해요. 돼지고기만 안 좋아해요. I like beef and chicken, but not pork.

- 이 음식은 서울에 없어요. 부산에만 있어요. This dish is available only in Busan, not in Seoul.

3 Particle for repetition or frequency 마다

The particle 마다 indicates each instance of a recurring event or the frequency of occurrences for a given period, often translating to "every" or "each" in English.

- 버스가 30분마다 있어요. Buses arrive every 30 minutes.

- 요즘 학생마다 핸드폰을 갖고 있어요. Nowadays, every student has a cellphone.

- 사람마다 좋아하는 음식이 달라요. Each person has a different favorite food.

4 Particle for surpassing expectations or alternative (이)나

The particle (이)나 is used to convey surprise by indicating that the amount or degree of something exceeds expectations or to introduce an alternative option that may not be ideal but is acceptable. The particle (이)나 attached to a noun; using 나 after a vowel-ending noun, and 이나 after a consonant-ending noun.

- 혼자 아이스크림을 10개나 먹었어요. I ate as many as ten ice creams by myself.

- 영화 예매 못 했어? 그럼, 우리 저녁이나 먹자! Couldn't book the movie? Then, let's at least have dinner!

5 Particle for exclusivity or limitation with a negative implication 밖에

The particle 밖에 is always used with negative expressions (e.g., 없다, 안, 못) to emphasize that only the preceding noun satisfies the condition. It highlights limitation, insufficiency, or that the number mentioned is small.

- 사람이 1명밖에 없어요. There is only one person.

- 집에서 공원까지 10분밖에 안 걸려요. It takes only 10 minutes from home to the park.

Tip

Combination of case particles and special particles

Special particles add special meanings and cannot be omitted when combined with case particles.

▶ **Combining special particles with subject and object particles**

When special particles combine with the subject particle 이/가 or the object particle 을/를, these case particles are omitted, and only the special particle is used. This simplification emphasizes the role of the special particle in conveying specific nuances or a special meaning conveyed by the special particle in the sentence.

- 음식이 싸요. 그런데 커피(가)는 비싸요. Food is cheap. But coffee is expensive.
- 갈비가 맛있어요. 비빔밥(이)도 맛있어요. Ribs are delicious. Bibimbap is also tasty.
- 친구들이 다 과자를 좋아해요. 그런데 유나 씨(가)만 과자를 안 좋아해요.
  All my friends like snacks. But Yuna alone does not.
- 제가 음악을 좋아해요. 그런데 영화(를)는 안 좋아해요. I like music. But I don't like movies.
- 친구를 만나요. 가족(을)도 만나요. I meet my friend. I also meet my family.
- 녹차를 마셔요. 커피(를)만 안 마셔요. I drink green tea. I only don't drink coffee.

▶ **Combining special particles with other case particles**

When special particles are combined with other case particles (e.g., 에, 에서, (으)로), both the case particle and the special particle are used together. This combination enriches the sentence by adding nuanced meanings or emphasizing specific aspects without altering the basic grammatical structure.

- 아침과 오후에 커피를 마셔요. 그런데 밤에는 커피를 안 마셔요.
  I drink coffee in the morning and afternoon. But I don't drink coffee at night.
- 병원에 가요. 시장에도 가요. I go to the hospital. I also go to the market.
- 좋은 물건이 가게에 없어요. 집에만 있어요. The good stuffs are not in the store. They are only at home.
- 이 빵은 버터로 만들었어요. 초콜릿으로도 만들 수 있어요.
  This bread is made with butter. It can also be made with chocolate.

4 Conjunctive particles for equally connecting nouns:

1 Particle for equal addition 하고

The particle 하고 connects nouns to imply shared activities or characteristics.

- 언니와 동생이 고향에 살아요. My older sister and younger sibling live in our hometown.
- 고향에 가면 저는 가족과 친구를 만나요. Visiting my hometown, I meet both my family and friends.

2 Particle for choices (이)나

The particle (이)나 is used to present options or alternatives among two or more equally listed items, from which only one is chosen.

- 주말에 친구나 가족하고 전화해요. On weekends, I call a friend or family.
- 신청할 때 여권이나 신분증이 필요해요. When applying, either a passport or ID is needed.

Grammar in Action

1 When using particles based on time, places, and person

In Korean, different particles are used to indicate starting points and destinations or endpoints.

	From	To
Time	작년부터 한국어를 배웠어요. I have learned Korean since last year.	이번 주까지 일을 끝내야 해요. I have to finish my work by this week.
Place/ Distance	저는 부산에서 왔어요. I am from Busan.	집에서 회사까지 30분 걸려요. It takes 30 minutes from home to work.
Person	동료한테서 문자가 왔어요. I got a text from a co-worker.	친구가 저한테 비밀을 얘기해요. My friend tells me a secret.

2 When using particles differently by context

In Korean, different particles are used depending on formal/informal situations or written/spoken languages.

	Informal/Spoken	Formal/Written
Recipient	저는 친구한테 전화했어요. I called a friend.	저는 동료에게 전화했습니다. I called a colleague.
Provider	친구한테서 소개받았어요. I was introduced to you by a friend.	동료에게서 소개받았습니다. I was introduced to you by a colleague.

The particle 하고 shares the same meaning as 와/과 and (이)랑 but is used in different contexts. 하고 is widely used in informal speech, 와/과 is used in formal contexts, and (이)랑 is used in casual speech.

	Vowel-ending noun	Consonant-ending noun
The particle 하고 Informal/Spoken	김치하고 밥을 먹어요. I eat kimchi and rice.	밥하고 김치를 먹어요. I eat rice and kimchi.
The particle 와/과 Formal/Written	서류와 펜을 준비했습니다. I prepared a document and a pen.	펜과 서류를 준비했습니다. I prepared a pen and a document.
The particle (이)랑 Casual	친구랑 동생이 집에 왔어. My friend and brother came home.	동생이랑 친구가 집에 왔어. My brother and friend came home.

3 When using particles for honorific vs. non-honorific contexts

In Korean, different particles are used depending on whether the noun before them is being honored (honorific) or not (non-honorific).

- When the subject is elevated, the subject particle 이/가 changes to the honorific particle 께서.
- When the recipient is elevated, the particle 에게 changes to the honorific particle 께.
- When the provider is elevated, the particle 에게서 changes to the honorific particle 께.

	Non-honorific	Honorific
Subject	동생이 집에 있어요. My sister is at home.	할머니께서 집에 계세요. My grandmother is at home.
Recipient	제가 친구에게 선물을 줬어요. I gave a gift to my friend.	제가 부모님께 선물을 드렸어요. I gave a gift to my parents.
Provider	동생한테서 소개를 받았어요. I was introduced by my brother.	사장님께 소개받았어요. I was introduced by my boss.

4 When using particles for animate vs. non-animated nouns

In Korean, different particles are used depending on whether it is animated or non-animated.

	Animated (Living beings such as people and animals)	Non-Animated (Non-Living)
Subject	제가 경기를 우승했어요. I won at the match.	우리 학교에서 경기를 우승했어요. My school won the match.
Recipient	제가 친구한테 전화했어요. I made a call to my friend.	제가 사무실에 전화했어요. I made a call to my office.
Provider	동료한테서 문자가 왔어요. I got a text from a colleague.	회사에서 문자가 왔어요. I got a text from work.

Quiz 10

Lesson

11

TOPIK I | SCK 1

Question words

Kor. 11

A 한국 문화 중에서 뭐 좋아해요? What do you like about Korean culture?

B 저는 K-Pop을 진짜 좋아해요. I really like K-Pop.

Grammar Essentials

1 Yes/No questions and WH-questions

Unlike in English, the word order of interrogative sentences in Korean remains the same as in declarative sentences. In Yes/No questions, the sentence structure does not change from a statement, but the intonation does. In statements, the intonation falls at the end, whereas in questions, it rises. The affirmative response is 네 (Yes), and the negative response is 아니요 (No).

- A 대니 씨가 한국 음식을 좋아해요? Does Danny like Korean food?

  B 네, 대니 씨가 한국 음식을 좋아해요. Yes, Danny likes Korean food.

- A 윤아 씨가 고기를 좋아해요? Does Yuna like meat?

  B 아니요, 윤아 씨가 채소를 좋아해요. No, Yuna likes vegetables.

- A 운동선수예요? Are you an athlete?

  B 아니요, 운동선수가 아니에요. No, I'm not an athlete.

  선생님이에요. I'm a teacher.

In WH-questions, question words are used, but the word order remains the same as in declarative sentences. Like Yes/No questions, the intonation falls at the end for statements and rises for questions. Depending on the context, a marker may or may not be attached to the question word.

- A 언제 회의가 끝나요? When does the meeting end?

  B 1시간 후에 회의가 끝나요. The meeting ends in an hour.

- A 지금 어디에 가요? Where are you going now?

  B 지금 공원에 가요. I am going to the park now.

- A 어떻게 회사에 가요? How do you get to work?

  B 지하철로 회사에 가요. I go to work by subway.

2 Question words

In Korean, as long as the predicate is at the end of the sentence, word order is flexible because particles indicate the function of each word within the sentence. Question words also take particles depending on whether the question refers to the subject or object, a person or a thing.

1 Asking about a person

누가	A 누가 한국 음식을 만들었어요? Who made Korean food? B 진수가 한국 음식을 만들었어요. Jinsu made Korean food.
누구를	A 어제 누구를 만났어요? Who did you meet yesterday? B 어제 사촌을 만났어요. I met my cousin yesterday.
누구한테	A 누구한테 이메일을 보냈어요? Who did you send the email to? B 동료한테 이메일을 보냈어요. I sent the email to a colleague.
누구한테서	A 누구한테서 얘기를 들었어요? Who did you hear this from? B 친구한테서 얘기를 들었어요. I heard it from a friend.
누구하고	A 누구하고 여행 갔어요? Who did you go on a trip with? B 친구하고 여행 갔어요. I went on a trip with a friend.
누구예요?	A 이분이 누구예요? Who is this person? B 제 친구예요. This is my friend.
누구 거	A 이게 누구(의) 거예요? Whose is this? B 친구 거예요. It's my friend's.

2 Asking about non-person subjects

뭐가 / 무엇이	A 한국어 공부에서 뭐가 어려워요? What's difficult about studying Korean? B 발음이 어려워요. The pronunciation is difficult.
뭐 / 무엇을	A 뭐 좋아해요? What do you like? B 코미디 영화를 좋아해요. I like comedy movies.
뭐/무엇에	A 무엇에 관심이 있어요? What are you interested in? B 한국 문화에 관심이 있어요. I'm interested in Korean culture.
무엇으로	A 무엇으로 이 음식을 만들어요? What is this food made with? B 닭고기로 이 음식을 만들어요. This food is made with chicken.
뭐하고	A 파전이 뭐하고 잘 맞아요? What pairs well with pajeon? B 파전이 막걸리하고 잘 맞아요. Pajeon pairs well with makgeolli (Korean rice wine).
뭐예요?	A 이게 뭐예요? What is this? B 한국 역사에 대한 책이에요. It's a book about Korean history.

3 Asking about places, destinations, or origins

어디가	A 어디가 아파요? Where does it hurt? B 허리가 아파요. My back hurts.
어디에 (with motion verbs 가다/오다)	A 지금 어디에 가요? Where are you going now? B 지금 회사에 가요. I'm going to the office now.
어디에 (with state verbs 있다/없다)	A 화장실이 어디에 있어요? Where is the bathroom? B 화장실이 2층에 있어요. The bathroom is on the second floor.
어디에서 (with action verbs)	A 어디에서 일해요? Where do you work? B 강남에서 일해요. I work in Gangnam.
어디에서 (with the verb 오다)	A 어디에서 왔어요? Where are you coming from? B 부산에서 왔어요. I'm from Busan.
어디를	A 어디를 구경했어요? Where did you visit? B 명동을 구경했어요. I visited Myeongdong.
어디부터	A 어디부터 공원이 시작해요? Where does the park start? B 여기부터 공원이 시작해요. The park starts from here.
어디예요?	A 여기가 어디예요? Where is this place? B 여기가 제 사무실이에요. This is my office.

4 Asking about time

언제	A 언제 한국어 공부를 시작했어요? When did you start studying Korean? B 작년에 한국어 공부를 시작했어요. I started studying Korean last year.
언제가	A 언제가 좋아요? When is good for you? B 금요일이 좋아요? Friday is good for me.
언제를	A 여행으로 언제를 생각하고 있어요? When are you considering for the trip? B 6월을 생각하고 있어요. I'm considering June.
언제부터	A 언제부터 배가 아팠어요? Since when have you had a stomach ache? B 어제부터 배가 아팠어요. I have had a stomach ache since yesterday.
언제까지	A 언제까지 일을 끝내야 해요? By when do you need to finish the work? B 내일까지 일을 끝내야 해요. I need to finish the work by tomorrow.
언제예요?	A 생일이 언제예요? When is your birthday? B 3월 29일이에요. It's on March 29th.

5 Asking about specific times

몇 년	A 이 집이 몇 년에 만들어졌어요? Which year was this house built? B 이 집이 2020년에 만들어졌어요. This house was built in 2020.
몇 월	A 학기가 몇 월에 시작해요? Which month does the semester start? B 학기가 3월에 시작해요. The semester starts in March.
며칠	A 오늘이 며칠이에요? Which day is the date today? B 9월 21일이에요. It's September 21st.
몇 시	A 회의가 몇 시에 끝나요? What time does the meeting end? B 회의가 3시에 끝나요. The meeting ends at 3 o'clock.
몇 시간	A 보통 몇 시간 운동해요? How many hours do you usually exercise? B 보통 1시간 운동해요. I usually exercise for an hour.
몇 분	A 집에서 지하철역까지 걸어서 몇 분 걸려요? How many minutes does it take to walk from home to the subway station? B 걸어서 10분 걸려요. It takes 10 minutes on foot.

6 Others

왜	A 왜 집에 일찍 가요? Why are you going home early? B 피곤해서 집에 일찍 가요. I'm going home early because I'm tired. A 왜 피곤해요? Why are you tired? B 잠을 못 자서 피곤해요. I'm tired because I couldn't sleep.
어떻게	A 어떻게 집에 가요? How do you get home? B 지하철로 집에 가요. I get home by subway. A 어떻게 그 사실을 알았어요? How did you find out about that fact? B 뉴스를 통해 그 사실을 알았어요. I found out about it through the news.
얼마	A 책이 얼마예요? How much is the book? B 책이 2만원이에요. The book is 20,000 won. A 침대를 얼마에 샀어요? How much did you buy the bed for? B 침대를 20만원에 샀어요. I bought the bed for 200,000 won.
얼마 동안	A 얼마 동안 한국어를 공부했어요? How long have you been studying Korean? B 1년 동안 한국어를 공부했어요. I've been studying Korean for a year.
얼마나	A 집에서 회사까지 시간이 얼마나 걸려요? How long does it take from home to work? B 시간이 30분 걸려요. It takes 30 minutes. A 월세가 얼마나 더 비싸요? How much more expensive is the rent? B 월세가 10만원 더 비싸요. The rent is 100,000 won more expensive.
얼마나 자주	A 얼마나 자주 운동해요? How often do you exercise? B 일주일에 3번 운동해요. I exercise three times a week.
어때요	A 한국 생활이 어때요? How is life in Korea? B 한국 생활이 재미있어요. Life in Korea is fun.

Grammar in Action

1 When asking about objects in formal and informal contexts

In Korean, 뭐 is used in informal settings, while 무엇 is used in formal contexts when asking about objects.

Informal	Formal
A 이름이 뭐예요? What's your name? B 제 이름이 김진수예요. My name is Jinsu Kim.	A 이름이 무엇입니까? What is your name? B 제 이름이 김진수입니다. My name is Jinsu Kim.
A 뭐 먹었어요? What did you eat? B 고기를 먹었어요. I ate meat.	A 무엇을 먹었습니까? What did you eat? B 고기를 먹었습니다. I ate meat.

2 When asking with question words that modify nouns

In Korean, the question words 어느, 무슨, and 어떤 are placed before a noun to modify it.

어느	어느 is used when choosing among options.	A 어느 선생님이 한국어 선생님이에요? Which teacher is the Korean teacher? B 오 선생님이 한국어 선생님이에요. Ms. Oh is the Korean teacher.
무슨	무슨 is used when inquiring about the kind or type of a noun.	A 김 선생님이 무슨 선생님이에요? What kind of teacher is Mr. Kim? B 김 선생님이 역사 선생님이에요. Mr. Kim is a history teacher.
어떤	어떤 is used when asking about the characteristics or properties of a noun.	A 김 선생님이 어떤 선생님이에요? What kind of teacher is Mr. Kim? B 김 선생님이 친절한 선생님이에요. Mr. Kim is a kind teacher.

3 When using 몇 to ask about numbers and quantities

The word 몇 is placed before a noun to ask about numbers. The way the number is read in the response depends on the context:

- For specific numbers, answers use Sino-Korean numerals.
- For quantity, answers use Native Korean numerals.

몇 What (Asking for a specific number)	몇 How many (Asking for a quantity)
A 번호가 몇 번이에요? What is your number? B 번호가 3(삼) 번이에요. My number is 3.	A 의자가 몇 개 있어요? How many chairs are there? B 의자가 3(세) 개 있어요. There are 3 chairs.
A 사무실이 몇 층에 있어요? On what floor is the office? B 사무실이 5(오) 층에 있어요. The office is on the 5th floor.	A 사람이 몇 명 있어요? How many people are there? B 사람이 5(다섯) 명 있어요. There are 5 people. Quiz 11

Regular and irregular conjugation

Kor. 12

닫다 ➡ 닫아요

식당이 8시에 문을 <u>닫아요</u>.
(닫다)

The restaurant closes at 8 o'clock.

듣다 ➡ 들어요

저는 음악을 자주 <u>들어요</u>.
(듣다)

I often listen to music.

1 Regular conjugation

Korean verbs and adjectives (e.g., 먹다, 좋다) consist of a stem (e.g., 먹-, 좋-) and an ending (-다). However, the infinitive form is not used in speech or writing; instead, verbs and adjectives are always conjugated.

Korean conjugation involves attaching various endings or grammatical patterns to the stem of verbs, adjectives, and the verb 이다 (to be).

Conjugation in Korean is divided into regular and irregular conjugations.

- Regular conjugation applies the same rules consistently without exceptions.
- The rules used in regular conjugation depend on the type of ending being attached to the stem.

Conjugation rules are classified into three types based on the ending or grammatical pattern:

1 Consonant-starting endings or grammatical patterns

When the ending or grammatical pattern starts with a consonant (e.g., -지 않다, -고 싶다, -지만), it attaches to the stem without any changes-regardless of whether the stem ends in a vowel or a consonant.

Stems ending in a vowel		Stems ending in a consonant	
보다	영화를 보지 않아요. I don't watch movies.	먹다	밥을 먹고 싶어요. I want to eat rice.
싸다	옷이 싸지 않아요. The clothes are not cheap.	좋다	날씨가 좋다고 했어요. They said the weather was nice.

2 Endings or grammatical patterns starting with -(으)-

When an ending or grammatical pattern starts with -(으)- (e.g., -으면, -으니까, -을 때):

- If the stem ends in a vowel, -으- is omitted, and the ending is attached directly.
- If the stem ends in a consonant, -으- is added before attaching the ending.

Stems ending in a vowel		Stems ending in a consonant	
보다	영화를 볼 때 When I see a movie	먹다	밥을 먹을 때 When I eat rice
싸다	옷이 싸면 If the clothes are cheap	좋다	날씨가 좋으면 If the weather is good

3 Endings or grammatical patterns starting with -아/어-

When an ending or grammatical pattern starts with -아/어- (e.g., -아서, -아/어요, -았/었어요):

- If the stem ends in 하, it changes to 해.
- If the stem ends in the vowels ㅏ or ㅗ, -아- is attached.
- For all other stems, -어- is attached.

Stems ending in 하		Stems ending in ㅏ or ㅗ		Stems ending in other vowels	
일하다	헬스장에서 일해요. I work at the gym.	보다	영화를 봐요. I watch a movie.	읽다	책을 읽어요. I read a book.
편하다	지하철이 편해요. The subway is convenient.	좋다	날씨가 좋아요. The weather is good.	길다	머리가 길어요. The hair is long.

2 Irregular conjugation

Irregular conjugation occurs when the stem and ending combine differently from regular conjugation under specific conditions. Unlike regular conjugation, certain consonants or vowels in the stem may change or be dropped when combined with endings.

1 ㄷ irregular conjugation

The ㄷ irregular conjugation occurs when a stem ending in ㄷ changes to ㄹ before an ending that starts with a vowel.

	Consonant-starting endings	Vowel-starting endings
듣다	듣 + -고 → 듣고	듣 + -어요 → 들어요
걷다	걷 + -지만 → 걷지만	걷 + -을 거예요 → 걸을 거예요

- 주말에 음악을 듣고 책을 읽어요. On weekends, I listen to music and read books.
- 저는 항상 음악을 들어요. I always listen to music.

2 ㅂ irregular conjugation

The ㅂ irregular conjugation occurs when a stem ending in ㅂ changes to 우 before an ending that starts with a vowel.

	Consonant-starting endings	Vowel-starting endings
춥다	춥 + -고 → 춥고	춥 + -어요 → 추워요
쉽다	쉽 + -지만 → 쉽지만	쉽 + -을 거예요 → 쉬울 거예요.

- 오늘 날씨가 춥고 비가 와요. Today's weather is cold and it's raining.
- 요즘 바람이 많이 불어서 추워요. Recently, it's very windy, so it's cold.

✳ Be careful!

Exception: For 돕다 (to help) and 곱다 (to be beautiful),
ㅂ changes to 오, not 우, before endings starting with -아/어-.
- 돕 + -을 거예요 → 도울 거예요 (O), 도왈 거예요 (✕)
- 곱 + -아요 → 고와요 (O), 고워요 (✕)

3 ㅅ irregular conjugation

The ㅅ irregular conjugation occurs when ㅅ in the stem is dropped before endings that start with a vowel.

	Consonant-starting endings	Vowel-starting endings
붓다	붓 + -고 → 붓고	붓 + -어요 → 부어요
낫다	낫 + -지만 → 낫지만	낫 + -을 거예요 → 나을 거예요

- 감기에 걸렸어요. 목이 붓고 기침이 나요. I caught a cold. My throat is swollen, and I keep coughing.
- 목이 부어서 노래를 부를 수 없어요. My throat is swollen, so I can't sing.

4 르 irregular conjugation

The 르 irregular conjugation occurs when the stem ends in 르, and the 으 is dropped, while an additional ㄹ is added before endings that start with -아/어-.

	Consonant-starting endings	Vowel-starting endings
다르다	다르 + -고 → 다르고	다르 + -아요 → 달라요
부르다	부르 + -지만 → 부르지만	부르 + -어요 → 불러요

- 나라마다 문화가 다르고 언어도 달라요. Every country has a different cultures and languages.

- 보통 혼자 노래를 부르지만 오늘은 친구하고 같이 노래를 불러요.
  Usually I sing alone, but today I sing with a friend.

※ Be careful!

For 르 irregular conjugation, changes depend on whether the following ending starts with -아/어-, regardless of whether it is a vowel-starting ending.

- 모르 + -아요 → 몰라요 (O)
- 모르 + -ㄹ 거예요 → 모를 거예요 (O),
  몰랄 거예요 (✕)

5 ㅎ irregular conjugation

The ㅎ irregular conjugation occurs when the stem ends in ㅎ, and the ㅎ is dropped before endings that start with ㄴ or a vowel. Vowel-starting endings -아/어- change to -애/에-.

	Consonant-starting endings	ㄴ or vowel-starting endings
하얗다	하얗 + -고 → 하얗고	하얗 + -아요 → 하야 + -애요 → 하얘요
그렇다	그렇 + -지만 → 그렇지만	그렇 + -어요 → 그러 + -애요 → 그래요
이렇다	이렇 + -지 → 이렇지	이렇 + -ㄴ → 이러 + -ㄴ → 이런

- 사과가 빨갛고 빛이 나요. The apple is red and shiny.

- 마크 씨가 수줍은 성격 때문에 쉽게 얼굴이 빨개져요.
  Mark easily blushes because of his shy personality.

- 날씨가 좋지 않아요. 그렇지만 운동할 거예요. The weather isn't good. But I will exercise.

- 목소리가 이상하죠? 감기에 걸려서 그래요. My voice is weird, right? It's because I caught a cold.

- 인터넷이 안 되죠? 이런 일이 자주 있어요. The internet isn't working, right? This happens often.

3 Elision

Elision refers to the dropping of certain vowels or consonants in a verb stem before an ending is attached.

1 으 Elision

The 으 elision occurs when a stem ends in 으, and 으 is dropped before an ending that starts with a vowel.

	Consonant-starting endings	Vowel-starting endings
바쁘다	바쁘 + -고 → 바쁘고	바쁘 + -아요 → 바ㅃ + -아요 → 바빠요
예쁘다	예쁘 + -지만 → 예쁘지만	예쁘 + -어요 → 예ㅃ + -어요 → 예뻐요

- 도시 생활은 항상 바쁘고 시간이 없어요. City life is always busy, and there's no time.
- 주중에 시간이 많은데 주말에 바빠요.
  I have a lot of time during the weekdays, but I'm busy on the weekends.
- 구두가 예쁘지만 너무 비싸요. The shoes are pretty but too expensive.
- 경치가 정말 예뻐요. The scenery is really pretty.

2 ㄹ Elision

The ㄹ elision occurs when a stem ends in ㄹ, and ㄹ is dropped before an ending that starts with ㄴ, ㅂ, ㅅ, or another ㄹ.

	Endings not starting with ㄴ, ㅂ, ㅅ, ㄹ	Endings starting with ㄴ, ㅂ, ㅅ, ㄹ
살다	살 + -아요 → 살아요	살 + -니까 → 사 + -니까 → 사니까
알다	알 + -아서 → 알아서	알 + -ㅂ니다 → 아 + -ㅂ니다 → 압니다
만들다	만들 + -고 → 만들고	만들 + -세요 → 만드 + -세요 → 만드세요
놀다	놀 + -지만 → 놀지만	놀 + -ㄹ 거예요 → 노 + -ㄹ 거예요 → 놀 거예요

- 한국에 사니까 한국 문화를 배워야 해요. Since I live in Korea, I should learn about Korean culture.
- 대학교에서 한국어를 전공해서 한국어 문법을 잘 압니다.
  I majored in Korean at university, so I know Korean grammar well.
- 한국 요리책을 보고 한국 음식을 만드세요. Look at a Korean cookbook and make Korean food.
- 시험이 끝났으니까 친구하고 놀 거예요. Since the exams are over, I'm going to play with friends.

> (✳) Be careful!
>
> When a stem ends in ㄹ, the 으 in endings that start with 으 is dropped.
> - 살 + -을 거예요 → 살을 거예요 → 살 거예요
> - 만들 + -을 수 있어요 → 만들을 수 있어요 → 만들 수 있어요

Grammar in Action

1 Regular vs. Irregular conjugation of ㄷ, ㅂ, ㅅ, ㄹ, and ㅎ

Verbs and adjectives ending in ㄷ, ㅂ, ㅅ, ㄹ, and ㅎ can follow either regular or irregular conjugation.

	Regular conjugation	Irregular conjugation
ㄷ	닫다: 닫 + -아요 → 닫아요 받다: 받 + -아요 → 받아요	듣다: 듣 + -어요 → 들어요 걷다: 걷 + -어도 → 걸어요
ㅂ	입다: 입 + -어요 → 입어요 좁다: 좁 + -아요 → 좁아요	춥다: 춥 + -어요 → 추워요 덥다: 덥 + -어요 → 더워요
ㅅ	웃다: 웃 + -어요 → 웃어요 씻다: 씻 + -어요 → 씻어요	붓다: 붓 + -어요 → 부어요 낫다: 낫 + -아요 → 나아요
ㄹ	치르다: 치르 + -어요 → 치러요 따르다: 따르 + -아요 → 따라요	다르다: 다르 + -아요 → 달라요 부르다: 부르 + -아요 → 불러요
ㅎ	좋다: 좋 + -아요 → 좋아요 넣다: 넣 + -어요 → 넣어요	빨갛다: 빨갛 + -아요 → 빨개요 그렇다: 그렇 + -어요 → 그래요

- 스트레스를 <u>받아서</u> 음악을 <u>들어요</u>. I listen to music because I'm stressed.
  (받다)　　　　(듣다)

- 코트를 <u>입었지만</u> 너무 <u>추워요</u>. I wore a coat but it's still too cold.
  (입다)　　　(춥다)

- 많이 <u>웃으니까</u> 병이 <u>나은</u> 것 같아요. It seems my illness healed because I laughed a lot.
  (웃다)　　　　(낫다)

- 선생님을 <u>따라서</u> 한국 노래를 <u>불러요</u>. I follow the teacher and sing Korean songs.
  (따르다)　　　　(부르다)

- 너무 짜요. 소금을 많이 <u>넣어서 그래요</u>. It's too salty. It's because too much salt was added.
  (넣다) (그렇다)

> **Note**
>
> Even if infinitive forms are different, their conjugated forms can be the same. The meaning of the infinitive form depends on the context.
>
> - 저는 가방을 삽니다.　사다　I buy a bag.
>   저는 서울에 삽니다.　살다　I live in Seoul.
>
> - 바닥을 깁니다.　　　기다　I am crawling on the floor.
>   머리가 깁니다.　　　길다　My hair grows long.

Quiz 12

저는 채소를 싫어해요.
그래서 채소를 안 먹어요.

I dislike vegetables.
That's why I don't eat vegetables.

저는 한자를 몰라요.
그래서 한자를 못 읽어요.

I don't know Chinese characters.
That's why I can't read Chinese characters.

Grammar Essentials

In Korean, to express the negation of an action or state, there are two types of negation:

- Short negation 안 or 못
- Long negation -지 않다 or -지 못하다

Generally, short negation (안, 못) is mainly used in colloquial or informal speech, while long negation (-지 않다, -지 못하다) is more common in written language or formal speech.

1 안 and -지 않다

In Korean, two forms of negation are used to express the negation of actions, states, or events:

- Short negation 안 is placed before verbs or adjectives.
- Long negation -지 않다 is attached directly to the verb or adjective stem.

While 안 is placed before verbs and adjectives, -지 않다 is attached directly to the verb or adjective stem, regardless of whether it ends in a vowel or consonant. This applies to both 하다 verbs and 하다 adjectives.

However, in 하다-verbs (e.g., 공부하다, 일하다), 안 is placed before 하다 (e.g., 공부 안 하다, 일 안 하다).

For 하다-adjectives (e.g., 유명하다, 따뜻하다), 안 is placed before the adjective without separating 하다 (e.g., 안 유명하다, 안 따뜻하다).

	Non 하다 verbs and adjectives	하다 verbs and adjectives
Verbs	저는 보통 아침을 안 먹어요. = 저는 보통 아침을 먹지 않아요. I usually don't eat breakfast.	토요일에 일 안 해요. = 토요일에 일하지 않아요. I don't work on Saturdays.
Adjectives	이 음식이 안 매워요. = 이 음식이 맵지 않아요. This food isn't spicy.	지금 안 피곤해요. = 지금 피곤하지 않아요. I'm not tired now.

Be careful!

In Korean, 필요하다 (to be necessary) is an adjective, not a verb. Therefore, when negating 필요하다, 안 must be placed before 필요하다.

- 신분증이 필요해요. An ID card is necessary. = I need an ID card.
  그런데 사진이 안 필요해요. But a photo is not necessary. = But I don't need a photo.

When expressing tense, the negation 안 is placed before verbs or adjectives without changing their form in the present, past, or future tense. On the other hand, -지 않다 is attached directly to the verb or adjective stem, and the tense marker is added afterward.

The conjugation of -지 않다 follows these patterns:

- Present: -지 않아요
- Past: -지 않았어요
- Future/Speculative: -지 않을 거예요

- 날씨가 안 좋아요. 그래서 운동하지 않아요. The weather is not good. So I am not exercising.

- 어제 몸이 안 좋았어요. 그래서 회사에 가지 않았어요.
  I was not feeling well yesterday. So I did not go to the office.

- 그 음식이 안 매울 거예요. 하지만 배가 아파서 아마 그 음식을 먹지 않을 거예요.
  That food will not be spicy. But my stomach hurts, so I probably will not eat that food.

2 Negation with adjectives containing 있다

In Korean, adjectives containing 있다 (e.g., 맛있다, 재미있다) cannot be negated using 안. Instead, they are either changed to adjectives containing 없다 (e.g., 맛없다, 재미없다) or negated with -지 않다.

- 이 음식이 안 맛있어요. (✗)　→　맛없어요. (O) This food is tasteless.

　　　　　　　　　　　　　　　　맛있지 않아요. (O) This food is not tasty.

- 이 영화가 안 재미있어요. (✗)　→　재미없어요. (O) This movie is boring.

　　　　　　　　　　　　　　　　재미있지 않아요. (O) This movie is not fun.

When tense is applied to the negation of adjectives containing 있다, it follows these forms:

- 어제 저녁 식사가 맛없었어요. Dinner yesterday was not delicious.

- 전에는 그 배우가 멋있지 않았어요. The actor wasn't cool before.

- 소금을 안 넣으면 음식이 맛없을 거예요. If you don't add salt, the food won't taste good.

- 많은 사람들이 안 오면, 파티가 재미있지 않을 거예요. If many people don't come, the party won't be fun.

3 Negation with nouns

The negation for nouns is expressed using 아니다. If the preceding noun ends in a vowel, the particle 가 is used, and if it ends in a consonant, the particle 이 is used.

- 제 고향이 제주도가 아니에요. My hometown is not Jeju Island.

- 저는 학생이 아니에요. I am not a student.

In the past tense, 아니다 becomes 아니었어요, and in the future or speculative form, it becomes 아닐 거예요.

- 저는 전문적인 요리사가 아니었어요. I was not a professional chef.

- 이것은 아마 한국 제품이 아닐 거예요. This is probably not a Korean product.

4 못 and -지 못하다

To express an inability to perform an action or achieve a state, Korean uses:

- Short negation 못 is placed before verbs.
- Long negation -지 못하다 is attached to the verb stem.

However, in 하다-verbs (e.g., 공부하다, 일하다), 못 is placed directly before 하다 (e.g., 공부 못하다, 일 못 하다).

For other verbs, 못 is simply placed before the verb (e.g., 밥을 못 먹어요).

- 배가 아파서 밥을 못 먹어요. = 밥을 먹지 못해요. I cannot eat because my stomach hurts.
- 운동한 지 한 시간도 못 돼요. = 한 시간도 되지 못해요. It has not been even an hour since I exercised.
- 노트북이 없어서 일 못 해요. = 일하지 못해요. I cannot work because I do not have a laptop.

(*) Be careful!

When 못 is used alone, it is pronounced [몯]. However, when combined with a verb, its pronunciation changes based on the following consonant or vowel:

못 before ㅂ, ㄷ, ㅈ, ㄱ	If 못 is followed by ㅂ, ㄷ, ㅈ, or ㄱ, the [ㄷ] sound in 못 is pronounced as [ㅃ, ㄸ, ㅉ, or ㄲ].	못 봐요 [몯빠요], 못 들어요 [몯뜨러요] 못 자요 [몯짜요], 못 가요 [몯까요]
못 before ㅎ	If 못 is followed by ㅎ, the [ㄷ] sound in 못 combines with ㅎ and is pronounced as [ㅌ].	못 해요 [모태요]
못 before ㄴ, ㅁ	If 못 is followed by ㄴ or ㅁ, the final consonant [ㄷ] in 못 is pronounced as [ㄴ] because of the influence of the following sound [ㄴ or ㅁ].	못 먹어요 [몬머거요] 못 나가요 [몬나가요]

When expressing tense, 못 is placed before verbs without changing their form in the present, past, or future tense. On the other hand, -지 못하다 is attached to the verb or adjective stem, with the tense marker added afterward.

The conjugation of -지 못하다 follows these patterns:

- Present: -지 못해요
- Past: -지 못했어요
- Future/Speculative: -지 못할 거예요

- 저는 피아노를 못 쳐요. I can't play the piano.
- 제 친구는 알레르기 때문에 땅콩을 먹지 못해요. My friend cannot eat peanuts because of an allergy.
- 어제 한 시간도 못 잤어요. I couldn't sleep even for an hour.
- 지난주에 축구 경기를 보지 못했어요. I couldn't watch the soccer game last week.
- 아마 진수가 우리와 같이 여행 못 갈 거예요. Jinsu probably won't be able to go on a trip with us.
- 준비하지 않으면 성공하지 못할 거예요. If you don't prepare, you won't succeed.

1 When expressing the negation of objective facts or states

To negate objective facts or states, use 안 or -지 않다.

- A 많이 아파요? Are you in a lot of pain?

  B 아니요, 안 아파요. No, I'm not in pain.

- A 핸드폰이 고장 났어요? Is your cellphone broken?

  B 아니요, 다행히 고장 나지 않았어요. No, fortunately, it's not broken.

- A 다음 주에 발표할 거예요? Will you present next week?

  B 아니요, 제가 발표하지 않을 거예요. 다른 사람이 할 거예요.

  No, I will not be presenting. Someone else will.

2 When expressing inability or impossibility

When someone lacks the ability to do something or when something is impossible, use 못 or -지 못하다.

- 저는 스키를 배우지 않았어요. 그래서 스키를 못 타요. I haven't learned to ski, so I can't ski.

- A 왜 전화 안 했어요? Why didn't you call?

  B 미안해요. 잊어버리고 전화 못 했어요. Sorry, I forgot and couldn't make the call.

- A 왜 배가 출발하지 않아요? Why isn't the boat leaving?

  B 날씨가 안 좋아요. 그래서 배가 출발하지 못해요. The weather is bad. So, the boat can't depart.

3 When expressing an unachieved state

못 or -지 못하다 is used to indicate that a certain state has not yet been achieved.

- 내 친구는 결국 대학교를 못 마쳤어요. 그만뒀어요.

  My friend eventually couldn't complete university and dropped out.

- 아직 제 꿈을 이루지 못했어요. 지금도 꿈을 위해 노력하고 있어요.

  I haven't achieved my dream yet. I'm still working towards it.

However, -지 못하다 is also used with a few specific adjectives to express failing to meet a certain level.

These exceptional adjectives only combine with -지 못하다, not 못.

- 그동안 바빠서 청소 못 했어요. 그래서 지금 방이 깨끗하지 못해요. (≠ 못 깨끗해요)

  I couldn't clean it because I was busy, so the room isn't clean now.

- 아름답지 못한 모습을 다른 사람에게 보이고 싶지 않아요. (≠ 못 아름다운)

  I don't want to show others an unattractive appearance.

4 When expressing negation in terms of perception or cognition

In Korean, perception or cognition verbs (such as 알다 (to know), 이해하다 (to understand), 알아보다 (to recognize), and 깨닫다 (to realize)) cannot be negated with 안. Instead, 못 is used.

- 그 사람은 제 이름을 <u>알지 않아요</u>. (✗) → 알지 못해요. (O)
  That person doesn't know my name.

- 저는 이 문법을 <u>이해 안 했어요</u>. (✗) → 이해 못 했어요. (O)
  I didn't understand this grammar.

- 화장을 해서 그 사람을 <u>알아보지 않았어요</u>. (✗) → 알아보지 못했어요. (O)
  I didn't recognize that person because of the makeup.

Perception verbs like 보다 (to see) and 듣다 (to hear) do not use 안 for negation. Instead, use 못:

- 유나 씨 얘기 <u>안 들었어요</u>. (✗) → 못 들었어요. (O) I haven't heard what Yuna said.

- 오늘 민수 씨를 <u>안 봤어요</u>. (✗) → 못 봤어요. (O) I havn't seen Minsu today.

 Be careful!

Using 안 with verbs like 보다 (to see) and 듣다 (to hear) means not seeing or hearing by choice.

Using 못 means being unable to see or hear, often due to circumstances.

- 저는 드라마를 안 좋아해요. 그래서 드라마를 안 봐요.
  I don't like dramas, so I don't watch them.

- 오늘 진수 씨를 못 봤어요. 다른 곳에 가 보세요.
  I haven't seen Jinsu today. Try looking somewhere else.

5 When asking for consent or confirming something uncertain

The negation -지 않다 is often used as a tag question to seek confirmation or agreement.

- A 오늘 날씨가 좋지 않아요? (= 오늘 날씨가 좋아요. 그렇죠?)
  Isn't the weather nice today? (= The weather is nice today, isn't it?)
  B 네, 날씨가 정말 좋아요. Yes, the weather is really nice.

- A 진수 씨가 집을 찾지 않아요? (= 마크 씨가 집을 찾아요. 맞죠?)
  Jinsu didn't find the house, did he? (= Mark found the house, right?)
  B 맞아요, 진수 씨가 집을 찾아요. Right, Jinsu found the house.

- A 지난 시험이 어렵지 않았어요? (= 지난 시험이 어려웠어요. 그랬죠?)
  Wasn't the last exam difficult? (= The last exam was difficult, wasn't it?)
  B 맞아요, 시험이 너무 어려웠어요. Right, the exam was too difficult.

- A 어제 파티에 사람들이 많이 오지 않았어요? (= 어제 파티에 사람들이 많이 왔어요. 그랬죠?)
  Didn't a lot of people come to the party yesterday?
  (= A lot of people came to the party yesterday, didn't they?)
  B 네, 사람들이 많이 왔어요. Yes, a lot of people came.

Quiz 13

Comparative and superlative

Kor. 14

로지 15살   유진 42살   지윤 28살

로지가 유진보다 **더** 키가 커요. Rosie is taller than Yujin.

하지만 로지가 유진보다 나이가 적어요. However, Rosie is younger than Yujin.

유진 씨가 **제일** 나이가 많아요. Yujin is the oldest.

하지만 유진 씨가 **제일** 키가 작아요. But, Yujin is the shortest.

지윤 씨가 **가장** 머리가 길어요. Jiyun has the longest hair.

그런데 로지 씨가 지윤 씨보다 **더** 키가 커요. Yet, Rosie is taller than Jiyun.

Grammar Essentials

1 Comparative

In Korean, to express comparisons, the particle 보다 (than) is attached to the object of comparison. Additionally, 더 (more) is placed before verbs, adjectives, or adverbs to indicate that someone or something has a greater degree of a characteristic. Unlike in English, the phrase containing 보다 can be placed flexibly in the sentence.

- 여름에 부산이 서울보다 더 더워요. (= 여름에 서울보다 부산이 더 더워요.)
  In summer, Busan is hotter than Seoul.

- 제 친구는 차를 커피보다 더 좋아해요. (= 제 친구는 커피보다 차를 더 좋아해요.)
  My friend likes tea more than coffee. (= My friend prefers tea more than coffee.)

When a verb alone cannot express a degree, 더 modifies adverbs to show a comparative meaning.

- 요즘에 저는 채소를 고기보다 더 많이 먹어요. These days, I eat vegetables more than meat.

- 버스가 지하철보다 시간이 더 오래 걸려요. The bus takes longer than the subway.

When the context is clear, the comparison object combined with 보다 and 더 can be placed flexibly.

- 커피가 라면보다 더 비싸요. Coffee is more expensive than ramyeon.

  = 커피가 (라면보다) 더 비싸요.

  = 커피가 라면보다 (더) 비싸요.

> **① Note**
>
> The adverb 더 (more) and 덜 (less) indicate comparative degrees in Korean.
> 덜 is used when something falls below a certain standard, while 더 is used when something exceeds it.
> - 운동화가 구두보다 더 싸요. Sneakers are cheaper than dress shoes.
>   = 구두가 운동화보다 덜 싸요. Dress shoes are less cheap than sneakers.
> - 지난주에 진짜 바빴어요. 이번 주에 덜 바빠요. I was really busy last week. This week is less busy.
> - 매운 음식을 잘 못 먹어요? 그럼, 이 음식이 덜 매워요. 이거 드세요.
>   Can't you eat spicy food well? Then, this food is less spicy. Try this.

2 Superlative

In Korean, the superlative is expressed using 제일 or 가장 (meaning "the most"). These adverbs are placed before verbs, adjectives, or adverbs.

- 항상 연말에 가장 바빠요. It's always the busiest at the end of the year.

- 한국 음악을 제일 좋아해요. I like Korean music the most.

Adverbs can also be modified by 제일 or 가장 before them.

- 제가 역에 제일 빨리 도착했어요. I arrived at the station the earliest.

- 토요일 아침에 가장 늦게 일어나요. I wake up the latest on Saturday mornings.

1 When expressing comparatives

80km/h

50km/h

지하철이 버스보다 더 빨라요
= 버스보다 지하철이 더 빨라요.
The subway is faster than the bus.

In Korean, the particle 보다 is attached to the object of comparison, and the adverb 더 is used to express the comparative degree. Here, 더 can modify verbs, adjectives, and adverbs.

- 빨래보다 청소를 더 싫어해요. I dislike cleaning more than doing laundry.

- 이 의자가 저 의자보다 더 편해요. This chair is more comfortable than that one.

- 말이 너무 빨라요. (이전보다) 더 천천히 말해 주세요.
  You speak too fast. Please speak more slowly (than before).

To specify a range between two objects in comparative statements, "A and B 중에서" is used.

- 사과하고 딸기 중에서 저는 사과를 딸기보다 더 좋아해요.
  Between apples and strawberries, I like apples more than strawberries. (= I prefer apples more.)

- 작년 여름하고 올해 여름 중에서 올해 여름이 더 더워요.
  Between last summer and this summer, this summer is hotter.

The adverb 훨씬 can be added before 더 to emphasize the comparative degree.

- 이 식당이 저 식당보다 음식이 훨씬 더 맛있어요.
  This restaurant's food is much tastier than that restaurant's.

- 겨울에 모자를 쓰면 훨씬 덜 추워요. Wearing a hat in winter makes it much less cold.

When expressing comparatives, particle usage varies depending on whether the comparison object is the subject, object, or adverb in the sentence.

Comparing subjects	만두보다 김밥이 맛있어요. Gimbap is tastier than dumplings.
Comparing objects	저는 버스보다 지하철을 더 많이 타요. I ride the subway more than the bus.
Comparing adverbial phrases	저는 토요일보다 금요일에 친구를 더 자주 만나요. I meet friends more on Fridays than Saturdays. 저는 헬스장보다 집에서 더 많이 운동해요. I exercise more at home than at the gym.

2 When expressing superlative

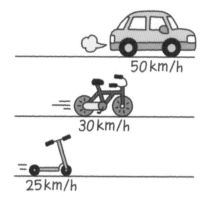

자동차가 제일 **빨라요.** The car is the fastest.
= 자동차가 가장 **빨라요.**

In Korean, the superlative is expressed by placing 제일 or 가장 before verbs, adjectives, or adverbs.

- 세계에서 이 빌딩이 제일 높아요. This building is the tallest in the world.

- 요즘 이 영화가 가장 인기가 많아요. This movie is currently most popular.

- 한국 사람들이 커피를 가장 많이 마셔요. Koreans drink coffee the most.

For superlative statements involving three or more objects, 중에서 (among) is used.

- 저는 스포츠 중에서 축구를 제일 좋아해요. Among sports, I like soccer the most.

- 한국 음식 중에서 비빔밥이 가장 맛있어요. Among Korean foods, bibimbap is the tastiest.

- 봄, 여름, 가을, 겨울, 중에서 봄에 제일 많이 여행 가요.
  Among spring, summer, autumn, and winter, I travel the most in spring.

When using superlatives, particle usage varies depending on whether the superlative functions as the subject, object, or adverb in the sentence.

Comparing with the subject	우리 반 학생들에서 <u>유진 씨</u>가 제일 운동을 잘해요. Among the students in our class, Yujin is the best at sports.
Comparing with the object	한국 음식 중에서 저는 <u>불고기</u>를 제일 좋아해요. Among Korean foods, I like bulgogi the most.
Comparing with the adverbial phrase	여름에 <u>카페</u>에 제일 자주 가요. I go to the cafe the most in the summer.

Quiz 14

PART

2

Meaning-Focused Endings and Expressions

Kor. 15

저는 노래를 못해요.

I can't sing.

저는 노래를 잘하고 싶어요.

I want to sing well.

Grammar Essentials

1 -고 싶다

-고 싶다 is used with verbs to express the speaker's desire or wish to perform a certain action. It can be attached to a verb stem regardless of whether the final syllable ends in a vowel or a consonant. In declarative sentences, the subject of -고 싶다 is typically limited to the first-person speaker. In interrogative sentences, it is used to ask about the second-person listener. In colloquial speech, the subject is often omitted when it is clear from the context.

- 지금 졸려요. (저는) 자고 싶어요. I'm sleepy. (I) want to sleep.

- A 배고파요? 밥을 먹고 싶어요? Are you hungry? Do you want to eat rice?

  B 아니요, 빵을 먹고 싶어요. No, I want to eat bread.

2 Conjugation

-고 싶다					
가다	가고 싶다	듣다	듣고 싶다	쓰다	쓰고 싶다
먹다	먹고 싶다	돕다	돕고 싶다	살다	살고 싶다
부르다	부르고 싶다	낫다	낫고 싶다	그렇다	그러고 싶다

3 Negation

To express an unwanted state, you can either place 안 before -고 싶다 or attach -지 않다 to the stem of 싶다, forming -고 싶지 않다.

- 오늘 저는 일하고 싶지 않아요. 쉬고 싶어요. Today, I don't want to work. I want to rest.

    (= 일 안 하고 싶어요.)

4 Tenses

To express a speaker's past desire or wish with -고 싶다, add -았/었- to 싶다, forming -고 싶었다.

- 어제 가족하고 전화하고 싶었어요. 그런데 못 했어요.
  I wanted to call my family yesterday, but I couldn't.

- 어렸을 때 운동선수가 되고 싶었어요. 그래서 운동선수가 됐어요.
  I wanted to be an athlete when I was young. So, I became an athlete.

To express a speculative future desire, add -(으)ㄹ 거예요 to 싶다, forming -고 싶을 거예요. This is used to indicate the speaker's or someone else's future desires or guesses. Since -고 싶을 거예요 conveys speculation, it can be used with first, second, or third-person subjects.

- 저는 나중에 다시 이곳에 여행 오고 싶을 거예요. I will want to visit this place again in the future.

- 마크 씨가 한국 음식을 먹고 싶을 거예요. Mark will probably want to eat Korean food.

1 When expressing the speaker's wishes or desires

나는 저 자동차를 사고 싶어.

I want to buy that car.

-고 싶다 is used in declarative sentences to express the speaker's wishes or desires and in interrogative sentences to ask about the listener's wishes or desires.

Asking about the listener's general desire

- A 한국어 공부가 끝나고 뭐 하고 싶어요?
  What do you want to do after you finish studying Korean?

  B 저는 한국 회사에서 일하고 싶어요. I want to work at a Korean company.

Asking about desired action in a specific situation

- A 핸드폰을 고치려면 수리비가 30만원이에요. 어떻게 하고 싶어요?
  It will cost 300,000 won to repair the phone. What do you want to do?

  B 저는 새 핸드폰을 사고 싶어요. I want to buy a new phone.

Tip

When -고 싶다 is used with a transitive verb, the object can take either the particle 을/를 or 이/가. 을/를 is used when the object functions as the direct object of the verb, while 이/가 is used when the object agrees with the adjective 싶다 rather than the verb. There is no difference in meaning whether 을/를 or 이/가 is used, though 을/를 is more common in standard usage.

- 저는 바다를 보고 싶어요. = 저는 바다가 보고 싶어요. I want to see the sea.

2   When expressing someone else's wishes or desires

진수도 저 자동차를 사고 싶어 해.

Jinsu also wants to buy that car.

In declarative sentences, -고 싶다 expresses the speaker's own desires and is only used with the first-person subject. To express the desires of a second or third person subject, -고 싶어 하다 should be used.

- A (나는) 저녁 사 먹고 싶어. I want to buy dinner.   First person

   B 너도 저녁 사 먹고 싶어 하고, 윤아도 저녁 사 먹고 싶어 해.
   You also want to buy dinner, and Yuna wants to buy dinner too.   Second person or third person

3   When asking about wishes or desires

In interrogative sentences, -고 싶다 is used to ask about the listener's desires (second person). For third-person desires, -고 싶어 하다 is used to inquire about what someone else wants.

- A 너는 뭐가 되고 싶어? What do you want to become?

   B 나는 축구선수가 되고 싶어. I want to become a soccer player.

- A 누가 이 일을 하고 싶어 해요? Who wants to do this job?

   B 진수가 이 일을 하고 싶어 해요. Jinsu wants to do this job.

> 🕐 **Note**
>
> **Incompatibility with adjectives or nouns**
>
> -고 싶다 can only be used with verbs. To express a desire with an adjective, convert it into a verb by adding -아/어지다 or -아/어 하다. For nouns, attach 되다 (to become).
>
> - 저는 더 예쁘고 싶어요. (✗)
>   → 예뻐지고 싶어요. (O) I want to become prettier.
> - 저도 여러분과 함께 기쁘고 싶어요. (✗)
>   → 기뻐하고 싶어요. (O) I want to be happy with you all.
> - 저는 가수이고 싶어요. (✗)
>   → 가수가 되고 싶어요. (O) I want to become a singer.

Quiz **15**

97

TOPIK I | SCK 3

-았/었으면 좋겠다 I wish / I hope

Kor. 16

저는 돈이 없어요.

I don't have money.

돈이 많았으면 좋겠어요.

I wish I had a lot of money.

1 -았/었으면 좋겠다 I wish / I hope

-았/었으면 좋겠다 is used to express the speaker's wish for something difficult or unlikely to happen or the speaker's hope for something feasible or realistic to occur. It is attached to verbs, adjectives, and "noun + 이다".

For verbs and adjectives ending in 하다, use -하면 좋겠다. If the verb or adjective stem contains ㅏ or ㅗ, use -았으면 좋겠다. Otherwise, use -었으면 좋겠다. For nouns, if the last syllable ends in a vowel, use -였으면 좋겠다, if it ends in a consonant, use -이었으면 좋겠다. In informal speech, 하다 is often replaced with 좋겠다, and -았/었으면 하다 is sometimes used.

- 세계여행을 갔으면 좋겠어요. I wish I could travel the world.

- 부모님이 건강하셨으면 좋겠어요. I hope my parents are healthy.

- 호텔이 편했으면 좋겠어요. I hope the hotel was comfortable.

- 룸메이트가 한국 사람이었으면 해요. I wish my roommate was Korean.

2 Conjugation

-았/었으면 좋겠다					
싸다	쌌으면 좋겠다	다르다	*달랐으면 좋겠다	쉽다	*쉬웠으면 좋겠다
먹다	먹었으면 좋겠다	듣다	*들었으면 좋겠다	낫다	*나았으면 좋겠다
예쁘다	*예뻤으면 좋겠다	살다	*살았으면 좋겠다	그렇다	*그랬으면 좋겠다

3 Negation

For verbs or adjectives, placing 안 or -지 않다 before -았/었으면 좋겠다 expresses the speaker's wish for something not to happen or for the situation to be different from what is expected. For 있다, the grammatical pattern 없었으면 좋겠다 is used to express the speaker's wish for something not to exist. For nouns, negation is expressed using 아니었으면 좋겠다.

- 내일 비가 안 왔으면 좋겠어요. I hope it doesn't rain tomorrow.

- 전쟁이 일어나지 않았으면 좋겠어요. I wish war wouldn't break out.

- 음식이 너무 맵지 않았으면 좋겠어요. I hope the food is not too spicy.

- 방에 소음이 없었으면 좋겠어요. I wish there was no noise in the room.

- 저 사람이 우리 팀이 아니었으면 좋겠어요. I wish that person wasn't on our team.

4 Persons

In a declarative sentence, -았/었으면 좋겠다 is limited to the first-person when expressing the speaker's desires. However, in an interrogative sentence, it is directed to the second-person when asking about the listener's desires.

Expressing what the speaker desires

- 나는 대학 입학 시험을 합격했으면 좋겠어. I wish I passed the college entrance exam.

Asking about what the listener desires

- 너는 생일 때 무슨 선물을 받았으면 좋겠어? What gift do you wish to receive for your birthday?

When speaking, the first-person subject of the sentence is often omitted. The subject of the wish can be first, second, or third person, depending on the context.

Expressing a wish for oneself

- (저는) (제가) 여자 친구가 있었으면 좋겠어요. I wish I had a girlfriend.

Expressing a wish for the listener

- (나는) 네가 좋은 회사에 취직했으면 좋겠어. I hope you get a job at a good company.

Expressing a wish about a third person

- (저는) 진수 씨가 행복했으면 좋겠어요. I hope Jinsu is happy.

5 Combination with -았/었-

-았/었으면 좋겠다 is used to express the speaker's wish in the present and cannot be combined with -았/었- to indicate past tense events. To express past wishes, you should rephrase the sentence differently.

- 노래를 잘했으면 좋겠었어요. (✗) → 노래를 잘했으면 좋겠다고 생각했어요. (O)
  I thought it would be good if I could sing well.

-았/었으면 좋겠다 can express a strong desire or wish for something impossible or unlikely to happen. On the other hand, -(으)면 좋겠다 can be used to indicate the speaker's preferences or conditions when choosing from multiple options.

- A 빨리 결혼했으면 좋겠어요. Expressing a wish without a partner
  I hope to get married soon.

  B 여자 친구부터 찾으세요. First, find a girlfriend.

- A 결혼식은 3월, 4월, 5월 중에서 몇 월이 좋아요?
  Which month is better for a wedding: March, April, or May?

  B 5월에 결혼하면 좋겠어요. Expressing a preference among provided options
  I would prefer to get married in May.

100

Tip

The difference between -았/었으면 좋겠다 and -고 싶다

Both -았/었으면 좋겠다 and -고 싶다 express the speaker's wish regarding their own state, accompanied by a first-person subject. However, -고 싶다 only combines with verbs, whereas -았/었으면 좋겠다 can be used with verbs, adjectives, and "noun + 이다". As a result, -았/었으면 좋겠다 can sometimes be replaced with -고 싶다, but only when the subject is first-person and the verb is used.

While the subject of -고 싶다 is limited to the first person in declarative sentences, -았/었으면 좋겠다 can also be used for the second or third person. Therefore, -았/었으면 좋겠다 is used to express a wish for an action or state concerning the listener or someone else.

- (제가) 한국 친구를 많이 사귀었으면 좋겠어요. (O) (I) wish I could make many Korean friends.

  = (제가) 한국 친구를 많이 사귀고 싶어요. (O) (I) want to make many Korean friends.

- (제가) 행복했으면 좋겠어요. (O) I wish that I were happy.

  = (제가) 행복하고 싶어요. (✕)

While the subject of -고 싶다 is limited to the first person in declarative sentences, -았/었으면 좋겠다 can also be used for the second or third person. Therefore, -았/었으면 좋겠다 is used to express a wish for an action or state concerning the listener or someone else.

- 생일 파티에 친구들이 많이 왔으면 좋겠어요. (O) I hope many of my friends come to my birthday party.

  ≠ 생일 파티에 친구들이 많이 오고 싶어요. (✕)

1 When expressing wishes for unlikely situations

할머니 병이 빨리 나았으면 좋겠어요.

I wish my grandmother would get better soon.

-았/었으면 좋겠다 expresses the speaker's strong wishes for a situation that is difficult or unlikely to happen. You can express your wishes using -았/었으면 좋겠다.

When asking about the listener's wishes in general, use "뭐 했으면 좋겠어요?" and if you are asking what kind of solution they would like in a specific situation, use "어떻게 했으면 좋겠어요?"

- A 돈이 생기면 뭐 했으면 좋겠어요? What do you wish to do if you have money?

  B 돈이 생기면 <u>다른 나라로 여행 갔으면 좋겠어요</u>. I wish to travel abroad if I have the money.

- A 환경 문제가 너무 심각해요. 어떻게 했으면 좋겠어요?
  The environmental issue is severe. What do you wish people to do?

  B <u>사람들이 환경 문제에 더 관심을 가졌으면 좋겠어요</u>.
  I wish people would become more aware of environmental issues.

2 When expressing the speaker's expectations

음식이 맛있었으면 좋겠어요.

I hope the food is delicious.

-았/었으면 좋겠다 is used to express positive expectations or desires regarding specific situations or outcomes.

- A 휴가 때 뭐 했으면 좋겠어요? What do you want to do on your holiday?

  B 휴가 때 집에서 <u>쉬었으면 좋겠어요</u>. I hope to rest at home during my holiday.

- A 올해 소망이 뭐예요? What is your wish for this year?

  B 올해에는 월급이 <u>올랐으면 좋겠어요</u>. I hope my salary goes up this year.

3 When indirectly expressing requests

화장실 문제를 빨리 해결해 주셨으면 좋겠어요.
I hope the staff can fix the bathroom issues quickly.

The grammatical pattern -았/었으면 좋겠다 is also used to politely express a request in formal settings by conveying the speaker's wish. When combined with the honorific -시- and -아/어 주다 (meaning "to help" or "to do something for someone"), -아/어 주시면 좋겠다 makes the request sound more formal and indirect than simply using -아/어 주세요.

- A 어떻게 계산해 드릴까요? How would you like to pay?

  B 카드로 계산했으면 해요. (= 카드로 계산해 주세요.)
  I'd prefer to pay with a card. (Card, please.)

- A 무슨 일로 오셨어요? What brings you here?

  B 지갑을 주웠어요. 주인을 찾아 주셨으면 좋겠어요. (= 찾아 주세요.)
  I've found a wallet. I hope you can help find its owner. (= Please, find the owner.)

- 결과를 이메일로 연락해 주셨으면 합니다. (= 연락해 주세요.)
  I would appreciate it if you could inform me of the results via email. (= Please, inform me of the results via email.)

When expressing formal requests, -았/었으면 좋겠다 is used in spoken language, while -기 바라다 is preferred in written language.

Subway station signage
- 계단에서 뛰지 않았으면 좋겠어요. Please do not run on the stairs.

  = 계단에서 뛰지 않기를 바랍니다.
  Please refrain from running on the stairs.

Quiz 16

Lesson
17

-(으)ㄹ 수 있다 can

마크는 수영할 수 있어요.

Mark can swim.

진수는 수영할 수 없어요.

Jinsu can't swim.

1 -(으)ㄹ 수 있다

-(으)ㄹ 수 있다 indicates that the subject has the ability to perform an action or that a certain situation is possible. Conversely, -(으)ㄹ 수 없다 expresses the lack of ability to act or the impossibility of a situation.

For verb or adjective stems ending in a vowel, -ㄹ 수 있다 is used, while for those ending in a consonant, -을 수 있다 is used. For nouns, 일 수 있다 is used regardless of whether the noun ends in a vowel or consonant.

Lesson 17

-(으)ㄹ 수 있다

- 저는 피아노를 칠 수 있어요. I can play the piano.

- 한자를 읽을 수 있어요? Can you read Chinese characters?

- 동생이 기타를 칠 수 없어요. My younger brother can't play the guitar.

- 저는 아랍어를 읽을 수 없어요. I can't read Arabic.

- 창문을 열면 추울 수 있어요. Opening the window may make it cold.

- 저 사람이 경찰일 수 있어요. That person could be a police officer.

2 Conjugation

-(으)ㄹ 수 있다					
타다	탈 수 있다	다르다	다를 수 있다	쉽다	*쉬울 수 있다
먹다	먹을 수 있다	듣다	*들을 수 있다	낫다	*나을 수 있다
쓰다	쓸 수 있다	만들다	*만들 수 있다	그렇다	*그럴 수 있다

3 Tenses

To express past abilities or possibilities, -(으)ㄹ 수 있었다 is used.

- 전에는 피아노를 칠 수 있었어요. 그런데 지금은 다 잊어버렸어요.
  I could play the piano before, but now I've forgotten everything.

- 지난주에 옷을 살 수 있었어요. 그런데 이번 주에 그 옷이 다 팔려서 옷을 살 수 없어요.
  I was able to buy clothes last week, but I can't this week because the clothes are sold out.

For future speculation about abilities or possibilities, -(으)ㄹ 수 있을 것이다 is used.

- 아마 유진 씨가 스키를 탈 수 있을 거예요. Maybe Yujin might be able to ski.

- 주말이니까 길이 막힐 수 있을 거예요. It's the weekend, so the roads might be congested.

1 When expressing one's ability

-(으)ㄹ 수 있다 indicates the ability to do something, while -(으)ㄹ 수 없다 indicates the inability. This pattern is only used with verbs.

- 저는 자동차를 운전할 수 있어요. 그런데 동생은 자동차를 운전할 수 없어요.
  I can drive a car, but my younger brother can't drive a car.

- A 피아노를 칠 수 있어요? Can you play the piano?

  B 어렸을 때 피아노를 배워서 칠 수 있어요. 그런데 잘 못 쳐요.
  I learned to play the piano when I was young and can play it. But I'm not good at it.

2 When expressing the possibility or probability of a situation

-(으)ㄹ 수 있다 is used to indicate that a specific situation is possible or likely to occur, while -(으)ㄹ 수 없다 expresses that there is no possibility or probability of a situation happening. When expressing possibility or probability, -(으)ㄹ 수 있다 can be used not only with verbs but also with adjectives and "noun + 이다".

- 이번 주말에 비가 올 수 있어요. 우산이 필요할 거예요.
  It might rain this weekend. You might need an umbrella.

- 그 식당은 주말에 사람이 많을 수 있어요. 그러니까 주중에 가 보세요.
  That restaurant might be crowded on weekends. You might want to try going during the week.

- 이게 정답일 수 있어요. 선생님한테 가서 물어봅시다.
  This might be the correct answer. Let's ask the teacher.

- 성수기에 여행 가면 방이 없을 수 있어요.
  If you travel during peak season, you might not find any rooms available.

- 기차는 오전 10시 전에 도착할 수 없어요. The train cannot arrive before 10 AM.

TIP

-(으)ㄹ 수 없다 and 못

When expressing impossibility, -(으)ㄹ 수 없다 can be changed to 못. However, remember that 못 is only combined with verbs.

- 진수 씨는 수영할 수 없어요. = 진수 씨는 수영 못 해요. (O) Jinsu cannot swim.
- 그 얘기는 지금 말할 수 없어요. = 그 얘기는 지금 말 못 해요. (O) I can't talk about that now.
- 술이 건강에 좋을 수 없어요. ≠ 술이 건강에 못 좋아요. (✗) Alcohol cannot be good for your health.

3 When suggesting or offering

-(으)ㄹ 수 있다 is often used with verbs in the interrogative form to suggest or offer something to someone else. To decline a suggestion, -(으)ㄹ 수 없다 is used.

- A 지금 잠깐 얘기할 수 있어요? Can I talk to you for a moment?

  B 그럼요, 무슨 일이에요? Sure, what's up?

- A 내일 같이 점심 먹을 수 있어요? Can we grab lunch together tomorrow?

  B 좋아요. 같이 점심 먹어요. That sounds great! Let's do it.

- A 우리 내일 만날 수 있어요? Can we meet tomorrow?

  B 미안해요. 다른 약속이 있어서 만날 수 없어요.
  I'm sorry. I can't meet tomorrow because I have other commitments.

4 When making a request

-(으)ㄹ 수 있다, when combined with -아/어 주다, is used to request a favor from someone else. This grammatical pattern is always combined with a verb to specify the action being requested. It conveys a polite request, often implying that the listener has the ability or willingness to fulfill the request.

- A 노트북을 빌려줄 수 있어요? Can you lend me your laptop?

  B 여기 있어요. 쓰세요. Here it is. Use it.

- A 저 좀 도와줄 수 있어요? Can you help me?

  B 그럼요, 도와드릴게요. Sure, I'll help you.

- A 자료 파일을 이메일로 보내줄 수 있어요? Could you email me the data file?

  B 네, 바로 보내 드릴게요. No problem, I'll send it right away.

5 When expressing prohibition

-(으)ㄹ 수 없다 is used with verbs to express that something is not allowed or prohibited.

- 16살은 가게에서 술을 살 수 없어요. 16-year-olds cannot buy alcohol at the store.

- 여기에 주차할 수 없어요. You can't park your car here.

- 시험 중에는 휴대 전화를 사용할 수 없습니다. You can't use your phone during the exam.

Quiz 17

-(으)ㄹ 줄 알다 know how to

Kor. 18

동생이 컴퓨터를 할 줄 알아요.

My brother knows how to use a computer.

할아버지가 컴퓨터를 할 줄 몰라요.

My grandfather doesn't know how to use a computer.

1 -(으)ㄹ 줄 알다

-(으)ㄹ 줄 알다 indicates that the subject possesses specific knowledge or skills necessary to perform an action, acquired through education or learning. Conversely, -(으)ㄹ 줄 모르다 indicates the absence of such knowledge or skills. This grammatical pattern is used only with verbs. If the verb stem ends in a vowel, -ㄹ 줄 알다 is used. If it ends in a consonant, -을 줄 알다 is used.

- 마크 씨는 한국어 자판을 칠 줄 알아요. Mark knows how to type in Korean.

  그런데 저는 한국어 자판을 칠 줄 몰라요. But I don't know how to type in Korean.

- 저는 한복을 입을 줄 알아요. I know how to wear a hanbok.

  그런데 로지 씨는 한복을 입을 줄 몰라요. But Rosie doesn't know how to wear a hanbok.

2 Conjugation

-(으)ㄹ 줄 알다			
고치다	고칠 줄 알다	듣다	*들을 줄 알다
읽다	읽을 줄 알다	열다	*열 줄 알다
쓰다	쓸 줄 알다	굽다	*구울 줄 알다
부르다	부를 줄 알다	짓다	*지을 줄 알다

3 Tenses

-(으)ㄹ 줄 알았다 indicates that the subject had the knowledge or skills to perform an action in the past.

- 전에 피아노를 칠 줄 알았어요. 그런데 지금은 다 잊어버렸어요.
  I knew how to play the piano before. But now I've forgotten everything.

- 어렸을 때 청소할 줄 몰랐어요. 그래서 청소 후에도 깨끗하지 않았어요.
  When I was young, I didn't know how to clean properly. So it wasn't clean even after cleaning.

-(으)ㄹ 줄 알 것이다 is used to assume that the subject will have the necessary knowledge or skills in the future.

- 아마 유진 씨가 김치를 만들 줄 알 거예요.
  Yujin probably might know how to make kimchi.

- 아마 제 친구가 한자를 읽을 줄 모를 거예요.
  My friend probably doesn't know how to read Chinese characters.

1 When indicating knowledge or skill for a specific action

A 이거 사용할 줄 알아요? Do you know how to use this?

B 네, 제가 도와드릴게요. Yes, I will help you.

-(으)ㄹ 수 있다 expresses whether the subject has knowledge and skills that can be acquired through education or training, such as using machines, playing sports, playing musical instruments, or cooking recipes.

• 저는 바이올린을 켤 줄 알아요. I know how to play the violin.

• A 개가 문을 열 줄 알아요? Does your dog know how to open the door?

  B 그럼요, 이 개가 똑똑해서 혼자 문을 열 줄 알아요.
    Of course, this dog is smart and knows how to open the door by herself.

• A 할아버지, 인터넷 할 줄 아세요? Grandpa, do you know how to use the internet?

  B 아니, 할 줄 몰라. 좀 도와줘. No, I don't know how to do it. Please help me.

2 When demonstrating comprehension of required skills

-(으)ㄹ 줄 알다 is used to show that one comprehends the necessary knowledge to execute an action. When combined with verbs like 놀다 (to play), 보다 (to see), 마시다 (to drink), 듣다 (to listen), these verbs are not interpreted in their primary meanings but suggest "understand" when used alongside -(으)ㄹ 줄 알다.

• 제 친구는 놀 줄 알아요. 그래서 그 친구하고 놀면 정말 재미있어요.
  My friend knows how to play, so it's really fun to play with him.

• 제 동생은 사람을 볼 줄 몰라요. 그래서 좋은 사람을 사귀기 어려워요.
  My younger brother doesn't know how to see people, so he has a hard time making good friends.

• 마크 씨는 한국 식으로 음식을 먹을 줄 알아요. 그래서 한국 사람들이 깜짝 놀라요.
  Mark knows how to eat Korean food, which is why Koreans are often surprised.

• 제 친구는 다른 사람의 말을 들을 줄 알아요. 그래서 문제가 있을 때 그 친구를 찾아요.
  My friend is a good listener, so I look for that friend when I have a problem.

The difference between -(으)ㄹ 줄 알다 and -(으)ㄹ 수 있다

-(으)ㄹ 줄 알다 indicates whether one possesses the knowledge or skills required to perform a specific action, whereas -(으)ㄹ 수 있다 indicates whether one has the ability or the possibility to execute a specific action. Essentially, -(으)ㄹ 줄 알다 refers to knowledge or proficiency, while -(으)ㄹ 수 있다 refers to ability.

However, for activities that can be learned and executed, such as sports or playing musical instruments, -(으)ㄹ 줄 알다 and -(으)ㄹ 수 있다 can often be used interchangeably without significant difference in meaning.

- 기타를 칠 줄 알아요. (O) I know how to play the guitar.

  = 기타를 칠 수 있어요. (O) I can play the guitar.

- 수영을 할 줄 몰라요. (O) I don't know how to swim.

  = 수영을 할 수 없어요. (O) I can't swim.

Perceptive verbs such as 보다 (to see), 듣다 (to hear) or daily routine verbs like 자다 (to sleep) are tasks that do not require special education or knowledge, and thus typically cannot be used with -(으)ㄹ 줄 알다.

- 저는 TV를 <u>볼 줄 몰라요</u>. (✕) → 저는 TV를 볼 수 없어요. (O) I can't watch TV.

- 밤에 시끄러워서 저는 <u>잘 줄 몰라요</u>. (✕) → 저는 잘 수 없어요. (O) I can't sleep.

Quiz 18

TOPIK I | SCK 2

-(으)세요 Please do something

Kor. 19

매일 운동하세요.
Exercise everyday.

물을 많이 드세요.
Drink water a lot.

담배를 피우지 마세요.
Don't smoke.

밤에 음식을 먹지 마세요.
Don't eat at night.

Grammar Essentials

1 The imperative -(으)세요

The ending -(으)세요 is a polite imperative form used with verbs to give instructions or commands to someone. When the verb stem ends in a vowel, -세요 is added directly; if it ends in a consonant, -으세요 is used instead.

- 여기에서 기다리세요. 금방 갔다 올게요. Please wait here. I'll be back soon.
- 한국 친구를 많이 사귀세요. Make a lot of Korean friends.
- 자주 웃으세요. 그러면 행복해져요. Smile often. Then you will be happy.
- 한국 음악을 많이 들으세요. Listen to a lot of Korean music.

Verbs used in everyday life, such as 먹다 (to eat), 마시다 (to drink), 자다 (to sleep), 있다 (to be), and 말하다 (to speak), take on special forms when combined with the imperative ending -(으)세요.

Infinitive form	Special form	Examples
먹다	잡수시다	천천히 잡수세요. Eat slowly.
	드시다	맛있게 드세요. Enjoy your meal.
마시다	드시다	커피를 드세요. Drink coffee.
자다	주무시다	안녕히 주무세요. Good night.
있다	계시다	안녕히 계세요. Goodbye.
말하다	말씀하시다	말씀하세요. Speak.

 Be careful!

The honorific marker -시- in the imperative ending -(으)세요 is a respectful form used to elevate the person being addressed. If honorifics are not required, -시- can be omitted, and the command can be given using -아/어요 instead. The ending -아/어요 can function in declarative, interrogative, imperative, and propositive sentences, with its meaning determined by context and intonation.

- 학교에 가요. I go to school. `Declarative`
- 학교에 가요. Go to school. `Imperative`
- 학교에 가요? Do you go to school? `Interrogative`
- 학교에 가요! Let's go to school! `Propositive`

2 Negation

The negative form of the imperative -(으)세요 is -지 마세요, which is used to politely tell someone not to do something. -지 마세요 is used regardless of whether the verb stem ends in a vowel or consonant.

	Ending in a vowel	Ending in a consonant
Affirmative	여기 보세요. Look here.	셀카를 찍으세요. Take a selfie.
Negative	이 영화를 보지 마세요. Don't watch this movie.	여기에서 사진을 찍지 마세요. Do not take pictures here.

3 Conjugation

	-(으)세요	-지 마세요		-(으)세요	-지 마세요
보다	보세요	보지 마세요	듣다	*들으세요	듣지 마세요
읽다	읽으세요	읽지 마세요	만들다	*만드세요	만들지 마세요
쓰다	쓰세요	쓰지 마세요	굽다	*구우세요	굽지 마세요
부르다	부르세요	부르지 마세요	짓다	*지으세요	짓지 마세요
받다	받으세요	받지 마세요	그렇다	*그러세요	*그러지 마세요

4 Combining with adjectives

In Korean, -(으)세요 or -지 마세요 cannot be directly combined with adjectives. To use these endings with adjectives, you must first convert the adjective into a verb and then apply the ending.

- 조용하세요. (✗) → 조용히 하세요. (O) Be quiet.

- 강하세요. (✗) → 강해 지세요. (O) Be strong.

- 무섭지 마세요. (✗) → 무서워하지 마세요. (O) Don't be scared.

Similarly, -(으)세요 cannot be combined directly with nouns. To express commands with nouns, the verb 되다 (to become) must be used.

- 동아리에 가입하고 회원이세요. (✗) → 동아리에 가입하고 회원이 되세요. (O)
  Join the club and become a member.

- 나쁜 사람하고 친구이지 마세요. (✗) → 나쁜 사람하고 친구가 되지 마세요. (O)
  Don't be friends with bad people.

Usually, -(으)세요 cannot be combined with adjectives. However, as an exception, "건강하세요 (Be healthy)" and "행복하세요 (Be happy)" are used as idiomatic expressions with -(으)세요.

- 항상 건강하세요. Always be healthy.
- 행복하세요. Be happy.

Grammar in Action

1 When giving instructions

비누로 깨끗이 손을 씻으세요.

Wash your hands thoroughly with soap.

수업 시간에 핸드폰을 보지 마세요.

Don't look at your phone during class.

-(으)세요 is used when instructing someone to do something, while -지 마세요 is used when instructing someone not to do something. To emphasize the instruction, -(으)세요 is often used together with the adverbs 꼭 (surely) or 반드시 (certainly), whereas -지 마세요 is often used with 절대로 (absolutely). The person receiving the instructions typically responds with -(으)ㄹ게 to indicate that they will follow the instructions.

- A 수업 시간에 한국어로 얘기하세요. Speak in Korean during class.

  B 네, 그럴게요. Yes, I will.

- A 엘리베이터가 위험해요. 엘리베이터를 절대 타지 마세요.

  The elevator is dangerous. Never take the elevator.

  B 알겠어요, 타지 않을게요. OK, I won't ride it.

2 When giving advice

-(으)세요 or -지 마세요 are used when giving advice or warnings to someone. A person who has received advice or a warning responds with -(으)ㄹ게 to indicate that they will follow the advice or warning.

- A 밤에 못 자요. 어떻게 해야 해요? I can't sleep at night. What should I do?

  B 오후에 커피를 마시지 마세요. 그리고 저녁에 가벼운 운동을 하세요.

  Don't drink coffee in the afternoon. And do light exercise in the evening.

  A 네, 그럴게요. Yes, I will.

3 When expressing permission

-(으)세요 is used when giving permission to someone to do something. If someone asks for permission using -아/어도 되다, you can grant permission by using -(으)세요. If you want to deny permission, you can use -지 마세요.

- A 화장실 좀 써도 돼요? Can I use the bathroom?

  B 그럼요, 쓰세요. Sure, use it. (= you can use it.)

- A 여기에 들어가도 돼요? Can I go in here?

  B 안 돼요, 들어가지 마세요. No, don't go in.

Quiz 19

115

-아/어 보세요 Try doing something

Kor. 20

FITTING ROOM

이 옷이 요즘 인기가 많아요. 한번 입어 보세요.

This outfit is popular these days. Try it on.

1 -아/어 보세요

The grammatical pattern -아/어 보세요 is a combination of -아/어 보다, which expresses the meaning of attempting or trying something, and the imperative ending -(으)세요. This pattern is always combined with a verb and is used to suggest or encourage someone to try a specific action or experience. It is often used in recommendations or invitations.

-아/어 보세요 is always combined with a verb. When the verb stem ends in 하다, it is combined with -해 보세요. If the last syllable of the verb stem contains ㅏ or ㅗ, it is combined with -아 보세요. In all other cases, it is combined with -어 보세요.

- 노래로 한국어를 연습해 보세요. Practice Korean with songs.

- 한강에 가 보세요. 야경이 정말 아름다워요. Go to the Hangang River. The night view is really beautiful.

- 한국 음식을 만들어 보세요. 정말 재미있어요. Try making Korean food. It's really fun.

For the verb 보다 (to see), instead of using 보다 twice, it is simply expressed as 보세요 when combined with -아/어 보세요.

- 이 영화가 진짜 재미있어요. 한번 이 영화를 <u>보세요</u>. (O)

  <u>봐 보세요</u>. (×)

  This movie is really fun. Please watch this movie once.

2 Conjugation

-아/어 보세요					
하다	해 보세요	부르다	*불러 보세요	입다	입어 보세요
오다	와 보세요	듣다	*들어 보세요	굽다	*구워 보세요
찍다	찍어 보세요	만들다	만들어 보세요	짓다	*지어 보세요
쓰다	*써 보세요	넣다	넣어 보세요	보다	*보세요

3 Negation

The negation of -아/어 보세요 is formed by adding -지 마세요 or -지 말아 보세요 to the verb stem to advise someone not to do something. These forms apply regardless of whether the verb stem ends in a vowel or a consonant. Both -지 마세요 and -지 말아 보세요 can be used to express negation, but -지 말아 보세요 often conveys a softer and more suggestive tone compared to -지 마세요, which sounds more direct and firm.

- 시간이 없어서 운동을 못 해요? 그러면 엘리베이터를 타지 마세요. 계단으로 올라가 보세요.
  Can't exercise because you don't have time? Then don't take the elevator. Go up the stairs.

- 국이 너무 짜요? 그러면 소금을 넣지 말아 보세요. 그리고 물을 더 넣어 보세요.
  Is the soup too salty? Then try not adding salt. And try adding more water.

1 When inviting or suggesting an action

시식 코너

이거 맛있어요. 한번 먹어 보세요.
This is tasty. Give it a try.

-아/어 보세요 is used to invite or suggest that someone try a specific action. When combined with the adverb 한번 (once), it conveys a gentle and encouraging suggestion. When responding to a suggestion, you can use -아/어 볼게요 to indicate your intention to follow it.

• A 한국 음식 레시피를 알려 주세요. Please tell me the Korean food recipe.

  B 이 앱을 사용해 보세요. 쉬운 레시피가 많이 있어요. Try this app. There are many easy recipes.

• A 이 차가 맛있으니까 한번 마셔 보세요. This tea is delicious, so try it.

  B 네, 마셔 볼게요. Yes, I will try it.

2 When recommending

-아/어 보세요 is used to recommend that someone try or do a certain action. The adverb 꼭 (definitely) indicates a strong recommendation, while 한번 (once) suggests a light recommendation. When a person accepts the recommendation, they respond with -아/어 볼게요.

• A 부산 경치가 정말 아름다워요. 부산에 꼭 가 보세요.
  The scenery in Busan is really beautiful. You should definitely visit Busan.

  B 네, 꼭 가 볼게요. Yes, I will definitely go.

• A 한국 음식을 아직 안 먹어 봤어요. I haven't tried Korean food yet.

  B 그래요? 한국 음식이 조금 맵지만 맛있어요. 한번 먹어 보세요.
  Really? Korean food is a little spicy but delicious. Give it a try.

  A 네, 한번 먹어 볼게요. Yes, I will try it.

To advise against an action, use -지 마세요.

• A 이 배가 조금 위험하니까 배를 타지 마세요. This boat is a bit dangerous, so don't get on it.

  B 네, 저는 수영 못 하니까 배를 타지 않을게요. Yes, I can't swim, so I won't go on the boat.

3 When giving advice in a gentle way

A 건강 때문에 고민이에요. 어떻게 해야 해요?
I'm worried about my health. What should I do?

B 하루에 30분씩 걸어 보세요.
Try walking for 30 minutes a day.

-아/어 보세요 is used to offer gentle advice, providing a softer tone compared to -(으)세요. When someone receives advice and intends to follow it, they respond with -아/어 볼게요 to indicate their intention to try it. For negative advice, use -지 마세요 or -지 말아 보세요 to advise against doing something.

- A 한국어 말하기를 잘하고 싶으면 어떻게 해야 해요? What should I do to speak Korean well?

  B 한국 친구를 사귀어 보세요. Make a Korean friend.

- A 내일 면접을 봐요. 너무 걱정돼요. 어떡하죠?
  I have an interview tomorrow. I'm so worried. What should I do?

  B 너무 걱정하지 마세요. 연습하면 돼요. 다시 연습해 보세요.
  Don't worry too much. You just need to practice. Try practicing again.

  A 알겠어요. 다시 해 볼게요. I understand. I'll try again.

- A 운동하고 싶은데 시간이 없어요. 어떻게 해야 해요?
  I want to exercise, but I don't have time. What should I do?

  B 그럼, 엘리베이터를 타지 말아 보세요. 계단으로 올라가 보세요.
  Then, try not taking the elevator. Go up the stairs.

  A 알겠어요. 그렇게 해 볼게요. I understand. I'll try that.

4 When giving warnings

-지 마세요 is used to warn someone not to do a certain action. When combined with the adverb 절대 (absolutely/never), it emphasizes the strength of the warning. When responding to a warning and expressing your commitment not to do the action, use -지 않을게요.

- A 밤에 못 자니까 오후에 커피를 마시지 마세요.
  Don't drink coffee in the afternoon because it can keep you up at night.

  B 알겠어요. 오후에 커피를 마시지 않을게요. I understand. I won't drink coffee in the afternoon.

- A 이 음식이 너무 매워요. 절대 먹지 마세요. This food is too spicy. Never try it.

  B 알겠어요. 절대 먹지 않을게요. OK, I will never eat it.

Quiz 20

Lesson 21

-아/어 주세요 Please do something for me

Kor. 21

A 저 좀 도와주세요. Please help me.

B 네, 제가 도와드릴게요. Yes, I will help you.

Grammar Essentials

1 -아/어 주세요

The grammatical pattern -아/어 주세요 is a combination of the imperative ending -(으)세요 and -아/어 주다, which indicates providing help or benefits. It is used to politely request someone to do something.

-아/어 주세요 is always combined with a verb and follows specific conjugation rules. If the verb stem ends in 하다, it combines with -여 주세요, forming 해 주세요. When the last syllable of the verb stem contains ㅏ or ㅗ, -아 주세요 is used. In all other cases, -어 주세요 is used.

- 통화하고 싶어요. 저한테 전화해 주세요. I want to talk on the phone. Please call me.

- 가방을 잃어버렸어요. 제 가방을 찾아 주세요. I lost my bag. Please find my bag.

- 진수 씨가 요리를 잘해요. 맛있는 음식을 만들어 주세요.
  Jinsu is good at cooking. Please make something delicious for me.

- 제 딸의 좋은 친구가 되어 주세요. Please be a good friend to my daughter.

When asking someone to give you a noun rather than requesting them to perform an action, use 주세요 directly after the noun.

- 물 주세요. Please give me water.

- 사과 하나 더 주세요. Please give me one more apple.

- 우유 대신에 두유 주세요. Please give me soy milk instead of milk.

2 Conjugation

-아/어 주세요					
하다	해 주세요	부르다	*불러 주세요	굽다	*구워 주세요
찾다	찾아 주세요	듣다	*들어 주세요	돕다	*도와 주세요
찍다	찍어 주세요	만들다	만들어 주세요	짓다	*지어 주세요
쓰다	*써 주세요	입다	입어 주세요	주다	*주세요

3 Negation

The negation of -아/어 주세요 is formed by adding -지 마세요 or -지 말아 주세요 to the verb stem to politely ask or request someone not to do something. This applies regardless of whether the verb stem ends in a vowel or a consonant.

Both -지 마세요 and -지 말아 주세요 have similar meanings, but -지 말아 주세요 often conveys a softer and more polite tone compared to -지 마세요, which sounds more firm and direct.

- 교실에서 핸드폰을 사용하지 말아 주세요.
  Please do not use cell phones in the classroom.

- 진수 씨한테 비밀을 말하지 말아 주세요. 비밀을 지켜 주세요.
  Please do not tell Jinsu my secret. Please keep it a secret.

- 바닥에 쓰레기를 버리지 마세요. 쓰레기통에 쓰레기를 버려 주세요.
  Do not throw trash on the floor. Please throw your trash in the trash can.

Tip

When the listener is older, has a higher status, or is someone you are meeting for the first time, use -아/어 주시겠어요 instead of -아/어 주세요 to make a more respectful request.

Similarly, when responding in such situations, use -아/어 드릴게요 instead of the more casual -아/어 줄게요 to offer a polite affirmation.

- A 실례합니다. 길 좀 가르쳐 주시겠어요? Excuse me, could you show me the way?
  B 네, 가르쳐 드릴게요. Yes, I will show you.

- A 네? 잘 못 들었어요. 다시 말해 주시겠어요? What was that? Could you say it to me again?
  B 알겠어요. 다시 말해 드릴게요. I understand. Let me say it again.

Grammar in Action

1 When making a request or asking for an action

-아/어 주세요 is used when politely asking someone to perform an action that would benefit the speaker. In conversational speech, the adverb 좀 (please) can be added to gently emphasize the request. 좀 can replace the object particle 을/를 or precede an adverb or verb when making a request without an object or to express an earnest plea. Additionally, the adverb 제발 (please, I beg you) can be used to intensify the request, showing a stronger sense of earnestness.

- 사진 좀 찍어 주세요. (= 사진을 찍어 주세요.) Please take a picture.

- 민수 씨한테 제 안부 좀 전해 주세요. (= 안부를 전해 주세요.) Please say hello to Minsu.

- 좀 천천히 말해 주세요. Please speak slowly.

- 다시 안 할게요. 제발 한 번만 봐 주세요. I won't do it again. Please forgive me once.

When someone receives a request and agrees to follow through, they respond with -아/어 줄게요 added to the verb stem. This response mirrors the conjugation of -아/어 주세요, applying it in the same manner.

- A 이 문법 좀 다시 설명해 주세요. Please, explain it again.

  B 네, 다시 설명해 줄게요. Okay, I will explain it again.

- A 나중에 저한테 시간을 알려 주세요. Please, let me know the time later.

  B 알겠어요. 문자로 알려 줄게요. I understand. I'll let you know by text.

2 When giving gentle instructions

-아/어 주세요 can replace the imperative ending -(으)세요 to give gentle instructions. It is commonly used when telling a taxi driver a destination, providing polite instructions in public settings, or assisting customers in service industries.

- In a taxi   A 강남에 가 주세요. Please go to Gangnam.

                 B 네, 알겠습니다. Yes, I understand.

- At the bank   A 비밀번호를 눌러 주세요. Please press your password.

                 B 네, 여기에 누르면 돼요? Yes, can I click here?

- At the airport   A 줄을 서 주세요. Please stand in line.

                 B 네, 알겠어요. Yes, I understand.

Quiz 21

-아/어야 하다 must, have to, need to, should

Kor. 22

핸드폰 배터리가 없어요. My phone is out of battery.

충전해야 해요. I need to charge it.

Grammar Essentials

1 -아/어야 하다

In Korean, -아/어야 하다 expresses that the subject must perform a certain action or be in a required state. It conveys necessity or obligation, similar to "must", "have to", "need to", or "should" in English, depending on the context.

-아/어야 하다 is used with both verbs and adjectives. If the verb stem ends in 하, it conjugates as -해야 하다. If the last syllable of the verb stem contains ㅏ or ㅗ, use -아야 하다. In all other cases, use -어야 하다.

- 신발이 편해야 해요. Shoes must be comfortable.

- 늦었어요. 집에 가야 해요. It's late; I must go home.

- 채소를 반드시 먹어야 해요. You must eat vegetables.

- 축제에 사람이 많아야 해요. There must be a lot of people at the festival.

The verb 하다 in -아/어야 하다 can be replaced with 되다 (-아/어야 되다) without changing the meaning. However, since 되다 has a slightly passive nuance, -아/어야 하다 is generally more formal and conveys a stronger sense of obligation than -아/어야 되다.

- 건강을 위해 하루에 30분씩 운동해야 합니다. You must exercise 30 minutes a day for your health.

- 보고서는 내일까지 완료되어야 합니다. The report should be completed by tomorrow.

- 내일 늦어도 9시에 출발해야 돼요. 그러니까 8시 30분까지 오세요.
  You have to leave by 9 o'clock tomorrow at the latest. So, please come by 8:30.

- 저녁 식사 전에 숙제를 끝내야 돼요. You need to finish your homework before dinner.

2 Conjugation

-아/어야 하다			
하다	해야 하다	듣다	*들어야 하다
보다	봐야 하다	살다	살아야 하다
읽다	읽어야 하다	굽다	*구워야 하다
바쁘다	*바빠야 하다	낫다	*나아야 하다
다르다	*달라야 하다	그렇다	*그래야 하다

3 Negation

To express that something should not be done or a state one should not be in, 안 or -지 않다 is placed before -아/어야 하다. The adverb 절대(로) can be used to add emphasis.

- 인스턴트 음식을 안 먹어야 해요. You should not eat instant food.

- 절대로 거짓말을 하지 않아야 해요. You must never lie.

To negate -아/어야 하다, use -지 않아야 하다 or -지 말아야 하다. Both convey prohibition or advice against an action, but -지 말아야 하다 typically emphasizes prohibition more strongly than -지 않아야 하다.

- 친구의 고마움을 잊지 말아야 해요. You must never forget to thank your friends.
  = 친구의 고마움을 잊지 않아야 해요. You should not forget to be thankful to your friends.

4 Combination with nouns

When attaching 이다 to a noun to express necessity, use -여야 하다 if the noun ends in a vowel and -이어야 하다 if it ends in a consonant. To negate this form, use 아니어야 하다.

- 파티에 노래가 필요해요. 노래는 빠른 노래여야 해요.
  I need a song for the party. The song must be fast.

- 아르바이트 직원이 꼭 학생이어야 돼요.
  Part-time employees must be students.

- 어떤 옷이든 상관없지만 검은색 옷이 아니어야 해요.
  Any clothes are fine, but they must not be black.

5 Tenses

To express that an action or state was necessary in the past, -았/었- is added to 하다 in -아/어야 하다, forming -아/어야 했다.

- 어젯밤 늦게까지 일해야 했어요. 그래서 오늘 아침에 늦게 일어났어요.
  I had to work late last night, so I woke up late this morning.

To predict that an action or state will be necessary in the future, use -아/어야 할 것이다.

- 아마 진수가 다음 주에 이사해야 할 거예요.
  Jinsu will probably have to move next week.

Grammar in Action

1 When emphasizing essential and obligatory actions or states

-아/어야 하다 is used to highlight rules, obligations, or unavoidable circumstances. The adverbs 꼭 (definitely) and 반드시 (necessarily) can further emphasize this necessity.

- 비행기 출발 2시간 전에 공항에 도착해야 해요. We must arrive at the airport two hours before the flight.

- 길을 건널 때 조심해야 돼요. You must be careful when crossing the street.

- A 어떤 집을 찾아요? 특별한 조건이 있어요?
    What are you looking for in a house? Any specific requirements?

    B 화장실이 꼭 깨끗해야 해요. The bathroom must be clean.

- A 시험을 볼 때 뭐가 필요해요? What do you need to take the test?

    B 반드시 신분증이 있어야 해요. You must have an ID card.

- A 내일 만날 수 있어요? Can we meet tomorrow?

    B 미안해요. 시험이 있어서 공부해야 해요. Sorry. I have an exam and must study.

2 When giving advice

-아/어야 하다 is used to give advice by suggesting that the listener should or needs to take a certain action. When advising against an action, use -지 않아야 하다 or -지 말아야 하다.

- A 한국어 말하기가 어려워요. 어떻게 공부해야 해요? Speaking Korean is difficult. How should I study?

    B 한국 사람하고 많이 말해야 해요. You need to speak a lot with Koreans.

- A 스트레스가 많아서 너무 피곤해요. 어떻게 해야 해요?
    I'm very stressed and tired. What should I do?

    B 일단 집에 가서 쉬어야 해요. 그리고 스트레스 받지 않아야 해요.
    First, you should go home and rest. And try not to get stressed.

- A 친구하고 싸웠어요. 어떻게 해야 해요? I fought with my friend. What should I do?

    B 친구한테 사과해야 해요. 그리고 심한 말을 하지 말아야 해요.
    You should apologize to your friend. And avoid saying anything offensive.

Quiz 22

-아/어도 되다 You may/can

Kor. 23

A 화장실을 써도 돼요? Can I use the bathroom?

B 그럼요, 화장실은 이쪽에 있어요. Sure, the bathroom is over here.

1 -아/어도 되다

-아/어도 되다 is used with verbs, adjectives, or 이다 to express that performing an action or being in a certain state is permissible or acceptable. It can also indicate that something is not a problem or does not need to meet a certain requirement.

- 조금 늦어도 돼요. 천천히 오세요. It's okay if you're a little late. Take your time.

- 음식을 남겨도 괜찮아요. It's okay to leave some food.

When conjugating -아/어도 되다, if the verb or adjective stem ends in 하다, it becomes 해도 되다. If the last syllable of the stem contains the vowel ㅏ or ㅗ, use -아도 되다; in all other cases, use -어도 되다. Additionally, 되다 in -아/어도 되다 can be replaced with 좋다 or 괜찮다 to mean "good" or "okay", respectively, without changing the overall meaning.

- 30분만 운동해도 좋아요. Exercising for just 30 minutes is okay.

- 언제든지 우리 집에 와도 돼요. You can come to my house anytime.

- 집이 회사에서 조금 멀어도 괜찮아요. It's okay if your home is a little far from work.

2 Conjugation

-아/어도 되다			
하다	해도 되다	듣다	*들어도 되다
많다	많아도 되다	멀다	멀어도 되다
먹다	먹어도 되다	굽다	*구워도 되다
쓰다	*써도 되다	붓다	*부어도 되다
다르다	*달라도 되다	그렇다	*그래도 되다

3 Negation

To express that it is okay not to do a certain action or not to be in a certain state, the negative 안 or -지 않다 is used before -아/어도 되다.

- 그 일을 하기 싫으면 안 해도 돼요. If you don't want to do it, you don't have to.

- 힘들면 말하지 않아도 돼요. You don't have to say anything if you're having a hard time.

- 방이 안 커도 돼요. 화장실만 깨끗하면 돼요.
  The room doesn't have to be big. All I need is a clean bathroom.

- 집이 지하철역에서 가깝지 않아도 돼요. Your house does not have to be close to the subway station.

- 항상 완벽하지 않아도 괜찮아요. It is okay not to be perfect all the time.

129

4 Combination with nouns

When -아/어도 되다 is combined with "noun + 이다", the form changes based on the final sound of the noun. If the noun ends in a vowel, use -라도 되다 or -여도 되다. If the noun ends in a consonant, use -이라도 되다 or -이어도 되다.

- 저는 무슨 영화든지 다 좋아해요. 재미없는 영화라도 괜찮아요. (= 재미없는 영화여도 괜찮아요.)
  I like all kinds of movies. Even if it's a boring movie, it's okay.

- 누구든지 괜찮아요. 학생이어도 돼요. (= 학생이라도 괜찮아요.)
  Anyone is okay. Being a student is fine.

To express negation, use 아니라도 되다 or 아니어도 되다.

- 무슨 말이든 말해 주세요. 정답이 아니라도 돼요. (= 정답이 아니어도 돼요.)
  Feel free to tell me anything. It doesn't have to be the correct answer.

- 자동차가 새 차가 아니어도 돼요. It's okay if that car isn't new.

5 Tenses

To express that an action or state was acceptable in the past, use -아/어도 됐다.

- 옛날에는 늦게 출근해도 괜찮았어요. 그런데 지금은 8시까지 와야 해요.
  In the past, it was okay to come to work late. But now, you have to be there by 8 o'clock.

- 전에는 운동 안 해도 괜찮았어요. 그런데 지금은 운동해야 해요.
  It was okay not to exercise before, but now you must exercise.

To speculate that an action or state will be acceptable in the future, use -아/어도 될 것이다.

- 아마 다음 주에 숙제를 내도 괜찮을 거예요.
  It would probably be okay to assign homework next week.

- 내일 등산할 때 등산화 아니라 운동화를 신어도 될 거예요.
  It's okay to wear sneakers instead of hiking shoes when you go hiking tomorrow.

Grammar in Action

1 When asking for permission

A 이거 입어 봐도 돼요?
Can I try this on?

B 그럼요, 저쪽에서 입어 보세요.
Sure, you can try it on over there.

When asking for permission, -아/어도 되다 is used in a question format to inquire whether an action is permissible. This grammatical pattern is typically spoken with a rising intonation at the end. In responses granting permission, it is common to use -(으)세요 instead of repeating -아/어도 되다.

- A 이거 좀 써도 돼요? Can I use this?

  B 그럼요, 쓰세요. Sure, go ahead.

- A 들어가도 돼요? Can I come in?

  B 들어오세요. Please come in.

- A 오늘 조금 늦게 전화해도 돼요? Can I call you a little later today?

  B 네, 괜찮아요. Yes, it's okay.

2 When expressing social and cultural acceptance

A 우리 회사는 집에서 재택근무해도 돼요.
You can work from home at our company.

B 정말요? 우리 회사는 사무실에서 일해야 해요.
Really? Our company requires us to work in the office.

-아/어도 되다 is used with the stem of a verb, adjective, and "noun + 이다" to indicate that certain actions or states are socially or culturally acceptable.

- 기숙사 식당에서 밥을 먹지 않아도 돼요. 밖에 있는 식당에서 밥을 먹어도 돼요.
  You don't have to eat in the dormitory cafeteria. You can eat at the restaurant outside.

- 낮에는 조금 시끄러워도 돼요. 하지만 밤에는 조용해야 해요.
  It can be a little noisy during the day. But you have to be quiet at night.

- 아르바이트 학생은 남자여도 되고, 여자여도 돼요. 성별은 상관없어요.
  Part-time students can be either male or female. The gender does not matter.

Quiz 23

-(으)면 안 되다 You must not/It's not allowed

실내에서 담배를 피우면 안 돼요.

You must not smoke indoors.

1 -(으)면 안 되다

-(으)면 안 되다 is used to indicate that certain actions must not be performed or specific states must not be maintained. It can be combined with verbs, adjectives, or "noun + 이다". If the verb or adjective stem ends in a vowel, use -면 안 되다. If it ends in a consonant, use -으면 안 되다. For "noun + 이다", if the noun ends in a vowel, use -면 안 되다, and if it ends in a consonant, use -이면 안 되다.

- 술을 마시고 운전하면 안 돼요. Drinking and driving is not allowed.

- 사무실이 너무 작으면 안 돼요. The office must not be too small.

- 중학생이면 안 돼요. 고등학생부터 할 수 있어요.
  Middle school students are not eligible. Eligibility starts from high school

-(으)면 안 되다 can be used with the adverb 절대(로) to emphasize prohibition. To emphasize necessity, use the adverbs 꼭 or 반드시.

- 꼭 운동해야 해요. Exercising is a must.

- 절대로 포기하면 안 돼요. You should never give up.

2 Conjugation

-(으)면 안 되다			
하다	하면 안 되다	듣다	*들으면 안 되다
많다	많으면 안 되다	멀다	*멀면 안 되다
먹다	먹어도 되다	굽다	*구우면 안 되다
쓰다	쓰면 안 되다	붓다	*부으면 안 되다
다르다	다르면 안 되다	그렇다	*그러면 안 되다

3 Tenses

To express that something was prohibited in the past, use -(으)면 안 됐다.

- 옛날에는 여자가 바지를 입으면 안 됐어요. 하지만 지금은 괜찮아요.
  Historically, women were not allowed to wear pants, but now it is acceptable.

To speculate that an action or state should be prohibited in the future, use -(으)면 안 될 것이다.

- 진수 씨가 요즘 몸이 안 좋아요. 그래서 무리하면 안 될 거예요.
  Jinsu hasn't been feeling well lately. Therefore, exerting himself too much should be avoided.

1 When expressing prohibitions and restrictions

A 사진을 찍어도 돼요?
Can I take a picture?

B 아니요, 여기에서 사진을 찍으면 안 돼요.
No, you can't take pictures here.

-(으)면 안 되다 is used when an action is not permitted or is generally restricted due to cultural customs or norms.

- A 마스크를 벗어도 돼요? Can I take off my mask?

  B 아니요, 실내에서 마스크를 벗으면 안 돼요. No, you cannot take off your mask indoors.

- A 핸드폰 사전을 사용해도 돼요? Can I use the cell phone dictionary?

  B 아니요, 시험에서 핸드폰 사전을 사용하면 안 돼요.
  No, you cannot use your phone dictionary during the test.

- A 여기 주차해도 돼요? Can I park here?

  B 아니요, 여기에는 주차하면 안 돼요. 공용 주차장을 이용해 주세요.
  No, you can't park here. Please use public parking.

- 한국에서는 신발을 신고 집에 들어가면 안 돼요.
  In Korea, you cannot enter a house with your shoes on.

Double negation -지 않으면 안 되다

-지 않으면 안 되다 contains double negation, expressing strong affirmation that an action must be done. It is often interchangeable with -아/어야 하다. To further emphasize necessity, use 꼭 (certainly) or 반드시 (definitely) with -아/어야 하다.

- 이 강의를 듣기 위해서는 이 책을 안 읽으면 안 돼요. = 이 책을 꼭 읽어야 해요.
  To enroll in this course, avoiding this book is not an option. = You must read this book.

- 이 쿠폰은 이번 주까지 쓰지 않으면 안 돼요. = 반드시 써야 해요.
  This coupon must be used within this week. = You must use it.

2 When expressing warnings

핸드폰에 개인 정보를 저장하면 안 돼요.
You should not store personal information on your cell phone.

-(으)면 안 되다 is used to warn someone not to do something.

- 여기에 쓰레기를 버리면 안 됩니다. You must not throw away trash here.

- 앞으로 또 지각하면 안 됩니다. You must not be late again in the future.

- 비밀번호를 다른 사람과 공유하면 안 돼요. You must not share your password with anyone.

3 When suggesting another option

When written as a question, -(으)면 안 돼요? can suggest an alternative option. This pattern is often used in casual relationships (family, friends, or lovers) when making a strong suggestion.

- A 오늘 불고기 먹어요! Let's eat bulgogi today!

  B 삼겹살 먹으면 안 돼요? Can't we eat samgyeopsal?

  A 좋아요. 그럼, 삼겹살 먹어요! Okay, then, let's eat samgyeopsal!

- A 우리 토요일에 만날까요? Shall we meet on Saturday?

  B 금요일에 만나면 안 돼요? Can't we meet on Friday?

  A 금요일은 다른 일이 있어서 안 돼요. 그럼, 일요일에 만나면 어때요?
  Friday is not an option because I have something to do. Then, how about meeting on Sunday?

- A 오늘 밤에 영화 보러 가자. Let's go to the movies tonight!

  B 내일 가면 안 돼? Can't we go tomorrow instead?

  A 그래, 그럼 내일 가자. Sure, we can go tomorrow.

Quiz 24

-(으)면 되다 just need to...

Kor. 25

A 이거 어떻게 사용해요? How do you use this?
잘 모르겠어요. I don't really get it.

B 이 버튼만 누르면 돼요. You just need to press this button.

1 -(으)면 되다

-(으)면 되다 is used to indicate that a certain action or state is sufficient to solve a problem or fulfill a condition. It can be combined with verbs, adjectives, and "noun + 이다". If the stem of a verb or adjective ends in a vowel, use -면 되다, and if it ends in a consonant, use -으면 되다.

- 문제가 있을 때 여기에 전화하면 돼요. When there's a problem, you can just call here.

- 추운 날씨에는 두꺼운 옷을 입으면 돼요. On cold days, just wear thick clothes.

- 창문이 크면 괜찮아요. It's okay if the window is big.

- 머리가 짧으면 돼요. It's fine if your hair is short.

- 석사 학위만 있으면 돼요. 박사 학위는 없어도 돼요.
  All you need is a master's degree. You don't need a doctorate.

For "noun + 이다", if the last syllable of the noun ends in a vowel, use -면 되다. If it ends in a consonant, use -이면 되다.

- 커피면 돼요. 다른 것은 필요 없어요. Coffee is fine. Nothing else is needed.

- A 어떤 서류를 더 내야 해요? What additional documents do I need to submit?

  B 여권이면 돼요. 다른 서류는 필요 없어요. A passport is sufficient. No other documents are needed.

Instead of 되다, 괜찮다 can also be used in the form of -(으)면 괜찮다, meaning "it's okay if...".

- 프로그램이 조금 비싸지만, 재미있으면 괜찮아요. The program is a little expensive, but it's okay if it's fun.

2 Conjugation

-(으)면 되다					
보다	보면 되다	다르다	다르면 되다	쉽다	*쉬우면 되다
많다	많으면 되다	듣다	*들으면 되다	짓다	*지으면 되다
바쁘다	바쁘면 되다	길다	길면 되다	그렇다	*그러면 되다

3 Negation

To negate the meaning of -(으)면 되다, use 안 or -지 않다 before -(으)면 되다. This structure expresses that an action is not required or that a specific condition does not need to be met. For verbs or adjectives, attach -지 않으면 되다 to the stem, and for nouns, use 아니면 되다.

- 소화가 안 돼요? 밀가루 음식을 먹지 않으면 돼요. (= 안 먹으면 돼요.)
  Having digestive issues? You just need to not eat gluten foods.

- 걱정하지 마세요. 다시 실수하지 않으면 돼요. (= 실수 안 하면 돼요.)
  Don't worry. You just need to not make the same mistake again.

- 너무 비싸지 않으면 돼요. (= 안 비싸면 돼요)
  It's fine as long as it's not too expensive.

- 아무거나 드세요. 술이 아니면 괜찮아요.
  Eat anything. As long as it's not alcohol, it's okay.

4 Tenses

To express that a condition was sufficient in the past, use -(으)면 됐다.

- 전에 취직을 위해서 영어 공부만 하면 됐어요. 그런데 지금은 자격증도 따야 해요.
  In the past, just studying English was enough to get a job. But now, you also need to obtain certifications.

- 코로나19 이전에 해외여행 갈 때 여권과 비자만 있으면 됐어요.
  Before COVID-19, to travel abroad, having a passport and visa was enough.

To speculate that a future action or state will be sufficient, use -(으)면 될 것이다.

- 그 식당이 인기가 많아요? 일주일 전에 미리 예약하면 될 거예요.
  Is that restaurant popular? You should make a reservation a week in advance, then it should be okay.

- 한국 문화를 배우고 싶어요? 그러면 이 책을 읽으면 될 거예요.
  Want to learn about Korean culture? Then reading this book should be sufficient.

Grammar in Action

1 When offering an easy solution

지도 앱을 설치하면 돼요.

You just need to install a map app.

-(으)면 되다 is often used to offer a simple or easy solution to someone worried about a problem. This grammatical pattern presents a non-forceful, practical solution compared to -아/어야 하다, which emphasizes obligation.

- A 친구들이 집에 올 거예요. 음식 준비를 어떻게 해야 해요?
  My friends are coming over. How should I prepare the food?

  B 걱정하지 마세요. 음식은 배달하면 돼요. Don't worry. You can just order delivery.

- A 노트북이 고장 났어요. 어떻게 해야 돼요? My laptop is broken. What should I do?

  B 서비스 센터에서 노트북을 수리하면 돼요. You can have it repaired at the service center.

2 When expressing minimum conditions

A 집에 뭐가 필요해요? What do we need at home?
B 에어컨만 있으면 돼요. We just need an air conditioner.

-(으)면 되다 is also used to express the minimum requirement needed to achieve a goal. To emphasize the minimum requirement, use the particle 만 (only) after the noun.

- A 무엇을 준비해야 해요? What do I need to prepare?

  B 신분증만 있으면 돼요. 다른 건 필요 없어요. You just need your ID. Nothing else is necessary.

- A 여행 준비로 뭐가 필요해요? What do we need for the trip?

  B 여권만 준비하면 돼요. You just need to prepare your passport.

When expressing minimal conditions with verbs or adjectives, attach -기만 하면 되다.

- 약은 필요 없어요. 잠이 부족하니까 푹 자기만 하면 돼요.
  You don't need medicine. You just need to get enough sleep.

- 신발 디자인이 예쁘지 않아도 돼요. 신발이 편하기만 하면 돼요.
  It doesn't matter if the shoe design isn't pretty. Shoes just need to be comfortable.

Quiz 25

TOPIK I | SCK 1

-아/어 봤다 have tried

스쿠버 다이빙을 해 봤어요.

I've tried scuba diving.

패러글라이딩을 못 해 봤어요.

I've never tried paragliding.

1 -아/어 봤다

-아/어 봤다 is derived from -아/어 보다, which conveys the meaning of attempting or trying something. It indicates that the subject has tried or experienced a specific action, often as a test or experiment.

This pattern can be used with any subject (first, second, or third person) and is attached to verbs to indicate an attempted action. If the verb contains 하다, the stem 하 combines with -여 봤다, forming 해 봤다. If the last syllable of the verb stem contains ㅏ or ㅗ, attach -아 봤다. For all other cases, attach -어 봤다.

- 저는 번지 점프를 해 봤어요. I have tried bungee jumping.
- 전에 케이블카를 한 번 타 봤어요. I have ridden a cable car before.
- 제 동생이 한복을 입어 봤어요. My sibling has tried wearing a hanbok.

The verb 보다 (to see) has the same form as 보다 (to try), which indicates an attempt or trial. When expressing the experience of having seen something in the past, 보다 is not combined with -아/어 봤다. Instead, it is used only once in its past tense form, 봤어요.

- 전에 한국 드라마를 **봤어요**. (O) I have watched a Korean drama before.

  봐 봤어요. (✕)

Cases where you cannot use -아/어 봤다

The grammatical pattern -아/어 봤다 indicates that the subject of the sentence has attempted or experienced a specific action as a trial. Therefore, -아/어 봤다 is not used with verbs that describe habitual, repetitive actions such as 자다 (to sleep), 밥을 먹다 (to eat a meal), or 집에 가다 (to go home). However, -아/어 봤다 can be used to describe experiences that are special or unusual for the subject.

- 자 봤어요. (✕) → 집에서 잤어요. (O) I slept at home.   `Routine action`
  텐트에서 자 봤어요. (O) I have tried sleeping in a tent.   `Specific experience`
- 아침을 먹어 봤어요. (✕) → 아침을 먹었어요. (O) I ate breakfast.   `Routine action`
  삼계탕을 먹어 봤어요. (O) I have tried samgyetang.   `Specific experience`

Since -아/어 봤다 includes 보다 (to try), it implies an intentional attempt or experience. As a result, -아/어 봤다 cannot express accidental or unintentional experiences, such as accidents or injuries.

- 교통사고가 나 봤어요. (✕) → 교통사고가 났어요. (O) I had a traffic accident.
- 다리를 다쳐 봤어요. (✕) → 다리를 다쳤어요. (O) I injured my leg.
- 길을 가다가 우연히 배우를 만나 봤어요. (✕) → 우연히 배우를 만났어요. (O)

  I bumped into an actor.

2 Conjugation

-아/어 봤다			
하다	해 봤다	듣다	들어 봤다
오다	와 봤다	만들다	만들어 봤다
읽다	읽어 봤다	굽다	*구워 봤다
쓰다	*써 봤다	짓다	*지어 봤다
부르다	*불러 봤다	보다	*봤다

3 Negation

The negation of -아/어 봤다 is formed by adding 안 or 못, resulting in 안 해 봤다 and 못 해 봤다.

안 해 봤다 is used when simply stating that an action was not attempted in the past.

- A 제주도에 가 봤어요? Have you been to Jeju Island?

  B 아니요, 안 가 봤어요. No, I haven't been there.

  A 그럼, 어디에 가 봤어요? Then, where have you been?

  B 부산에 가 봤어요. I've been to Busan.

못 해 봤다 is often used with the adverb 아직 (yet) to indicate that one wants to try something but hasn't had the opportunity.

- A 제주도에 가 봤어요? Have you been to Jeju Island?

  B 아니요, 아직 못 가 봤어요. No, I haven't had the chance to go yet.

  A 제주도에 꼭 가 보세요. 정말 좋아요. You should definitely go to Jeju Island. It's really nice.

  B 네, 가 볼게요. Yes, I'll go.

Grammar in Action

1 When expressing an intentionally attempted experience

A 한복을 입어 봤어요?
Have you ever tried wearing a hanbok?

B 아니요, 아직 못 입어 봤어요.
한복을 입어 보고 싶어요.
No, I haven't had the chance to wear one yet.
I want to try wearing a hanbok.

-아/어 봤다 is used to indicate that the subject of the sentence has intentionally attempted or experienced a specific action in the past.

• A 닭갈비를 먹어 봤어요? Have you tried dakgalbi?

  B 네, 몇 번 먹어 봤어요. 진짜 맛있었어요. Yes, I've tried it a few times. It was really delicious.

 Note

Usage of 몇 in sentences

The word 몇 is used before a unit noun, but its meaning changes depending on the type of sentence. In declarative sentences, 몇 conveys an indefinite small number, while in interrogative sentences, it is used to ask about a specific quantity.

• 저도 대기업에서 몇 년 일해 봤어요. I also worked at a large company for several years.

• A 빵 몇 개 드릴까요? How many pieces of bread would you like?
  B 두 개 주세요. Two, please.

-아/어 봤다 is used to express that the subject of the sentence intentionally attempted a specific action in the past. However, once an attempt has been confirmed in a conversation, -아/어 봤다 should not be repeated. Instead, the past tense marker -았/었- is used in follow-up questions and responses.

• A 한강에서 자전거를 타 봤어요? Have you tried riding a bicycle at Hangang River?

  B 네, 한 번 타 봤어요. Yes, I've tried it once.

  A 언제 타 봤어요? (✕) → 언제 탔어요? (O) When did you ride it?

  B 지난달에 탔어요. 정말 재미있었어요. I rode it last month. It was really fun.

Quiz 26

143

27 -(으)ㄴ 적이 있다 have experienced

TOPIK I | SCK 2

Kor. 27

길을 잃어버린 적이 많이 있어요.

I have often gotten lost.

저는 길을 잃어버린 적이 한 번도 없어요.

I have never gotten lost.

Grammar Essentials

1 -(으)ㄴ 적이 있다

-(으)ㄴ 적이 있다 is used to express that the subject has experienced a certain action or state in the past, while -(으)ㄴ 적이 없다 indicates the absence of such experience. The particle 이 in -ㄴ 적이 있다 can sometimes be omitted, resulting in -(으)ㄴ 적 있다.

- 저는 전에 한복을 입은 적이 있어요. I have worn a hanbok before.
- 동생이 수술한 일이 없어요. My younger sibling has not had a surgery.

-(으)ㄴ 적이 있다 can be combined with verbs, adjectives, and "noun + 이다" to indicate past experiences. If the verb or adjective stem ends in a vowel, attach -ㄴ 적이 있다; if it ends in a consonant, attach -은 적이 있다. For nouns, attach 인 적이 있다.

- 전에 김치를 만든 적이 있어요. I have made kimchi before.
- 우울한 적이 있어요? Have you ever felt depressed?
- 스트레스가 많은 적이 있어요. I have been through a lot of stress.
- 저는 졸업 후에 사업을 시작했어요. 직장인인 적이 없어요.
  I started my own business after graduation. I have never been an employee.

Since -ㄴ in -ㄴ 적이 있다 already indicates the past, the past tense marker -었/았- is unnecessary. The noun 적 refers to a specific time in the past but implies an action or state when used with a verb. Therefore, -ㄴ 적이 있다 can sometimes be replaced with -ㄴ 일이 있다.

- 옛날에 친구하고 한국 음식을 만든 적이 있어요. (O) I have made Korean food with a friend in the past.
  만든 적이 있었어요. (×)

To emphasize that something has never been experienced, adverbs such as 전혀 (never) or 한 번도 (not even once) can be used with -(으)ㄴ 적이 없다.

- 그 얘기를 전혀 들은 적이 없어요. I have never heard of that.
- 저는 한국 음식을 먹은 적이 한 번도 없어요. I have never eaten Korean food.

To express an experience of not taking a specific action, use 안 or -지 않다 before -(으)ㄴ 적이 있다.

- 저는 친구의 문자를 읽고 답장하지 않은 적이 있어요.
  I once read a text message from a friend and did not reply.
- 회사 동료가 회의 때 저한테 연락 안 한 적이 있어요.
  There was a time when a coworker did not contact me during a meeting.

When -지 않은 적이 없다 is used, it creates double negation, which emphasizes that a certain action has always been performed.

- 저 사람은 항상 약속에 늦어요. 제 기억에 그 사람이 늦지 않은 적이 없어요.
  That person is always late for his appointments. Based on my memory, he has never been late before.

2 Conjugation

	-(으)ㄴ 적이 있다					
가다	간 적이 있다	부르다	부른 적이 있다	가깝다	*가까운 적이 있다
먹다	먹은 적이 있다	듣다	*들은 적이 있다	붓다	*부은 적이 있다
아프다	아픈 적이 있다	힘들다	*힘든 적이 있다	그렇다	*그런 적이 있다

3 -아/어 본 적이 있다

-아/어 본 적이 있다 is a grammatical pattern that combines -아/어 보다, which conveys the meaning of attempting or trying, with -(으)ㄴ 적이 있다, which expresses that the subject has intentionally attempted an experience.

While -(으)ㄴ 적이 있다 can be combined with verbs, adjectives, and "noun + 이다?", -아/어 본 적이 있다 is only used with verbs. If you want to express an attempted experience with an adjective, use -(으)ㄴ 적이 있다 instead.

- 혼자 여행해 본 적이 있어요. I have traveled alone before.

- 한국 절에 가 본 적이 없어요. I have never been to a Korean temple.

- 불고기를 먹어 본 적이 몇 번 있어요. I have eaten bulgogi several times before.

To express the experience of trying something, rather than repeating the verb 보다 with -아/어 보다, simply use 보다 once in the pattern 본 적이 있다.

- 자막 없이 한국 영화를 <u>본 적이 있어요</u>. (O) I have watched a Korean movie without subtitles.
  봐 본 적이 있어요. (×)

To express the presence or absence of experience using adjectives, use -(으)ㄴ 적이 있다/없다 instead of -아/어 본 적이 있다.

- 시험이 쉬워 본 적이 없어요. (×) → 시험이 쉬운 적이 없어요. (O) I have never had an easy exam.

4 Conjugation

	-아/어 본 적이 있다		
가다	가 본 적이 있다	살다	*살아 본 적이 있다
오다	와 본 적이 있다	굽다	*구워 본 적이 있다
쓰다	써 본 적이 있다	짓다	*지어 본 적이 있다
부르다	*불러 본 적이 있다	그렇다	*그래 본 적이 있다
듣다	*들어 본 적이 있다	보다	*본 적이 있다

Grammar in Action

1 When expressing the presence or absence of experience

A 한국 앱으로 음식 배달을 주문해 본 적이 있어요?
Have you ever ordered food for delivery using a Korean app?

B 아니요, 아직 없어요. 한번 해 보고 싶어요.
No, not yet. I'd like to try it sometime.

While -(으)ㄴ 적이 있다 can broadly be used to express an experience the subject has had, -아/어 본 적이 있다 is used when emphasizing an experience that was intentionally attempted. When replying, you can omit repetition and respond concisely with 있다 or 없다.

- 아프리카를 여행한 적이 있어요. 그때 정말 재미있었어요.
  I have traveled to Africa. It was really fun then.

- 그 친구하고 성격이 잘 맞아요. 그래서 그 친구와 싸운 적이 한 번도 없어요.
  I get along well with that friend. That's why I've never fought with her.

- 피아노를 배워 본 적이 있어요. 그런데 피아노 치는 것이 어려웠어요.
  I have tried learning the piano. But playing piano was really difficult.

- A 한국의 전통 술을 마셔 본 적이 있어요? Have you ever tried traditional Korean alcohol?

- B 아니요, 없어요. 맛이 어때요? No, I haven't. What does it taste like?

2 When expressing an accidental and unintentional experience

A 교통사고가 난 적이 있어요?
Have you ever been in a traffic accident?

B 아니요, 교통사고가 난 적이 없어요.
No, I have never been in a traffic accident.

When expressing accidental or unintentional experiences, -(으)ㄴ 적이 있다 is used instead of -아/어 본 적이 있다. This form is applied regardless of the subject's intention, particularly for negative experiences such as accidents, injuries, or failures. Even for positive experiences like winning the lottery, if the event occurred unintentionally, -(으)ㄴ 적이 있다 is still used instead of -아/어 본 적이 있다.

- 기차를 잘못 탄 적이 있어요. 그때 고생했어요.
  I have taken the wrong train before. I had a hard time back then.

- 10년 전에 복권에 당첨된 적이 있어요. 그때를 잊을 수 없어요.
  I won the lottery ten years ago. I can't forget that time.

- A 전에 다리를 다친 적이 있어요? Have you ever injured your leg before?

  B 네, 그런 적 있어요. Yes, I have.

Quiz 27

-고 있다 be ...ing [Action]

민수가 의자에 앉아 있어요. Minsu is sitting in a chair.

민수가 핸드폰을 보고 있어요. Minsu is looking at his cell phone.

진호가 소파에 누워 있어요. Jinho is lying on the sofa.

진호가 자고 있지 않아요. Jinho is not sleeping.

음악을 듣고 있어요. He is listening to music.

1 -고 있다

-고 있다 is combined with an action verb to indicate that an action is currently in progress. Regardless of whether the verb stem ends with a vowel or a consonant, -고 있다 is used. The subject of -고 있다 can be in the first, second, or third person.

- 친구가 지금 자고 있어요. My friend is sleeping right now.

- 지금 밥을 먹고 있어요. 이따가 전화할게요. I'm eating food now. I'll call you later.

- 저는 요즘 학원에서 태권도를 배우고 있어요. I am learning taekwondo at an academy these days.

2 Conjugation

-고 있다							
보다	보고 있다	쓰다	쓰고 있다	걷다	걷고 있다	굽다	굽고 있다
먹다	먹고 있다	부르다	부르고 있다	살다	살고 있다	짓다	짓고 있다

3 Negation

To express the negative form of -고 있다, place 안 before -고 있다 or use -고 있지 않다 (-고 있다 + -지 않다). Note that -고 없다 is not used as the negation of -고 있다.

- 지금 이메일을 <u>안 쓰고 있어요</u>. (O) I'm not writing an email right now.
  쓰고 없어요. (✕)

- 친구가 책을 <u>읽고 있지 않아요</u>. (O) My friend is not reading a book.
  읽고 없어요. (✕)

4 Tenses

To express an action that was in progress in the past, attach -았/었- before -고 있다.

- 어제 9시에 자고 있었어요. 그래서 동료 전화를 못 받았어요.
  I was sleeping at 9 o'clock yesterday. So I couldn't answer my colleague's phone call.

- 조금 전에 책을 읽고 있었어요. 그래서 지나가는 사람을 못 봤어요.
  I was reading a book a little while ago. So I didn't see anyone passing by.

To express that an action will likely be in progress in the future, attach -(으)ㄹ 것이다 to -고 있다, forming -고 있을 것이다.

- 아마 마이클 씨가 지금 회사에서 일하고 있을 거예요. Michael is probably working at the company now.

Be careful!

-고 있었다 expresses an action that was in progress at a specific point in time. For an extended duration, use the simple past tense -았/었- instead of -고 있었다.

- 제가 어렸을 때 <u>아르바이트하고 있었어요</u>. (✕) I worked part-time when I was young.
  → 아르바이트했어요. (O)

Lesson 28

-고 있다

149

Grammar in Action

1 When expressing an action in progress at a specific point

A 지금 뭐 하고 있어요?
What are you doing now?

B 운동하고 있어요.
I'm exercising.

-고 있다 expresses an action in progress at a specific point in time. When describing actions currently in progress, it is often used with the adverb 지금 (now). When describing actions that were in progress in the past, it is used with time expressions referring to a specific past moment (e.g. "at 9 o'clock yesterday").

- A 지금 뭐 하고 있어요? What are you doing now?

  B 지금 핸드폰을 찾고 있어요. I'm looking for my cell phone right now.

- A 어젯밤 9시에 뭐 하고 있었어요? What were you doing at 9 o'clock last night?

  B 어젯밤 9시에 집에서 자고 있었어요. I was sleeping at home at 9 o'clock last night.

In Korean, the informal polite present tense -아/어요 can also be used with 지금 (now) to express an ongoing action, similar to -고 있다.

- A 지금 어디에 가요? (= 가고 있어요?) Where are you going now?

  B 친구 만나러 가요. (= 가고 있어요.) I'm going to meet a friend.

- A 지금 뭐 해요? (= 하고 있어요?) What are you doing now?

  B 내일 시험이 있어서 지금 공부해요. (= 공부하고 있어요.) I have a test tomorrow, so I'm studying now.

2 When expressing a repetitive action over a specific period

요즘 한국 노래를 듣고 있어요.
I'm listening to Korean songs these days.

-고 있다 is used with the adverb 요즘 (these days) to express an action that is repeatedly occurring over a specific period.

- 요즘 시간이 날 때마다 집을 찾고 있어요. These days, whenever I have time, I am looking for a house.

- A 요즘 부산에서 뭐 하고 있어요? What are you doing in Busan these days?

  B 한국 회사에서 일하고 있어요. I work at a Korean company.

3 When expressing wearing attire

제임스가 흰색 티셔츠하고 청바지를 입고 있어요.
James is wearing a white t-shirt and jeans.

그리고 운동화를 신고 있어요. 모자를 쓰고 있어요.
And he's wearing sneakers. He's wearing a hat.

하지만 안경을 쓰고 있지 않아요. (= 안 쓰고 있어요.)
But he's not wearing glasses.

-고 있다 is used with wearing verbs such as 입다 (to wear clothes), 신다 (to wear shoes), 쓰다 (to wear headgear), 차다 (to wear accessories like a watch), 끼다 (to wear gloves/rings), and 하다 (to wear necklaces, ties, makeup, etc.) to indicate that the result of a completed action is continuing.

- To describe something currently being worn, use -고 있다.
- To indicate that something was previously worn, add the past tense marker -았/었-.

- 로지 씨가 치마를 <u>입고 있어요</u>. Rosie is wearing a skirt.

    (= 입었어요)

- 유진 씨가 목걸이를 <u>하고 있어요</u>. Yujin is wearing a necklace.

    (= 했어요)

- 진수 씨가 시계를 <u>차고 있지 않아요</u>. Jinsu is not wearing a watch.

    (= 차지 않았어요)

Tip

-고 있다 can indicate both the progress of an action and the state after the action is completed. When used with wearing verbs, the meaning depends on the context:

▶ Action: Describes the moment of putting on the clothing or accessory.
▶ State: Describes the fact that the clothing or accessory is already being worn.

진수 씨가 지금 자켓을 입고 있어요. [Action]
Jinsu is currently in the process of putting on his jacket.

진수 씨가 지금 자켓을 입고 있어요. [State]
Jinsu is already wearing his jacket.

Quiz 28

TOPIK II | SCK 2

-아/어 있다 be ...ing [State]

Kor. 29

유진 씨 방에 창문이 열려 있어요.
The window in Yujin's room is open.

그런데 문이 닫혀 있어요.
But the door is closed.

벽에 그림이 걸려 있어요.
There's a picture hanging on the wall.

탁자 위에 커피가 놓여 있어요.
There is coffee on the table.

유진 씨가 의자에 앉아 있어요.
Yujin's is sitting on a chair.

진수 씨 방에 창문이 닫혀 있어요.
The window in Jinsu's room is closed.

그런데 문이 열려 있어요.
But the door is open.

벽에 시계가 걸려 있어요.
There is a clock hanging on the wall.

탁자 위에 책이 놓여 있어요.
There is a book on the table.

진수 씨가 앉아 있지 않아요.
Jinsu is not sitting.

서 있어요.
He is standing.

1 -아/어 있다

The grammatical pattern -아/어 있다 indicates that the result of an action continues after it has been completed. While -고 있다 expresses an ongoing action, -아/어 있다 shows the state that remains once the action is finished.

- 진수 씨가 지하철로 집에 가고 있어요. Jinsu is going home by subway.   Action

  진수 씨가 집에 가 있어요. Mr. Jinsu has arrived at home.   Result of action

- 진수 씨가 문을 열고 있어요. Mr. Jinsu is opening the door.   Action

  문이 열려 있어요. The door is open.   Result of action

-아/어 있다 is only used with verbs that do not require an object, such as intransitive verbs or passive expressions. As a result, verbs combined with -아/어 있다 cannot be used with the object particle 을/를 and must always be paired with the subject particle 이/가.

- 가방이 걸고 있어요. (✕) → 가방이 걸려 있어요. (○) The bag is hanging.
- 가방을 걸려 있어요. (✕) → 가방을 걸고 있어요. (○) I'm hanging my bag.

The grammatical pattern -아/어 있다 is also used with verbs like 서다 (to stand), 앉다 (to sit), 눕다 (to lie down) to describe a state that continues.

- 동생이 자고 있지 않아요. 그냥 침대 위에 누워 있어요.
  My younger brother is not sleeping. He's just lying on the bed.

- 계속 의자에 앉아 있으면 허리에 좋지 않아요.
  Continuously sitting on a chair is not good for your back.

When verbs like 서다 (to stand), 앉다 (to sit), or 눕다 (to lie down) are used with -고 있다, they express an action taking place over a short period of time.

- 진수가 교실 의자에 앉고 있을 때 선생님이 교실에 왔어요.   In the process of sitting down
  The teacher came to the classroom while Jinsu was sitting on the classroom chair.

- 진수가 수업 시간에 계속 의자에 앉아 있어요.   State after sitting down
  Jinsu keeps sitting on his chair during class.

2 Conjugation

-아/어 있다					
앉다	앉아 있다	닫히다	닫혀 있다	들다	들어 있다
서다	서 있다	놓이다	놓여 있다	눕다	*누워 있다
열리다	열려 있다	걸리다	걸려 있다	붓다	*부어 있다

3 Negation

To express the negation of -아/어 있다, place 안 before it or use -아/어 있지 않다 (a combination of -아/어 있다 and -지 않다).

- 책에 이름이 <u>안 쓰여져</u> 있어요. (O) The name is not written in the book.
   쓰여져 없어요. (✕)

- 방에 불이 <u>꺼져 있지 않아요</u>. (O) The light in the room is not turned off.
   꺼져 없어요. (✕)

> **Note**
>
> The negation of -아/어 있다 is not -아/어 없다.
> - 책에 이름이 <u>안 쓰여져</u> 있어요. (O) The name is not written in the book.
>   쓰여져 없어요. (✕)
> - 방에 불이 <u>꺼져 있지 않아요</u>. (O) The light in the room is not turned off.
>   꺼져 없어요. (✕)

4 Tenses

To express that a state was continuing in the past, add the past tense marker -았/었- to 있다 in -아/어 있다, forming -아/어 있었다.

- 어젯밤에 진수 방에 불이 켜져 있었어요. 아마 진수 씨가 공부하는 것 같았어요.
   Last night, the light was on in Jinsu's room. It seemed like Jinsu was probably studying.

- 10분 전에 윤아가 교실에 앉아 있었어요. 지금도 아마 교실에 있을 거예요.
   Yuna was sitting in the classroom 10 minutes ago. She's probably still in class now.

To express the speaker's guess that a certain state is continuing or will occur in the future, use -아/어 있을 것이다, a combination of -아/어 있다 and -(으)ㄹ 것이다.

- 마이클 씨가 아파요. 아마 집에서 침대에 누워 있을 거예요.
   Michael is sick. He's probably lying in bed at home.

> **Tip**
>
> **The difference between -고 있다 and -아/어 있다**
>
> ▷ -고 있다 is combined with action verbs and cannot be used with stative verbs like 앉다 (to sit) and 서다 (to stand).
>
> ▷ -아/어 있다 is used with stative verbs to express that a state is continuing.
>
> - 민수 씨가 3시간 동안 의자에 <u>앉고 있어요</u>. (✕) → 앉아 있어요. (O)
>   Minsu has been sitting on the chair for 3 hours.
> - 오늘 아침부터 저녁까지 계속 <u>서고 있었어요</u>. (✕) → 서 있었어요. (O)
>   I was standing there from morning to evening today.

Grammar in Action

1 When describing the continuation of a state

책상 위에 노트북하고 컵하고 스피커가 놓여 있어요.
There is a laptop, a cup, and a speaker on the desk.

컴퓨터가 켜져 있지 않아요. 꺼져 있어요.
The computer is not turned on. It's off.

컵에 커피가 들어 있어요.
스피커에서 음악이 나오고 있어요.
There is coffee in the cup. Music is coming from the speaker.

The grammatical pattern -아/어 있다 is used to describe the ongoing state of an object or person after an action has already been completed. In contrast, -고 있다 is used to express an action that is currently in progress. When asking about a certain state, you can say: "어떻게 되어 있어요?".

- A 핸드폰이 어떻게 되어 있어요? What is your cell phone like?

  B 핸드폰이 깨져 있어요. My cell phone is broken.

2 When describing the result of a completed action

남자가 식당에 가고 있어요.
A man is on his way to the restaurant.
(= A man is going to the restaurant.)

여자는 벌써 식당에 가 있어요.
The woman is already at the restaurant.
(= The woman has arrived at the restaurant.)

-아/어 있다 is mainly used with passive verbs or intransitive verbs to describe a state that continues after an action has been completed.

- 회의실에 사람들이 다 모여 있어요. All the people are gathered in the meeting room.

- 접시 위에 음식이 남아 있어요. Food remains on the plate.

-아/어 있다 is used with action verbs like 가다 (to go) and 오다 (to come) to distinguish between an action in progress and the state after its completion. When combined with -고 있다, it expresses the ongoing progress of the movement. In contrast, when combined with -아/어 있다, it expresses the state that remains after the movement has been completed.

- 일주일 전에 주문한 물건이 아직도 오고 있어요. The item I ordered a week ago is still on its way.

- 집 앞에 물건이 와 있어요. The item has arrived in front of my house.

Quiz 29

155

Lesson

30

TOPIK I | SCK 1

-겠- will / must be

Kor. 30

이번 경기는 꼭 이기겠습니다.

I will definitely win this match.

저 선수가 많이 아프겠어요.

That player must be very hurt.

A 케이크가 맛있겠어요!

The cake must be delicious!

B 케이크가 달겠어요!

The cake must be sweet!

1 -겠- Expressing intention

The pre-final ending -겠- expresses the speaker's or listener's intention at the moment of speaking. In declarative sentences, it shows the speaker's determination or willingness to perform a future action. In interrogative sentences, it is used to inquire about the listener's intention or preference regarding a future action.

-겠- can be attached to verbs, regardless of whether the verb stem ends in a vowel or a consonant. To express the intention not to perform an action or to indicate refusal, the negation 안 or -지 않다 is placed before -겠-.

- 내일까지 이 일을 끝내겠습니다. I will finish this work by tomorrow.

- 창가와 복도 중에서 어떤 좌석을 하시겠습니까? Which seat would you prefer, window or aisle?

- 이 얘기를 다른 사람에게 말하지 않겠습니다. I won't tell this to anyone else.

> **TIP**
>
> **The difference between -겠- and -(으)ㄹ 것이다, when expressing intention**
>
> Both -겠- and -(으)ㄹ 것이다 express the speaker's intention, but they differ slightly in meaning and usage. -겠- is used when the speaker shows determination or resolve to take a specific action at the moment of speaking. In contrast, -(으)ㄹ 것이다 is used when the speaker expresses their intention based on the belief that a certain action or state will naturally occur.
>
> - 우리 팀이 반드시 이기겠습니다. Our team will definitely win.
>   Expresses determination to win as a player
> - 우리 팀이 반드시 이길 거예요. Our team will definitely win.
>   Expresses belief that the team will win as a supporter

2 Conjugation

-겠-					
보다	보겠어요	부르다	부르겠어요	춥다	춥겠어요
먹다	먹겠어요	듣다	듣겠어요	붓다	붓겠어요
아프다	아프겠어요	힘들다	힘들겠어요	그렇다	그렇겠어요

3 -겠- Expressing a guess

The pre-final ending -겠- indicates the speaker's or listener's guess about an event or state at the moment of speaking. In declarative sentences, it expresses the speaker's guess, while in interrogative sentences, it asks about the listener's guess.

이 케이크를 보세요. (제가 추측하기에) 케이크가 맛있겠어요.

　　　　　　　　　　Subject of speculation　Contents of speculation

Look at this cake. (I guess) the cake must be delicious.

(네가 추측하기에) 한국 축구 팀이 이기겠어?

　Subject of speculation　Contents of speculation

(Can you predict whether) the Korean soccer team will win?

When -겠- is used for guessing, the subject can be in the first, second, or third person. However, when -겠- expresses intention, it typically applies to the first person in statements and the second person in questions.

Unlike -겠- for expressing intention, -겠- for guessing can be combined with verbs, adjectives, and "noun + 이다". This distinguishes it from its use in intentional statements, where it is only attached to verbs to indicate determination or intent.

- 이 일을 하면 제가 스트레스를 받겠어요.　　　　The speaker's guess about oneself
  I will be stressed if I do this job.

- 넘어졌어요? 많이 아프겠어요.　　　　　The speaker's guess about the second person
  Did you fall? It must hurt a lot.

- 동생이 이제 대학생이겠어요.　　　　　The speaker's guess about the third person
  Your younger brother is now a college student.

- 숙제가 너무 많아요. 학생들이 좋아하겠어요?　　Listener's guess about the third person
  There is too much homework. Will your students like it?

TIP

The difference between -겠- and -(으)ㄹ 것이다 when expressing a guess

Both -겠- and -(으)ㄹ 것이다 express the speaker's guess about an event or situation, but they differ in subtle ways. -겠- is used when the guess is based on clear evidence or logical reasoning. In contrast, -(으)ㄹ 것이다 is used when the guess is more general, vague, or relies on personal belief rather than concrete evidence.

- 진수가 정말 열심히 공부해요. 진수가 이번 시험을 잘 보겠어요.

  　Logical basis for inference　　　Inference based on evidence

  Jinsu studies really hard. Jinsu will do well on this exam.

- 화장품을 선물해 보세요. 아마 어머니가 좋아할 거예요. Give cosmetics as a gift. Maybe your mom will like it.

  　Guess based on personal belief rather than evidence

4 Person

-겠- indicating intention is used with the first person in declarative sentences and the second person in interrogative sentences. When used for guessing, -겠- can apply to the first, second, or third perosn. A first person subject with -겠- can indicate either intention or a guess, depending on the context. However, with second or third person subjects, it always indicates a guess.

- 저는 내일 9시까지 오겠습니다.   First-person intention
  I will be there by 9 o'clock tomorrow.

- 일이 너무 많아요. 저는 오늘도 하루 종일 일하겠어요.   First-person guess
  There is too much work. I will work all day today again.

- 내일 너도 집에 있겠다.   Second-person guess
  You will be home tomorrow too.

- 선생님이 내일도 숙제를 많이 주겠어요.   Third-person guess
  The teacher will give us a lot of homework tomorrow as well.

5 Combinations

-겠-, when expressing intention, is used only with verbs. For guessing, it can combine with verbs, adjectives, and "noun + 이다". Thus, when -겠- is used with a verb in the first person, it may indicate either intention or a guess, depending on the context. However, when -겠- is combined with an adjective or "noun + 이다", it expresses a guess rather than intention.

- 오늘은 많이 준비했어요. 꼭 맛있는 음식을 만들겠어요.   Verb indicating intention
  I prepared a lot today. I will definitely make delicious food.

- 바람이 많이 불어요. 코트가 없으면 감기에 걸리겠어요.   Verb indicating guess
  It's very windy. If I don't have a coat, I'll catch a cold.

- 주말에 일도 없고 친구하고 약속도 없어요. 진짜 심심하겠어요.   Adjective indicating guess
  I have no work or plans with friends on the weekend. I must be really bored.

- 유진 옆에 있는 사람이 유진의 남자 친구겠어요.   Noun indicating guess
  The person next to Yujin is probably her boyfriend.

6 Tenses

-겠- expresses the speaker's or listener's intention at the moment of speaking and does not combine with -았/었-. To express a past intention, attach -(으)려고 했다 to the verb stem.

- 어제 제가 운동했겠어요. (✗) → 어제 제가 운동하려고 했어요. (○)   Intention
  I tried to exercise yesterday.

When -겠- is used for guessing, it can combine with the past tense marker -았/었-, forming -았/었겠-, to express speculation about past events or states.

- 친구들하고 여행한 것이 재미있었겠어요.   Past guess
  It must have been fun traveling with friends.

1 When expressing the speaker's commitment or determination

앞으로 밤에 야식을 먹지 않겠어요.
I won't eat late at night from now on.

-겠- is used to express the speaker's commitment or determination, often conveying aspirations in formal settings. In casual speech, -(으)ㄹ게 may be used instead, offering a less formal way to express intent while also considering the listener.

• 앞으로 열심히 하겠습니다. = 앞으로 열심히 할게요. I will work hard from now on.

• 올해는 꼭 대학교에 입학하겠습니다. I will definitely enter university this year.

• 무슨 일이 있어도 여러분 곁에 있겠습니다. No matter what happens, I will be by your side.

2 When asking about the listener's intentions

A 뭐 드시겠습니까?
What would you like to eat?

B 저는 스테이크를 주문하겠습니다.
I will order steak.

C 저도 같은 걸로 주문할게요.
I will order the same thing.

-겠- in questions probes the listener's intentions. In polite contexts, especially customer service, the form -(으)시겠습니까 is commonly used. For informal inquiries, -(으)ㄹ래 can be used instead, while -(으)ㄹ게 often expresses personal intent in response.

• A 어떻게 가시겠습니까? How would you like to get there?

  B 저는 택시로 가겠습니다. I will go by taxi.

• 이번 게임이 끝났습니다. 계속 하시겠습니까? This game is over. Do you want to continue?
                    (= 계속 할래요?)

3 When making guesses about an event or condition

A 요즘 잠을 못 자요.
I can't sleep these days.

B 그래요? 정말 피곤하겠어요.
Really? You must be really tired.

-겠- is used to infer outcomes based on observed conditions. For present events or states, -겠- is used, while for past events or completed conditions, -았/었겠- is used to indicate speculation.

- A 오늘 아무것도 못 먹었어요. I couldn't eat anything today.

  B 그래요? 배고프겠어요. Really? You must be hungry.

- 진수가 아르바이트를 시작했어요. 이제 진수를 자주 못 만나겠어요.
  Jinsu started working part-time. I won't be able to see Jinsu often anymore.

4 When announcing future actions in public

다음으로 표를 보겠습니다.

Next, let's look at the charts.

In formal settings such as public presentations or meetings, -겠- is commonly used to announce upcoming content or actions. Facilitators or speakers often use -겠- to indicate the next steps or progression of a presentation.

- 지금부터 회의를 시작하겠습니다. We will start the meeting now.

- 이상으로 발표를 마치겠습니다. This concludes the presentation.

5 When expressing or asking an opinion in a polite manner

-겠- is used to politely and indirectly express opinions or ask questions, similar to saying "I believe", "I think", or "Might you" in English. For added politeness, it can be combined with expressions like -(으)면 좋겠다 or -(으)ㄹ 수 있다. However, omitting -겠- in these contexts does not significantly change the overall meaning.

- A 컴퓨터가 고장 났어요. The computer is broken.

  B 잠깐만요, 제가 고치면 되겠어요. (= 고치면 돼요.) Just a moment, I suppose I could fix it.

- A 여기 물이 너무 깊어요. The water here is too deep.

  B 이 정도면 저도 수영할 수 있겠어요. (= 수영할 수 있어요.)
    It's okay. I can swim at this depth.

Quiz 30

-(으)ㄹ까? Shall we? / Would it be?

Kor. 31

A 우리 같이 점심 먹을까요?

B 좋아요. 같이 점심 먹어요!

A Shall we have lunch together?
B Sounds good. Let's have lunch together!

A 저 사람이 몇 살일까요?

B 글쎄요, 아마 20대일 거예요.

A How old is that person?
B Well, probably in his 20s.

Grammar Essentials

1 -(으)ㄹ까 Expressing intention

When using the ending -(으)ㄹ까 to express intention, attach -ㄹ까 if the verb stem ends in a vowel and -을까 if it ends in a consonant. This form is typically accompanied by a rising intonation, indicating that the speaker is asking for the listener's opinion or thoughts about performing a certain action.

- A 오늘 내가 저녁을 준비할까? Should I prepare dinner today?
  B 그래. 네가 해 줘. Yes. You do it.

- A 같이 사진 찍을까요? Shall we take a picture together?
  B 좋아요. 같이 사진 찍어요! Good. Let's take a picture!

2 -(으)ㄹ까 Expressing a guess

When expressing a guess with -(으)ㄹ까, it can be used with verbs, adjectives, and "noun + 이다". For verbs and adjectives, attach -ㄹ까 if the stem ends in a vowel and -을까 if it ends in a consonant. For nouns followed by 이다, attach -일까 regardless of the noun's final syllable. In responses, guesses are typically answered using -(으)ㄹ 것이다 to indicate probability.

- A 내일 비가 올까요? Will it rain tomorrow?
  B 글쎄요, 아마 비가 안 올 거예요. Well, it probably won't rain.

- A 저 사람이 선생님일까요? Will that person be a teacher?
  B 제 생각에, 저 사람은 아마 학생일 거예요. In my guess, that person is likely a student.

혹시 (perhaps) is used in questions or hypothetical sentences, while 아마 (probably) is used in declarative sentences. Thus, -(으)ㄹ까 is frequently paired with 혹시 to ask about a possibility, whereas -(으)ㄹ 것이다 is typically used with 아마 in responses to express probability.

- A 혹시 저 사람이 한국어를 할 수 있을까요? Might that person be able to speak Korean?
  B 네, 아마 한국어를 할 수 있을 거예요. Yes, he probably can speak Korean.

3 Conjugation

-(으)ㄹ까?					
보다	볼까?	부르다	부를까?	돕다	*도울까?
먹다	먹을까?	듣다	*들을까?	붓다	*부을까?
쓰다	쓸까?	살다	*살까?	그렇다	*그럴까?

163

4 Negation

When -(으)ㄹ까 is used in negation, it expresses the speaker's concern or expectation about a particular situation. The negation is formed using -지 않을까 for verbs or adjectives and 아닐까 for nouns.

- A 지금 택시를 타면 길이 막히지 않을까요? If I take a taxi now, won't the road be blocked?

  B 맞아요. 지금 택시를 타면 길이 막힐 거예요. That's right. If you take a taxi now, the road will be blocked.

- A 내일 파티에 음식이 부족하지 않을까요? Won't there be a shortage of food at the party tomorrow?

  B 제 생각에 음식이 충분할 거예요. I think there will be enough food.

- A 환경이 가장 큰 문제가 아닐까요? Isn't the environment the biggest problem?

  B 네, 제 생각도 환경이 가장 큰 문제예요. Yes, in my opinion, the environment is the biggest problem.

5 Tenses

To express a guess about something that occurred or was happening in the past, -았/었을까 is used by incorporating the past tense marker -았/었-. For verbs or adjectives ending in 하다, use 했을까. If the last vowel in the verb or adjective stem is ㅏ or ㅗ, use -았을까; for all other cases, use -었을까. When attaching the form to nouns, use -이었을까 if the final syllable ends in a consonant, and -였을까 if it ends in a vowel. Typically, when responding to a question with -았/었을까, speakers use -았/었을 것이다 to indicate a guess.

- A 비행기가 제주도에 벌써 도착했을까요? Has the plane already arrived in Jeju Island?

  B 아니요, 아직 도착 안 했을 거예요. No, it probably hasn't arrived yet.

- A 민수가 어렸을 때도 키가 컸을까요? Was Minsu tall when he was young?

  B 네, 민수가 어렸을 때도 아마 키가 컸을 거예요. Yes, even when Minsu was young, he was likely tall.

For "noun + 이다", attach -였을까 if the final syllable ends in a vowel, and -이었을까 if it ends in a consonant.

- A 유진 씨 3년 전 직업이 무엇이었을까요? What might have been Yujin's job 3 years ago?

  B 글쎄요. 잘 모르겠어요. I'm not sure. I really don't know.

Grammar in Action

1 When making proposals

-(으)ㄹ까 is used when making a soft suggestion to engage in an activity together, using "we" as the subject in the first-person plural. A positive response is often an agreement, while a negative response typically includes a reason for refusal.

- ■ **Accepting an offer**
  - A 우리 같이 산책할까요? Shall we take a walk together?

    B 좋아요. 같이 산책해요! Good. Let's take a walk together!

- ■ **Rejecting an offer**
  - A 오늘 같이 만날까요? Shall we meet today?

    B 미안해요. 오늘 시간이 없어요. 다음에 같이 만나요! I'm sorry. I don't have time today. See you next time!

When asking about the listener's opinion on not doing a certain action, -지 않을까 or -지 말까 is added to the verb stem, regardless of whether it ends in a vowel or consonant. Note that -지 말까 has a stronger negative implication than -지 않을까.

- A 점심을 배달할까요? Shall we deliver lunch?

  B 오늘도요? 오늘은 배달하지 말까요? Today too? Should we not deliver today?

  A 그래요. 그럼, 밖에 나가서 식사해요! Yes. Well then, let's go out and eat!

When suggesting multiple options, -(으)ㄹ까 can be used sequentially.

- A 지하철을 탈까요? 아니면 택시를 탈까요? Shall we take the subway? Or should we take a taxi?

  B 길이 막히니까 지하철 타요! The road is congested, so let's take the subway!

-(으)ㄹ까 and 말까 are used to propose whether or not to undertake a certain action.

- A 밤 10시인데 배고파요. 우리 야식 먹을까요? 말까요? (= 먹지 말까요?)

  It's 10 o'clock at night and I'm hungry. Shall I have a late-night snack or not?

  B 야식 먹지 말아요! 조금만 참으세요. Don't eat late-night snacks! Please be patient.

2 When giving indirect instructions

-(으)ㄹ까 can also softly direct someone to perform a certain action using a second-person subject, acting as an indirect command. If the listener agrees to the suggestion, they respond with -(으)ㄹ게.

- A 네가 먼저 얘기를 시작할까? Should you start talking first?

  B 알았어. 나부터 얘기할게. Okay. Let me talk first.

- A 이번에는 민수 씨가 음식을 준비할까요? Will you prepare food this time?

  B 네, 이번에는 제가 준비할게요. Yes, I will make preparations this time.

- A 네가 먼저 발표해 볼까? Should you present first?

  B 네, 선생님, 제가 먼저 발표할게요. Yes, teacher, I will present first.

3　When offering to help

A 제가 사진 찍어 줄까요?
Shall I take a picture for you?

B 고마워요. 여기요. 예쁘게 찍어 주세요.
Thank you. Please, go ahead and take a nice picture.

When offering help or services to the listener, -(으)ㄹ까 is often combined with -아/어 주다, forming -아/어 줄까 in an interrogative sentence. This is a polite way to volunteer assistance by asking if the listener would like the speaker to perform an action for their benefit.

• 제가 문법을 다시 설명해 줄까요? Shall I explain the grammar again?

• 내가 집까지 태워줄까? Shall I give you a ride home?

In more formal or respectful situations, -아/어 줄까 can be replaced with -아/어 드릴까, where 드리다 is the honorific form of 주다. This form is used when speaking to someone of higher status, older age, or in formal contexts, showing extra politeness.

• A (제가) 도와드릴까요? Shall I help you?　　　　Honorific

　B 네, 부탁합니다. Yes, please.

• A (제가) 짐을 들어 드릴까요? Shall I carry your luggage?　　Honorific

　B 고마워요. 이거 좀 들어 주세요. Thanks, please do.

4　When asking for opinions based on doubts

-(으)ㄹ까 is used when the speaker has doubts about an event or situation and is asking for opinions. It conveys the speaker's uncertainty and does not assume the listener has the answer.

• 이게 정말 사실일까요? 저는 사실이 아닌 것 같아요.　　Expressing doubt
  Is this really true? I don't think that's true.

• 이상해요. 왜 한국 사람들이 아파트를 좋아할까요?　　Questioning oneself
  It's strange. Why do Korean people like apartments?

• A 앞으로 한국 경제가 좋아질까요?　　Prompting a guess
  Will the Korean economy improve in the future?

  B 아마 좋아질 거예요. It will probably get better.

5 When asking about the listener's intentions or preferences

-(으)ㄹ까 is used with a first-person subject to ask about the other person's intentions or preferences regarding the speaker's actions. In particular, -(으)ㄹ까 is used when the speaker expects the listener to express their intention or preference in response.

- A 제가 밥을 살까요? Shall I buy food?

  B 아니요, 제가 밥을 살게요. No, I will buy food.

- A 어두우니까 (제가) 불을 켤까요? Since it's dark, shall I turn on the light?

  B 네, 불 좀 켜 주세요. Yes, please turn on the light.

When -(으)ㄹ까 and 말까 appear together in a declarative sentence, they express indecision or hesitation about taking action. -(으)ㄹ까 and 말까 are particularly useful when the speaker is offering choices or asking if a specific action should be taken or avoided.

- A 김민수 씨 계세요? Is Minsu Kim here?

  B 지금 잠깐 나갔어요. He just stepped out for a moment.

  A 나중에 다시 올까요? 아니면 여기에서 기다릴까요? Shall I come back later, or should I wait here?

  B 금방 올 거예요. 여기에서 잠깐 기다려 주세요. He'll be back soon. Please wait here for a moment.

- A 이 옷 어때? 살까? 말까? What do you think of this outfit? Should I buy it? Or not?

  B 이 옷 사. 너한테 잘 어울려. Buy it. It suits you well.

- A 손님, 커피에 시럽 넣을까요? 말까요? Should I add syrup to your coffee, or should I not?

  B 시럽 넣어 주세요. Please add syrup.

> ✽ **Be careful!**
>
> When -(으)ㄹ까 and 말까 appear together in a declarative sentence, they express indecision or hesitation about taking action.
>
> - 그 사람에게 고백할까 말까 고민 중이에요. I'm hesitating whether to confess to that person or not.

6 When euphemistically asking for opinions

-(으)ㄹ까 is used to make a question sound less direct and more polite by easing the listener's burden. It seeks an estimation rather than directly asking for information, making it suitable when addressing someone older or of higher status. This courteous expression keeps the intent clear, even when -(으)ㄹ까 is not explicitly stated.

- A 같이 저녁 먹어요! Let's have dinner together!

  B 좋아요. 언제가 좋을까요? (= 언제가 좋아요?) Good. When would be a good time?

  A 금요일 저녁 어때요? How about Friday evening?

- A 저, 부탁 하나 해도 될까요? (= 부탁 하나 해도 돼요?) Can I ask you a favor?

  B 네, 말씀하세요. Yes, please tell me.

Quiz 31

-(으)ㄹ게 I will...

A 이따가 다시 전화할게요. I'll call you back later.

B 네, 알겠어요. Okay, I understand.

Grammar Essentials

1 -(으)ㄹ게

The ending -(으)ㄹ게 is used to express the speaker's intention to perform a certain action at the moment of speaking in an informal setting. It is limited to first-person subjects and conveys a sense of decision or commitment. This ending is only used with verbs: attach -ㄹ게 if the verb stem ends in a vowel and -을게 if it ends in a consonant.

- 제가 밥을 살게요. 같이 점심 먹어요! I will buy food. Let's have lunch together!
- 저는 커피 대신에 주스를 마실게요. I will drink juice instead of coffee.
- 저는 여기에 있을게요. 갔다 오세요. I will stay here. Come back.

Since -(으)ㄹ게 is always used with a first-person subject, even if the subject is omitted in the sentence, it is understood that the speaker is referring to themselves.

- (저는) 커피 마실게요. I will drink coffee.
- (내가) 너한테 줄게. I will give it to you.

To express the speaker's intention not to perform an action, the negation -지 않다 is added before -(으)ㄹ게, forming -지 않을게 to mean "I will not do."

- 다른 사람한테 말하지 않을게요. 약속해요. I won't tell anyone else. I promise.
- 미안해요. 다시는 약속에 늦지 않을게요. I'm sorry. I won't be late again.

> **Tip**
>
> **The difference between -(으)ㄹ게 and -(으)ㄹ 것이다**
>
> -(으)ㄹ게 is used with a first-person subject to indicate an immediate intention at the moment of speaking, often implying a promise to the listener.
>
> - 걱정하지 마. 내가 도와줄게. Don't worry. I will help you.　　　　Intent
>
> -(으)ㄹ 것이다 can be used with first, second, or third-person subjects to describe planned actions, expectations, or guesses.
>
> - 저는 내일 친구를 만날 거예요. I will meet a friend tomorrow.　　Planned/Expected
> - 주말에 길이 많이 막힐 거예요. The roads will be very congested on the weekend.　　Guess

2 Conjugation

-(으)ㄹ게					
하다	할게	부르다	부를게	굽다	*구울게
먹다	먹을게	듣다	*들을게	짓다	*지을게
쓰다	쓸게	만들다	*만들게	그렇다	*그럴게

Grammar in Action

1 When making a promise to another person

A 금방 올게. 조금만 기다려. I'll be right back. Please wait.

B 알겠어요. 기다릴게요. I understand. I'll wait.

The ending -(으)ㄹ게 is used by a first-person speaker to indicate their willingness to fulfill the listener's request or expectation. It is often used when making promises, showing the speaker's commitment to an action requested or expected by the listener.

- A 9시 30분에 버스가 출발해요. 그러니까 9시까지 꼭 오세요.
  The bus leaves at 9:30. So, make sure to come by 9 o'clock.

  B 네, 9시까지 꼭 올게요. Yes, I will definitely be there by 9 o'clock

- A 담배가 건강에 안 좋아요. 담배를 피우지 마세요. Smoking is bad for your health. Don't smoke.

  B 알겠어요. 담배를 안 피울게요. I understand. I won't smoke.

2 When expressing the speaker's intention

A 어떤 것을 할래? What would you like to do?

B 내가 청소할게. I will do the cleaning.

C 그럼, 나는 빨래할게. Then, I will do the laundry.

The ending -(으)ㄹ게 expresses the speaker's intention to perform an action, emphasizing their decision at the moment of speaking. It is not used in questions directed at the listener's intentions. -(으)ㄹ래 is used to inquire about the listener's intention, while -겠- is used in formal situations.

Informal	Formal
• A 뭐 보실래요? What would you like to see? B 저는 코미디 영화를 볼게요. I will watch a comedy movie.	• A 뭐 보시겠습니까? What do you want to see? B 저는 코미디 영화를 보겠습니다. I'm going to watch a comedy movie.
• A 과자 먹을래요? Do you want some snacks? B 아니요, 안 먹을게요. No, I won't eat.	• A 과자 드시겠습니까? Would you like some snacks? B 아니요, 안 먹겠습니다. No, I won't eat it.

Tip

The difference between -(으)ㄹ게 and -겠-

▶ **Usage Context**

제가 먼저 발표할게요. I will present first.

제가 하겠습니다. I will do it.

The ending -(으)ㄹ게 is used in informal, casual speech, typically for immediate decisions or promises. In contrast, -겠- is used in more formal speech and is suitable for official settings.

- 제가 연락할게요. = 제가 연락하겠습니다. I will contact you.
- 제가 식당을 찾을게요. = 제가 식당을 찾겠습니다. I will find a restaurant.

▶ **Person & Sentence Type**

The ending -(으)ㄹ게 is only used for first-person statements and cannot be used in questions. On the other hand, -겠- is used for first-person statements but can also be used to ask about the second person's intention.

- A 오늘 점심 뭐 먹을래요? (O) Do you want to have lunch today?
  먹을게요? (✗)
  B 저는 비빔밥을 먹을게요. (O) I will eat bibimbap.
- A 진수 씨는 어떻게 하겠습니까? (O) What would Jinsu do?
  B 저는 혼자 준비하겠습니다. (O) I will prepare by myself.

▶ **Meaning & Function**

The ending -(으)ㄹ게 expresses an immediate decision or promise at the moment of speaking. In contrast, -겠- not only expresses intention but also conveys guesses, assumptions, or speculation.

	-(으)ㄹ게	-겠-
Intention	저는 책을 읽을게요. I will read a book.	저는 책을 읽겠습니다. I will read a book.
Guess		나도 다음 주에 바쁘겠다. I will be busy next week too. 너는 그 책을 다 읽겠다. You will read the whole book. 저 남자도 웃겠습니다. That man will laugh too.

Quiz 32

33

-(으)ㄹ래 I want to

Kor. 33

A 우리는 산책 갈 거야. We are going to take a walk.

너도 갈래? Do you want to come too?

B 어, 나도 갈래. Yes, I want to go too.

Grammar Essentials

1 -(으)ㄹ래

The ending -(으)ㄹ래 expresses the intention or will of the speaker or listener and is mainly used in informal speech. In declarative sentences, it indicates the speaker's intention, while in interrogative sentences, it asks about the listener's intention. This ending is only used with verbs: attach -ㄹ래 if the verb stem ends in a vowel and -을래 if it ends in a consonant.

- A 너도 같이 영화 볼래? Do you want to watch a movie with me?

  B 응, 나도 볼래. Yes, I want to watch it too.

- A 진수 씨도 먹을래요? Would you like to eat too?

  B 저는 안 먹을래요. I don't want to eat.

- A 우리 음악 들을래요? Shall we listen to music?

  B 좋아요. 음악 들어요. Yes, let's listen to music.

The ending -(으)ㄹ래 cannot be used to ask about the speaker's own intention in interrogative sentences. Additionally, it cannot be used to express the listener's intention when the subject is in the second person in declarative sentences.

- 너는 경영학을 전공할래. (✕)

  → 나는 경영학을 전공할래. (O)

  I will major in business.

- 내가 여행을 갈래? (✕)

  → 네가 여행을 갈래? (O)

  Do you want to go on vacation?

2 Conjugation

-(으)ㄹ래					
보다	볼래	부르다	부를래	줍다	*주울래
먹다	먹을래	걷다	*걸을래	짓다	*지을래
쓰다	쓸래	만들다	*만들래	그렇다	*그럴래

3 Negation

To express the intention not to perform a certain action, place 안 before -(으)ㄹ래 or use -지 않을래 instead.

- 이제부터 술 안 마실래. I won't drink alcohol from now on.

- 이 선물은 받지 않을래요. 마음만 받을래요. I don't want to accept this gift. I'll just accept the thought.

Grammar in Action

1 When asking about the listener's intention

-(으)ㄹ래 is used in interrogative sentences to ask about the listener's intention. When responding with one's own intention, both -(으)ㄹ래 and -(으)ㄹ게 can be used, but -(으)ㄹ래 conveys a more personal choice than -(으)ㄹ게.

- A 뭐 먹을래? What do you want to eat?

  B 난 국수 먹을래. I want to have noodles.

-(으)ㄹ래 can also be used sequentially to ask about preferences between choices. Responding with -겠- or -(으)ㄹ게 makes the response more polite than just using -(으)ㄹ래.

- A 나중에 다시 올래? 아니면 여기 있을래? Do you want to come again later or do you want to stay here?

  B 여기 있을게. I want to stay here.

When asking whether the listener intends to do something or not, use "-(으)ㄹ래? 안 -(으)ㄹ래?" or "-(으)ㄹ래? 말래?". When responding, it is more natural to say "안 할래" rather than just "말래".

- A 우리는 게임할 거야. 너도 할래? 말래? We are going to play a game. Do you want to join or not?

  B 말래. (✗) → 안 할래. (O) I don't want to play.

Tip

1. The difference between -(으)ㄹ래 and -(으)ㄹ게

Both -(으)ㄹ래 and -(으)ㄹ게 express the first-person speaker's intention in informal situations. However, -(으)ㄹ게 implies that the speaker is considering the listener, such as responding to a request or expectation, making it more polite. In contrast, -(으)ㄹ래 reflects the speaker's own will or preference without considering the listener's influence.

A 오늘 꼭 운동하세요. Please exercise today. B 네, 꼭 운동할게요. (O) 　Yes, I will definitely exercise. 네, 꼭 운동할래요. (✗)	A 오늘 꼭 운동하세요. Please exercise today. B 아니요, 운동 안 할게요. (✗) 　아니요, 운동 안 할래요. (O) No, I won't exercise.

2. The difference between -(으)ㄹ래 and -겠-

Both -(으)ㄹ래 and -겠- express intention, but they are used in different contexts. -(으)ㄹ래 is typically used in informal speech, while -겠- is more formal and suitable for official settings. Additionally, -겠- can express guesses or speculation, whereas -(으)ㄹ래 is strictly limited to expressing intention only.

Informal	Formal
A 밥 먹을래? Do you want to eat? B 아니, 안 먹을래. No, I don't want to eat. 　= 먹지 않을래.	A 밥 먹겠습니까? Do you want to eat? B 아니요, 안 먹겠습니다. No, I won't eat. 　= 먹지 않겠습니다.

2   When asking for a favor in informal situations

-아/어 줄래 is a phrase that combines -(으)ㄹ래 with -아/어 주다, which means to give or do something for someone. It is used in informal settings when requesting someone's help. When agreeing to such a request, -(으)ㄹ게 is used instead of -(으)ㄹ래.

- A 핸드폰 좀 빌려 줄래? Can you lend me your cell phone?

   B 빌려 줄게. 여기 있어. Sure, here it is.

- A 사진 좀 찍어 줄래? Can you take a picture for me?

   B 그래. 사진 좀 찍어 줄래. (✕)

   → 찍어 줄게. (○) Sure, I'll take the picture for you.

3   When making a suggestion to someone

-(으)ㄹ래 is used with the first-person plural subject "우리" to suggest doing something together. However, it is only used for making suggestions and cannot be used to accept one.

- A 오늘 같이 영화 볼래? Do you want to watch a movie together today?

   B 그래. 영화 볼래. (✕) → 영화 보자. (○) Okay, let's watch a movie.

- A 같이 점심 먹을래? Do you want to have lunch together?

   B 미안해. 오늘 다른 약속이 있어. Sorry, but I have other plans today.

-(으)ㄹ래 can be interchanged with -(으)ㄹ까 for suggestions. However, while -(으)ㄹ래 directly asks about the listener's intention, -(으)ㄹ까 is more indirect and makes the tone softer.

- A 커피 마실래? (= 마실까?) Do you want coffee? (= Shall we have coffee?)

   B 그래. 같이 영화 보자. Sure. Let's have coffee.

Adding 안 or -지 않을래 makes the suggestion stronger. -지 말래 is not used to make suggestions.

- A 오늘 콘서트 있어. 같이 안 갈래? There is a concert today. Don't you want to go together?

   B 좋아. 같이 가자. Sure, let's go together.

- A 나 게임기 샀어. 해 보지 않을래? (≠ 말래?) I bought a game console. Don't you want to try it?

   B 그래. 해 볼래. Okay. I want to try it.

Quiz 33

-(으)려고 하다 plan / try to, be about / going to...

A 휴가 때 뭐 할 거예요? What are you going to do during your vacation?

B 여행 가려고 해요. I'm planning to travel.

조심하세요. Be careful.

책장이 넘어지려고 해요. The bookshelf is about to fall over.

1 -(으)려고 하다 Expressing intention

The grammatical pattern -(으)려고 하다 is used to describe the subject's intention or plan to perform an action and can be applied to first, second, or third person subjects. It attaches to the verb stem by using -려고 하다 if the verb stem ends in a vowel and -으려고 하다 if the verb stem ends in a consonant.

- 저는 휴가 때 집에서 쉬려고 해요. I plan to rest at home during my vacation.

- 제 친구가 회사를 그만두려고 해요. My friend is planning to quit their job.

- 너는 매일 검은색 옷만 입으려고 해. You always try to wear only black clothes.

- 오늘 저녁에는 제가 국수를 만들려고 해요. I plan to make noodles tonight.

2 Conjugation

-(으)려고 하다					
보다	보려고 하다	부르다	부르려고 하다	줍다	*주우려고 하다
먹다	먹으려고 하다	듣다	*들으려고 하다	붓다	*부으려고 하다
쓰다	쓰려고 하다	만들다	*만들려고 하다	그렇다	*그러려고 하다

3 Negation

To express the intention not to perform a certain action, 안 or -지 않다 is attached before -(으)려고 하다.

- 아기가 안 자려고 해요. The baby is trying not to sleep.

- 이 문제를 부모님께 말하지 않으려고 해요. I am trying not to tell my parents about this problem.

To express that there was no intention to perform a certain action, -지 않다 is attached to 하다 in -(으)려고 하다 to form -(으)려고 하지 않다.

- 동생이 이상해요. 웃으려고 하지 않아요. My younger sibling is strange. She is not trying to laugh.

- 제 친구가 제 얘기를 들으려고 하지 않아요. My friend does not try to listen to what I say.

4 -(으)려고 하다 Expressing a guess

The grammatical pattern -(으)려고 하다 indicates that an event is about to happen or a state is about to change. While it can be used with any subject, when expressing a guess, -(으)려고 하다 is typically used with a third person subject.

- 비가 오려고 해요. 집에 빨리 들어가세요! It looks like it's about to rain. Let's quickly go inside the house!

- 저 사람이 넘어지려고 해요. 저 사람을 도와주세요. That person is going to fall. Please help him.

5 Tenses

To express that the subject of a sentence had an intention to perform an action in the past, or that an event was about to happen or a state was about to change, the past tense marker -았/었- is attached to 하다 in -(으)려고 하다, forming -(으)려고 했다. Using -(으)려고 했다 implies an intended action or a predicted event that ultimately did not happen or was uncertain.

- 저도 전화하려고 했어요. 그런데 배터리가 떨어져서 전화 못 했어요.
  I was trying to call you too, but my battery died and I couldn't call.

- 처음에는 친구가 음식을 안 먹으려고 했어요. 그런데 결국 배고파서 다 먹었어요.
  Initially, my friend didn't try to eat the food, but eventually, she was too hungry and ate it all.

- 전에 나도 여드름이 생기려고 했어. (그런데 지금은 괜찮아.)
  Before, I also was about to have an acne breakout. (But now I'm okay.)

To indicate that a certain action or event will happen in the future, -(으)려고 하다 is combined with -(으)ㄹ 것이다, forming -(으)려고 할 것이다.

- 지금 천장을 수리해야 해요. 안 그러면 천장이 무너지려고 할 거예요.
  We need to repair the ceiling now, or else it's going to collapse.

> **Tip**
>
> **The difference between -(으)ㄹ래 and -(으)려고 하다**
>
> The ending -(으)ㄹ래 is always used with a first-person subject to indicate the speaker's intention and cannot be used with a third person subject. In contrast, -(으)려고 하다 can express the intention of a third person, allowing it to be used with first, second, or third person subjects.
>
> - 동생이 대학원에 갈래요. (✕)
>   → 동생이 대학원에 가려고 해요. (O) My younger sibling is planning to go to graduate school.
>
> Like -겠-, -(으)ㄹ래 expresses the speaker's or listener's intention at the moment of speaking. However, -(으)ㄹ래 cannot express past intentions and cannot be combined with the past tense marker -았/었. Instead, -(으)려고 했다 is used to indicate past intentions.
>
> - 1년 전에 나도 운동을 시작했을래. (✕)
>   → 1년 전에 나도 운동을 시작하려고 했어. (O) I also tried to start exercising a year ago.

Grammar in Action

1 When expressing plans or attempts

A 진수가 졸업 후에 뭐 할 거예요?
What is Jinsu going to do after graduation?

B 진수는 개인 사업을 하려고 해요.
Jinsu plans to start his own business.

그래서 대학원에 안 갈 거예요.
So, he is not going to graduate school.

-(으)려고 하다 is used to express someone's plans or attempts. It can describe a plan or intention of a first, second, or third person subject.

In questions, phrases like "뭐 하려고 해요?" or "뭐 할 거예요?" can be used.

- A 내일 뭐 하려고 해요? What are you planning to do tomorrow?

  B 몸이 안 좋아요. 그래서 내일 집에서 쉬려고 해요. I'm not feeling well, so I plan to rest at home tomorrow.

- A 민수가 왜 안 밥을 안 먹어요? Why isn't Minsu eating?

  B 민수가 살을 빼려고 해요. 그래서 밥을 안 먹어요. Minsu is trying to lose weight, so he is not eating.

2 When expressing an imminent situation

빨리 오세요. 기차가 출발하려고 해요.
Hurry up. The train is about to leave.

-(으)려고 하다 is also used to express a situation that is about to happen very soon. It is typically used with third person or inanimate subjects. Even when personal subjects are used, the same form applies when the verb does not convey the subject's intention.

- 단추가 떨어지려고 해요.   Pointing at a button on clothing

  The button is about to come off.

- A 언제 회의가 시작해요? When does the meeting start?

  B 지금 시작하려고 해요. It is about to start now.

- 조용히 해 주세요. 아기가 잠에서 깨려고 해요.

  Please be quiet. The baby is about to wake up.

Quiz 34

179

TOPIK I | SCK 2

-기로 하다 decide / determine / promise to...

오늘부터 운동하기로 했어요.

I decided to start exercising today.

우리 결혼하기로 했어요.

We decided to get married.

Grammar Essentials

1 -기로 하다

The grammatical pattern -기로 하다 indicates that the subject of the sentence has decided to undertake a certain action. It can be used with first, second, or third person subjects and combines with a verb, regardless of whether the verb stem ends in a vowel or a consonant.

In -기로 하다, the verb 하다 can be replaced with more specific verbs such as 결정하다 (to decide), 결심하다 (to resolve), or 약속하다 (to promise), depending on the context.

- 친구가 승진해서 밥을 사기로 했어요. My friend got a promotion and has decided to treat us to a meal.

- 올해 친구하고 같이 제주도에 여행 가기로 결정했어요.
  This year, my friend and I have decided to go on a trip to Jeju Island together.

- 가족과 이제부터 식사 후에 같이 걷기로 약속했어요.
  My family and I have promised to go for a walk together after meals from now on.

- 앞으로 고기를 덜 먹기로 결심했어요. I have resolved to eat less meat going forward.

The difference between -기로 하다 and -(으)려고 하다

Both -기로 하다 and -(으)려고 하다 describe the subject's resolution or plan. However, -기로 하다 expresses a firmly made resolution, with less uncertainty and a more definitive nature. In contrast, -(으)려고 하다 describes plans that are still being considered and may change depending on the situation.

- A 언제 진수 씨하고 결혼할 거예요? When are you going to marry Jinsu?

  B 다음 달에 결혼하기로 했어요. We have decided to marry next month.

  A 축하해요. 저는 아직 모르겠어요. 2-3년 후에 결혼하려고 해요.
    Congratulations. I'm not sure yet. I plan to marry in 2-3 years.

2 Conjugation

-기로 하다					
가다	가기로 하다	부르다	부르기로 하다	돕다	돕기로 하다
먹다	먹기로 하다	걷다	걷기로 하다	짓다	짓기로 하다
쓰다	쓰기로 하다	살다	살기로 하다	그렇다	그렇기로 하다

3 Negation

When the negation 안 or -지 않다 is added before -기로 하다, it indicates that the subject has decided not to engage in a certain action.

- 이제부터 담배를 안 피우기로 했어요. From now on, I have decided not to smoke.

- 앞으로 약속에 늦지 않기로 했어요. I have decided not to be late for appointments anymore.

- 다리를 다쳤으니까 움직이지 않기로 했어요. Since I injured my leg, I have decided not to move it.

4 Tenses

When -았/었- is combined with 하다 in -기로 하다, forming -기로 했다, it expresses that the subject of the sentence has already decided to perform a certain action.

내일 같이 점심 먹기로 했어요. We have decided to have lunch together tomorrow.

Expresses a future action   Expresses that it has already been decided

Even if the action discussed is planned for the future, if the decision was made before the moment of speaking, it should be expressed using -기로 했다. Since -기로 하다 indicates future actions, the past tense markers -았/었- cannot be added before it.

- 전에 엄마하고 앞으로 게임을 2시간 이상 안 했기로 약속해요. (✕)

  → 안 하기로 약속했어요. (O)

  I previously promised my mom that I would not play games for more than two hours from now on.

- 이제부터 아침에 일찍 일어났기로 어제 결심해요. (✕)

  → 일어나기로 어제 결심했어요. (O)

  I decided yesterday that from now on, I will get up early in the morning.

-기로 하다 is used to express making a promise or decision at the moment of speaking, whereas -기로 했다 indicates that a decision or promise was made before the current time. Therefore, -기로 하다 is used for making new commitments, and -기로 했다 is used to describe decisions or promises that were already made.

- A 내일부터 우리 같이 운동하기로 해요.   Making a promise

  Let's start exercising together from tomorrow.

  B 그래요. 같이 운동해요. Yes, let's exercise together.

- A 내일부터 유진 씨하고 같이 운동하기로 했어요.   Talking about a promise

  I have already promised to start exercising with Eugene from tomorrow.

  B 그래요? 어디에서 운동할 거예요? Really? Where are you going to exercise?

Tip

The difference between -기로 하다 and -(으)ㄹ게

Both -기로 하다 and -(으)ㄹ게 can be used when making promises, but they differ in context. -기로 하다 is used when making a promise to someone, while -(으)ㄹ게 is used when responding to someone's request or expectation.

- A 우리 이제부터 한국어로 말하기로 해요. Let's agree to speak in Korean from now on.
  B 좋아요. 한국어로 말할게요. Okay, I will speak in Korean.

- A 우리 서로에게 거짓말을 하지 않기로 해요. Let's agree not to lie to each other.
  B 알겠어요. 거짓말을 하지 않을게요. Okay. I won't lie.

Grammar in Action

1 When expressing a decision or resolution

A 요즘 담배를 안 피워요?
Have you stopped smoking recently?

B 이제부터 담배를 끊기로 했어요.
I have decided to stop smoking from now on.

-기로 하다 is used when the subject of a sentence expresses a decision or resolution that has already been made. It can be used with first, second, and third person subjects to express the decision or resolution of oneself or someone else.

• 저는 회사를 그만두기로 했어요. I have decided to quit my job.

• A 이번 파티에 무슨 옷을 입어요? What are you going to wear to the party?

  B 검은색 옷을 입기로 했어요. I have decided to wear black.

• 사라 씨가 한국에서 취직하기로 했어요. Sarah has decided to get a job in Korea.

2 When expressing a promise

A 오늘 같이 저녁 먹을 수 있어요?
Can we have dinner together tonight?

B 미안해요. 같이 못 먹어요.
Sorry. I can't.

친구를 만나기로 했어요.
I have promised to meet a friend.

-기로 하다 is used when the subject of a sentence mentions a promise made based on mutual agreement. This pattern can be used with first, second, and third person subjects to indicate someone else's set plans or promises.

• 저는 친구하고 같이 운동하기로 했어요. I have promised to exercise with a friend.

• 어제 네가 저녁을 만들기로 했어. 기억 안 나? You promised to cook dinner yesterday, remember?

• A 진수 씨가 무슨 일을 하기로 했어요? What has Jinsu agreed to do?

  B 진수 씨가 서류를 정리하기로 했어요. Jinsu has agreed to organize the documents.

Quiz 35

TOPIK I | SCK 2

-(으)ㄴ/는 것 같다 seem to, look like

Kor. 36

밖에 비가 오는 것 같아요.
It looks like it's raining outside.

사람들이 우산을 쓰고 있어요.
People are using umbrellas.

이 음식이 진짜 맛있는 것 같아요.
The food seems to be delicious.

진수 씨가 케이크를 먹은 것 같아요.
I think Jinsu ate the cake.

우리 팀이 이길 것 같아요.
I think our team will win.

1 -(으)ㄴ/는 것 같다

-(으)ㄴ/는 것 같다 is used when the speaker makes a guess or speculation about an event or state. The subject of the guess is always the speaker, but the speaker is typically omitted from the sentence. This pattern can be used with first, second, or third person subjects.

Current speculation

(제 생각에) 비가 오는 것 같아요. (I think) it looks like it's raining.

Speaker   Content of speculation

-(으)ㄴ/는 것 같다 can be used with verbs, adjectives, and "nouns + 이다". The endings vary depending on the word type (verb, adjective, or noun) and the tense.

- 이 가게가 저 가게보다 물건이 싼 것 같아요. This store seems cheaper than that one.

- 저분이 사장님인 것 같아요. 항상 가게에 나와 있어요.
  That person seems to be the boss. She is always at the store.

2 Tenses

❶ Speculation about the present

When speculating about a current event or state, the conjugation form changes based on the part of speech. For verbs, -는 것 같다 is attached regardless of whether the stem ends in a vowel or consonant. For adjectives, -ㄴ 것 같다 is used if the stem ends in a vowel, and -은 것 같다 if it ends in a consonant. For adjectives like 있다/없다 (e.g., 있다, 맛있다, 재미있다), -는 것 같다 is used. For "noun + 이다", 인 것 같다 is attached regardless of whether the noun ends in a vowel or consonant.

	When ending in a vowel	When ending in a consonant
Verbs	**-는 것 같다** 윤아 씨가 요즘 못 자는 것 같아요. Yuna seems to have been unable to sleep lately.	**-는 것 같다** 유진 씨한테 좋은 일이 있는 것 같아요. It seems like something good happened to Yujin.
Adjectives	**-ㄴ 것 같다** 진수 씨가 요즘 아픈 것 같아요. Jinsu seems sick lately.	**-은 것 같다** 요즘 K-Pop이 인기가 많은 것 같아요. It seems like K-Pop is very popular lately.
Noun + 이다	**인 것 같다** 저 사람이 운동선수인 것 같아요. That person seems to be an athlete.	**인 것 같다** 그 사람이 프랑스 사람인 것 같아요. That person seems to be a French person.

2 Speculation about the past

When speculating about a past event or state, the conjugation changes depending on the word type. For verbs, -ㄴ 것 같다 is attached if the stem ends in a vowel, and -은 것 같다 if it ends in a consonant. For adjectives, -았/었던 것 같다 is used, depending on whether -았/었- is applied in conjugation. For "noun + 이다", 였던 것 같다 is attached if the noun ends in a vowel, and 이었던 것 같다 if it ends in a consonant.

	When ending in a vowel	When ending in a consonant
Verbs	**-ㄴ 것 같다** 유진 씨가 전에 중국에 산 것 같아요. 중국어를 잘해요. Yujin seems to have lived in China before. She speaks Chinese well.	**-은 것 같다** 진수 씨가 이 책을 읽은 것 같아요. 이 책에 대해 잘 알아요. Jinsu seems to have read this book. He knows a lot about this book.
Adjectives	**-았/었던 것 같다** 어제 먹은 음식이 많이 매웠던 것 같아요. 어제 속이 안 좋았어요. The food we ate yesterday seems to have been very spicy. I felt sick yesterday.	**-았/었던 것 같다** 이전 모델이 지금 모델보다 인기가 많았던 것 같아요. The previous model seems to have been more popular than the current one.
Noun + 이다	**였던 것 같다** 어렸을 때 밝은 아이였던 것 같아요. It seems like I was a bright child when I was young.	**이었던 것 같다** 그때 그 사람이 학생이었던 것 같아요. That person seems to have been a student at that time.

3 Speculation about the future

When speculating about a future event or state, -(으)ㄹ 것 같다 is used. For verbs and adjectives, -ㄹ 것 같다 is attached if the stem ends in a vowel, and -을 것 같다 if it ends in a consonant. For "noun + 이다", 일 것 같다 is attached regardless of whether the noun ends in a vowel or consonant.

	When ending in a vowel	When ending in a consonant
Verbs	**-ㄹ 것 같다** 30분 후에 회의가 끝날 것 같아요. The meeting seems like it will end in 30 minutes.	**-을 것 같다** 이번 휴가 때 보너스를 받을 것 같아요. It seems like I will receive a bonus during this vacation.
Adjectives	**-ㄹ 것 같다** 다음 주에 바쁠 것 같아요. It seems like next week will be busy.	**-을 것 같다** 내일 날씨가 좋을 것 같아요. The weather seems like it will be nice tomorrow.
Noun + 이다	**일 것 같다** 저 사람이 부자일 것 같아요. That person seems like they might be wealthy.	**일 것 같다** 저 사람이 대학생일 것 같아요. That person seems like they might be a college student.

3 Negation

-(으)ㄴ 것 같다 can be combined with the negation markers 안 or -지 않다. The conjugation varies depending on whether the speculation is about the present, past, or future. It also changes based on how it is combined with a verb, adjective, or noun.

1 Present

Verbs: -지 않는 것 같다

- 진수 씨는 주말에 일찍 일어나지 않는 것 같아요. It seems like Jinsu does not wake up early on weekends.

Adjectives: -지 않은 것 같다

- 유진 씨가 요즘 바쁘지 않은 것 같아요. It seems like Yujin has not been busy lately.

Nouns: 아닌 것 같다

- 이 책이 제 책이 아닌 것 같아요. It seems like this book is not mine.

2 Past

Verbs: -지 않은 것 같다

- 진수 씨가 어제 한 시간도 자지 않은 것 같아요. It seems like Jinsu did not sleep at all yesterday.

Adjectives: -지 않았던 것 같다

- 전에는 문제가 이렇게 심하지 않았던 것 같아요. It seems like the problem was not this severe before.

Nouns: 아니었던 것 같다

- 옛날에는 공무원이 인기 직업이 아니었던 것 같아요.
  It seems like being a civil servant was not a popular job in the past.

3 Future

Verbs/Adjectives: -지 않을 것 같다

- 비가 와서 사람이 많이 오지 않을 것 같아요. Because it's raining, it seems like not many people will come.
- 내일 날씨가 좋지 않을 것 같아요. It seems like the weather will not be good tomorrow.

Nouns: 아닐 것 같다

- 저분이 한국어 선생님이 아닐 것 같아요. It seems like that person will not be a Korean teacher.

> **Tip**
>
> **The difference between 인 것 같다 and 같다**
>
> "noun + 인 것 같다" expresses the speculation that the subject is (something), while "noun + 같다" is used for a metaphorical comparison with the noun.
>
> The content of the speaker's speculation is "He is British."
> - 저분 영어 발음을 들어 보니까 영국 사람인 것 같아요.
>   Listening to his English accent, he seems to be British.
>
> Metaphorically compared to: "An angel."
> - 저분은 마음이 정말 착해요. 천사 같아요.
>   He has a really kind heart. He's like an angel.

Grammar in Action

1 When expressing the speaker's uncertainty or assumption

-(으)ㄴ/는 것 같다 is used to express uncertainty or to make assumptions about an event or state based on the speaker's observations or guess.

- 민수 씨가 집에 간 것 같아요. It seems like Minsu has gone home.

- 저 사람이 우리 회사 사람인 것 같아요. That person seems to be from our company.

-(으)ㄴ/는 것 같다 is also used to express guesses based on the speaker's subjective experiences. These guesses may vary among individuals, and the accuracy of the guess is not crucial.

- A 진수 씨가 힘이 없어요. 요즘 진수 씨가 몸이 안 좋은 것 같아요.
  Jinsu has no strength. He seems to be unwell lately.

  B 그래요? 제가 보기에 진수 씨가 요즘 걱정이 있는 것 같아요.
  Really? To me, it seems like Jinsu has been worried lately.

- 이 자판기가 고장 난 것 같아요. 안 되네요. This vending machine seems to be broken. It's not working.

- 사무실에서 회의하고 있는 것 같아요. 문이 닫혀 있어요.
  It seems like they are having a meeting in the office. The door is closed.

When asking about the listener's guess, -(으)ㄴ/는 것 같다 is used to form a question. Conversely, when both the speaker and listener are unsure about the information, -(으)ㄹ까 is used.

- A 왜 진수 씨가 전화를 안 받는 것 같아요? Why do you think Jinsu isn't answering the phone?

  B 요즘 바빠서 전화를 안 받는 것 같아요. He seems to be busy and not taking calls lately.

- A 왜 진수 씨가 전화를 안 받을까요? Why might Jinsu not be answering the phone?

  B 글쎄요, 저도 잘 모르겠어요. I'm not sure either.

-(으)ㄴ/는 것 같다 can also be used to express a vague feeling without any solid basis for the thought.

- 저 사람이 나를 좋아하는 것 같아요. I feel that person likes me.

- 왠지 모르겠지만, 오늘 나쁜 일이 생길 것 같아요.
  For some reason, I feel like something bad is going to happen today.

2 When expressing the speaker's thoughts or feelings softly

-(으)ㄴ/는 것 같다 softens the expression of the speaker's thoughts or feelings. This indirect form may be inappropriate in formal or direct situations.

Omitting -(으)ㄴ/는 것 같다 does not change the sentence's meaning. When gently inquiring about the listener's thoughts or feelings, phrases like "어떻게 생각해요?" or " 어떤 것 같아요?" are used.

- A 이 모자가 어때요? How do you like this hat?

  B 제 생각에 조금 비싼 것 같아요. (= 조금 비싸요.) I think it's a bit expensive. (= It's a bit expensive.)

- A 한국 지하철에 대해서 어떻게 생각해요? What do you think about the Korean subway?

  B 한국 지하철이 정말 깨끗하고 편리한 것 같아요. (= 편리해요.)
  In my opinion, the Korean subway is really clean and convenient. (= It's convenient.)

- A 이 영화가 어떤 것 같아요? How does this movie seem to you?

  B 지루한 것 같아요. (= 지루해요.) I think it's boring. (= It's boring.)

3 When talking about past guesses, thoughts, or feelings

-(으)ㄴ/는 것 같았다 is used when expressing guesses, thoughts, or feelings that the speaker had in the past. It is mainly used to recount past events or states and express the thoughts or feelings at that time.

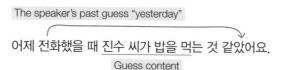

The speaker's past guess "yesterday"

어제 전화했을 때 진수 씨가 밥을 먹는 것 같았어요.

Guess content

When I called Jinsu yesterday, it seemed like he was eating.

- 제가 어렸을 때는 우리 아버지가 진짜 키가 큰 것 같았어요. 그런데 나중에 보니까 보통 키였어요.
  When I was young, it seemed like my father was really tall, but later I realized he was of average height.

- 작년에는 유진 씨가 건강이 좋지 않은 것 같았어요. 유진 씨는 항상 피곤해 보였어요.
  Last year, I thought Yujin wasn't well. She always looked tired.

- A 주사 맞을 때 어땠어요? How was it when you got the injection?

  B 주사 맞을 때 아파서 죽을 것 같았어요. When I got the injection, it felt like I was going to die.

Quiz 36

-아/어지다 become / get

지금

3년 전

동생이 키가 커졌어요.

My brother has grown taller.

2월

6월

날씨가 더워졌어요.

The weather has gotten warmer.

1 -아/어지다

The ending -아/어지다 is combined with an adjective to express a change in the state indicated by the adjective. For adjectives ending in 하다, the stem 하 combines with -어지다 to form -해지다. If the final syllable of the stem contains the vowels ㅏ or ㅗ, -아지다 is used; in all other cases, -어지다 is used. Additionally, the adverb 점점 (meaning "more and more") can be used with this form to express the degree of change, indicating whether something has increased or decreased.

- 스마트폰 때문에 생활이 편리해졌어요. Smartphones have made life more convenient.

- 퇴근 시간 후에 자동차가 점점 많아졌어요. There are more and more cars after work hours.

- 갑자기 날씨가 추워졌어요. 감기 조심하세요.
  Suddenly, the weather has become cold. Be careful of the cold.

-아/어지다: Changes in state vs. Passive meaning

When expressing change with -아/어지다, adjectives are only used. To express that a certain situation or state has been reached with a verb, use -게 되다.

- 열심히 연습해서 수영을 잘해졌어요. (✕) → 잘하게 됐어요. (O)
  I practiced hard and became good at swimming.

- 옛날에는 피아노를 잘 쳤는데 지금은 잘 못해졌어요. (✕) → 못하게 됐어요. (O)
  I used to be good at playing the piano, but now I'm not so good at it.

The form -아/어지다 combined with an adjective indicates a change to a certain state, while -아/어지다 combined with a verb indicates the passive meaning of a certain state in Korean.

느끼다 (to feel)

- 말하지 않아도 어머니의 마음이 따뜻하게 느껴졌어요.
  I felt my mother's warm heart without her saying anything.

믿다 (to believe)

- 그 사람의 말이 믿어지지 않아요. I don't believe what that person said.

2 Conjugation

-아/어지다			
편하다	편해지다	다르다	*달라지다
많다	많아지다	길다	길어지다
적다	적어지다	쉽다	*쉬워지다
바쁘다	*바빠지다	그렇다	*그래지다

3 Negation

To indicate that a state has not changed, place the negation marker 안 before -아/어지다 or add -지 않다 after it, forming -아/어지지 않다.

- 많이 잤지만, 컨디션이 안 좋아져요. I slept a lot, but my condition is not improving.

- 작년보다 생활비가 더 비싸지지 않았어요. 하지만 여전히 비싸요.
  The cost of living has not increased compared to last year, but it's still expensive.

4 Tenses

To describe a general state of change happening under certain conditions in the present, use -아/어지다 without -았/었-.

- 여름이 되면 낮이 길어져요. In summer, the days get longer.

- A 피부가 안 좋아요. 어떻게 하면 돼요? I have bad skin. What should I do?

  B 매일 물을 많이 마시면 피부가 좋아져요. If you drink a lot of water every day, your skin will get better.

To indicate that a change has already occurred, use -아/어지다 with the past tense marker -았/었-.

- 그는 매일 운동을 해서 건강이 좋아졌어요. He exercised every day, so his health has improved.

To express the speaker's guess about what state will change, -아/어지다 is combined with -(으)ㄹ 것이다 to form -아/어질 것이다.

- 할인 쿠폰을 사용하면, 값이 더 싸질 거예요. If you use a discount coupon, the price will become cheaper.

- A 한국어 말하기가 어려워요. 어떻게 공부해야 돼요? It's too difficult to speak Korean. How should I study?

  B 매일 한국 사람하고 얘기하면, 말하기가 쉬워질 거예요.
  If you talk to Korean people every day, speaking will become easier.

Tip

Adjectives becoming verbs with -아/어지다

Although -아/어지다 is attached to an adjective, the resulting form functions as a verb. For example, when used before -(으)ㄴ/는 것 같다, the conjugation changes depending on whether the word is treated as an adjective or a verb.

- 요즘 날씨가 <u>따뜻한</u> 것 같아요. The weather seems warm these days.
  Adjective
- 요즘 날씨가 <u>따뜻해지는</u> 것 같아요. The weather seems to be getting warmer these days.
  Verb

In Korean, there are grammatical patterns that can only be combined with verbs (e.g., -고 싶다, -고 있다). To use these patterns while expressing the meaning of an adjective, -아/어지다 must first be added to the adjective stem to convert it into a verb.

- 예쁘고 싶어서 다이어트를 시작했어요. (✕)
  → 예뻐지고 싶어서 다이어트를 시작했어요. (○) I started dieting because I wanted to become prettier.
- 요즘 운동해서 몸이 좋고 있어요. (✕)
  → 요즘 운동해서 몸이 좋아지고 있어요. (○) I've been working out lately and my body is getting better.

Grammar in Action

1 When expressing a change to a certain state

A 폴 씨가 달라졌어요.
Mr. Paul has changed.

B 어떻게 달라졌어요?
How has he changed?

A 건강해졌어요. 그리고 성격도 밝아졌어요.
He has become healthier. And his personality
became brighter.

To express that a change has already been completed, -아/어지다 is combined with the past tense marker -았/었- to form -아/어졌어요. When asking about the change, "뭐가 달라졌어요? (What has changed?)" is used to inquire about what specifically changed, while "어떻게 달라졌어요? (How has it changed?)" is used to ask how the change occurred.

- 봄이 돼서 날씨가 따뜻해졌어요. It's spring and the weather has become warmer.

- 친구하고 연락 안 해서 사이가 멀어졌어요.
  I became distant from my friend because I stopped communicating with him.

- A 한국어를 공부하고 뭐가 달라졌어요? What changed after studying Korean?

  B 한국 생활이 편해졌어요. Life in Korea has become easier.

2 When expressing an already changed state

-아/어지다 can also emphasize that a state has already changed. In this case, the question "어때요? (How is it?)" is used to inquire about the current state after the change.

- 슬픈 영화를 보면 저도 울고 싶어져요. I also want to cry when I watch a sad movie.

- A 방이 어때요? How is your room?

  B 에어컨을 켰지만, 방이 시원해지지 않았어요.
  I turned on the air conditioner, but my room did not cool down.

- 잊어버리려고 노력했지만, 마음이 편해지지 않았어요. I tried to forget it, but I couldn't feel at ease.

Quiz 37

-게 되다 end up ...ing, come to

A 어떻게 두 사람이 만났어요?

How did you two meet?

B 같은 회사에서 일하다가 사귀게 됐어요.

We ended up dating while working at the same company.

Grammar Essentials

1 -게 되다

-게 되다 indicates that the subject did not act intentionally but eventually ended up in a particular situation or condition. It can be used with verbs and adjectives and is attached to their stems regardless of whether they end in a vowel or a consonant.

- 한국에 여행하러 왔다가 한국에서 살게 됐어요. I came to Korea for a trip and ended up living here.

- 대학교에서 아내를 만나서 결혼하게 됐어요. I met my wife in college, and we ended up getting married.

- 소금을 중간에 넣었더니 음식이 짜게 됐어요. I added salt in the middle, and the food became salty.

To express a change with a noun, use the grammatical pattern 이/가 되다.

- 혼자 노래 연습하다가 드디어 <u>가수이게 됐어요</u>. (✕) → 가수가 됐어요. (O)
  I practiced singing alone and finally became a singer.

2 Conjugation

-게 되다					
가다	가게 되다	부르다	부르게 되다	맵다	맵게 되다
먹다	먹게 되다	듣다	듣게 되다	낫다	낫게 되다
아프다	아프게 되다	멀다	멀게 되다	그렇다	그렇게 되다

3 Negation

To express that someone ends up not doing something unintentionally, place 안 before -게 되다 or use -지 않게 되다.

- 전에는 술을 자주 마셨는데, 요즘은 술을 자주 마시지 않게 됐어요.
  I used to drink a lot, but these days I don't drink as much.

- 가구를 바꿨는데, 집이 저하고 어울리지 않게 됐어요.
  I changed the furniture, but the house no longer suits me.

- 저 사람은 첫날에 친구들과 인사 못 해서 결국 친하지 않게 됐어요.
  He couldn't greet my friends on the first day, so we ended up not becoming close.

To express that something does not lead to a certain situation or outcome, -지 않다 is combined with -게 되다 to form -게 되지 않다.

- 전에는 책을 많이 읽었는데 요즘에는 책을 읽게 되지 않아요.
  I used to read a lot of books, but these days I don't get to read anymore.

- 왜 그런지 잘 모르겠지만, 요즘 아침 일찍 일어나게 되지 않아요.
  I'm not sure why, but I can't wake up early in the morning these days.

4 Tenses

-게 됐다 (with -았/었-) indicates that a situation has already happened. In contrast, -게 되다 (without -았/었-) suggests that a situation typically occurs under certain conditions.

General facts	Results already reached
• 그 사람 얘기를 들으면 계속 듣게 돼요. When I hear that person's story, I keep listening. • 저녁을 안 먹으면 밤에 음식을 먹게 돼요. If you don't eat dinner, you end up eating at night.	• 우연히 그 사람 얘기를 듣게 됐어요. I happened to hear about that person. • 참다가 배고파서 음식을 먹게 됐어요. After holding it in, I got hungry and ended up eating.

To express the speaker's guess that a certain result will be reached under certain conditions, -(으)ㄹ 것이다 is combined with -게 되다 to form -게 될 것이다.

• 이 노래를 들으면 이 가수를 좋아하게 될 거예요. If you listen to this song, you will like this singer.

• 한국 사람을 자주 만나면 한국 문화에 빨리 적응하게 될 거예요.
If you meet Korean people often, you will quickly adapt to Korean culture.

> **Tip**
>
> ### The difference between -아/어지다 and -게 되다
>
> -아/어지다 and -게 되다 can both be combined with adjectives to express a change in state. While -아/어지다 highlights the process of change, -게 되다 emphasizes the result.
>
> The change
> • 한 달 동안 못 본 사이에 예쁘게 됐어요. (?) → 예뻐졌어요. (O)
> Even though we haven't seen each other for a month, you have become prettier.
>
> The result of the change
> • 오늘 화장이 예뻐졌어요. (×) → 예쁘게 됐어요. (O)
> My makeup turned out pretty today.

Grammar in Action

1 When expressing the result of a certain situation

A 어떻게 그 가수를 만났어요?
How did you meet that singer?

B 길을 걷다가 우연히 가수를 보게 됐어요.
As I was walking down the street,
I happened to see the singer.

-게 되다 is used to describe how an action or situation unintentionally leads to a certain outcome. It is often used when talking about changes that occur by chance or due to external circumstances, rather than the subject's direct intention. When describing an action or state that results from a process happening by chance, -게 되다 is combined with -다가.

• A 어떻게 한국어를 배우게 됐어요? How did you learn Korean?

　B 한국 친구가 있어서 한국어를 배우게 됐어요. Because I have a Korean friend, I started learning Korean.

• A 어떻게 하다가 남자 친구하고 헤어지게 됐어요? How did you end up breaking up with your boyfriend?

　B 멀리 살면서 연락하다가 남자 친구와 헤어지게 됐어요.
　I ended up breaking up with my boyfriend since we live far away from each other.

2 When emphasizing a difference in the result with -게 되다

A 전하고 뭐가 달라졌어요?
What has changed since before?

B 전에는 매운 음식을 못 먹었는데
요즘은 매운 음식을 잘 먹게 됐어요.
I couldn't eat spicy food before,
but I can eat spicy food well these days.

-게 되다 expresses a change in state by comparing it to a previous state. It highlights how something has changed over time or how a situation has developed differently from before. If the state has already changed, -게 됐다 is used, and if the change is expected to happen, -게 될 것이다 is applied.

• 어렸을 때는 매주 친구들하고 시간을 보냈는데, 요즘은 가족하고 시간을 보내게 됐어요.
　When I was young, I spent time with my friends every week, but these days, I spend time with my family.

• 처음에는 한국어를 할 수 없었는데 지금은 할 수 있게 됐어요.
　At first I couldn't speak Korean, but now I can.

• A 요리를 배우면 뭐가 달라져요? What will change if you learn to cook?

　B 집밥을 좋아하게 될 거예요. You will come to like home-cooked food.

Quiz 38

A 한국 음식이 맵지요?

Korean food is spicy, right?

B 네, 정말 매워요.

Yes, it's really spicy.

A 늦게 일어났지요?

You woke up late, didn't you?

B 네, 늦게 일어났어요.

Yes, I woke up late.

Grammar Essentials

1 -지

The ending -지 is used at the end of a sentence to indicate that the speaker is already aware of a fact or situation and is confirming that information.

-지 can be combined with verbs, adjectives, and "noun + 이다". For verbs and adjectives, attach -지 to the stem, regardless of whether it end in a vowel or consonant. For "noun + 이다", attach 지 if the noun ends in a vowel, and attach 이지 if the noun ends in a consonant.

In casual speech, -지요, which includes the polite form -요, is often shortened to -죠. When -지 is used in a question, it implies that the speaker already knows some fact or situation and assumes the listener does as well, asking for confirmation.

- 시장 물건이 싸죠? Market items are cheaper, right?

- 한국 사람들은 아파트에 많이 살지요. Many Koreans live in apartments, don't they?

- A 주말에 한강 공원에 사람이 많죠? There are a lot of people at Hangang Park on weekends, right?
  B 네, 날씨가 좋으면 사람이 더 많아요. Yes, there are even more when the weather is nice.

- 민수 씨 친구죠? 맞죠? You're Minsu's friend, right?

-지 can also be used at the end of other grammatical patterns like -고 싶다, -(으)ㄹ 수 있다, -아/어야 하다.

- A 지금 자고 싶죠? You want to sleep now, don't you?
  B 네, 자고 싶어요. 어떻게 알았어요? Yes, I do. How did you know?

- 미국에서 태어났지만 한국어를 잘할 수 있지.
  He was born in the USA, but he can speak Korean well, can't he?

- A 오늘 늦게까지 일해야 하죠? You have to work late today, right?
  B 맞아요. 오늘 밤까지 일해야 해요. Yes, I have to work until tonight.

2 Conjugation

-지					
피곤하다	피곤하지	부르다	부르지	쉽다	쉽지
먹다	먹지	듣다	듣지	짓다	짓지
바쁘다	바쁘지	살다	살지	그렇다	그렇지

3 Negation

When the negation marker 안 is added before -지, or -지 않다 is combined before -지, forming -지 않지, it indicates that the speaker already knows where an action is not taken or where some state is not present. 안 or -지 않지 combines with verb or adjective stems. The negation of a noun attaches as 아니지.

- A 음식을 해 먹지 않죠? You don't cook your meals, do you?

  B 맞아요. 귀찮아서 음식을 사 먹어요. Right, I buy food because it's cumbersome.

- A 회식에 안 왔죠? 왜 안 왔어요? You didn't come to the dinner yesterday, did you? Why not?

  B 어제 몸이 안 좋아서 일찍 집에 갔어요. I wasn't feeling well yesterday, so I went home early.

- A 마크 씨가 학생이 아니죠? Mark isn't a student, is he?

  B 네, 마크 씨는 학생이 아니에요. No, Mark is not a student.

4 Tenses

To express that the speaker knows about and is confirming an event or state that occurred in the past, the past marker -았/었- is added before -지 to form -았/었지.

- A 어제 저한테 전화했지요? You called me yesterday, didn't you?

  B 맞아요. 저녁에 전화했어요. Yes, I called you in the evening.

- 어렸을 때 민수는 좋은 학생이었지. Minsu was a good student when he was young, wasn't he?

To express the speaker's premise or confirmation about something that will happen in the future, -(으)ㄹ 것이다 is combined with -지 to form -(으)ㄹ 거지. To express the speaker's assumption or guess about a future event or state, -(으)ㄹ 테지 is used.

- A 내일 집에 있을 거죠? You will be at home tomorrow, right?

  B 네, 집에 있을 거예요. Yes, I will be at home.

- A 친구가 이 사실을 알면 기분 나쁠 테지? If your friend finds out about this, they'll be upset, won't they?

  B 그럼, 기분 많이 나쁠 거야. Yes, they'll be very upset.

Tip

-지 is used in declarative, interrogative, imperative, and propositive sentences. The intonation varies depending on the sentence type.

- 날씨는 봄이 좋지요. The weather in spring is nice, isn't it? Declarative
- A 저분이 미국 사람이죠? That person is American, isn't he? Interrogative
  B 네, 미국 사람 맞아요. Yes, they are.
- A 청소는 네가 좀 하지. You should do some cleaning. Imperative
  B 알았어. 내가 할게. Okay, I'll do it.
- A 회의는 식사 후에 하죠. Let's have the meeting after lunch. Propositve
  B 좋아요. 그렇게 해요. Okay, let's do that.

Grammar in Action

1 When the speaker seeks confirmation

-지 is used in interrogative sentences when the speaker already knows about an event or state and seeks confirmation from the listener. The response typically omits -지.

- A 단 음식을 좋아하죠? You like sweet foods, don't you?

  B 네, 좋아해요. 어떻게 알았어요? Yes, I do. How did you know?

- A 너 머리 잘랐지? You got a haircut, didn't you?

  B 어, 맞아. 머리 잘랐어. 어때? Yeah, I did. What do you think?

2 When stating known information softly

-지 is used in declarative sentences when the speaker already knows something and wishes to convey it softly. It is often used to introduce familiar topics in conversation. Omitting -지 does not change the meaning.

- 아이들이 아이스크림을 좋아하죠. Children like ice cream.

- 책 읽기는 글 쓰기에 도움이 돼요. 물론 재미없는 책도 많지요.
  Reading books helps you write. Of course, many books are not enjoyable.

3 When the speaker seeks agreement or consent

-지 is used when the speaker expresses or seeks agreement about an event or state. When responding, one may use -지 or omit it.

- A 오늘 날씨가 정말 좋죠? The weather is really nice today, isn't it?

  B 네, 날씨가 정말 좋아요. Yes, the weather is really nice.

- A 외국어 공부가 쉽지 않죠. (= 쉽지 않아요.) Studying a foreign language isn't easy, is it?

  B 맞아요. 쉽지 않죠. (= 쉽지 않아요.) Yes, it isn't easy.

Quiz 39

PART

3

Clause-Connecting Endings and Expressions

-고 and

엠마는 일하고 마크는 책을 읽고 있어요.
Emma is working, and Mark is reading a book.

지연은 커피를 마시고 민지는 얘기하고 있어요.
Jiyeon is drinking coffee, and Minji is talking.

그런데 유나는 얘기를 듣지 않고 창문 밖을 보고 있어요.
But Yuna is not listening to her and is looking out the window.

Grammar Essentials

1 -고

The ending -고 is a connective ending used to link two clauses that could be connected by 그리고 (which means "and" in English).

> 이 음식이 싸요. 그리고 이 음식이 맛있어요.
> = 이 음식이 싸고 맛있어요. This food is cheap and delicious.

When -고 is combined with a verb or adjective, it is added regardless of whether the stem ends with a vowel or a consonant.

- 가방이 커요. 그리고 무거워요. → 가방이 크고 무거워요. The bag is big and heavy.

- 비가 와요. 그리고 바람이 불어요. → 비가 오고 바람이 불어요. It's raining and the wind is blowing.

- 보통 주말에 친구하고 점심을 먹어요. 그리고 커피를 마셔요.
  → 보통 주말에 점심을 먹고 커피를 마셔요. I usually have lunch and drink coffee on the weekend.

When -고 follows a noun, it becomes -이고. However, in spoken language, if the final syllable of a noun is a vowel, -고 is often used.

- 라이언은 친구예요. 그리고 운동선수예요. → 라이언은 제 친구이고(= 친구고) 운동선수예요.
  Ryan is my friend and an athlete.

- 제 친구는 영국 사람이에요. 그리고 대학생이에요. → 제 친구는 영국 사람이고 대학생이에요.
  My friend is from England and is a college student.

 Be careful!

In Korean, when two sentences are connected with 그리고 (to form one sentence), verbs and adjectives combine using the ending -고, whereas nouns combine using the particle 하고, 와/과, or (이)랑.

- 보통 밥을 먹고 커피를 마셔요. I usually eat rice and drink coffee. Verb + Verb
- 여동생이 예쁘고 귀여워요. My younger sister is pretty and cute. Adjective + Adjective
- 엄마하고 형이 고향에 살아요. My mom and older brother live in our hometown. Noun + Noun
  = 엄마와 형이 고향에 살아요. = 엄마랑 형이 고향에 살아요.
  = 형과 엄마가 고향에 살아요. = 형이랑 엄마가 고향에 살아요.

2 Conjugation

-고					
보다	보고	다르다	다르고	덥다	덥고
읽다	읽고	듣다	듣고	붓다	붓고
크다	크고	살다	살고	그렇다	그렇고

Lesson 40

1 When enumerating actions or descriptions

진우 씨는 키가 크고 멋있어요. Jinwoo is tall and cool.
= 진우 씨는 멋있고 키가 커요. = Jinwoo is cool and tall.

The ending -고 is used to list actions, situations, or states. It can be attached to the stem of verbs, adjectives, and "noun + 이다". The meaning remains the same even if the order of the clauses before and after -고 is switched. In spoken Korean, -고 is sometimes pronounced as [gu].

• 제 친구는 친절하고 착해요. My friend is nice and kind.

= 제 친구는 착하고 친절해요.

• 저는 한식을 좋아하고 엠마는 일식을 좋아해요. I like Korean food, and Emma likes Japanese food.

= 엠마는 일식을 좋아하고 저는 한식을 좋아해요.

-고 can emphasize the meaning of a list by adding the particle 도 (also) to both the preceding and following clauses.

• 나중에 한국에서 일도 하고 싶고 결혼도 하고 싶어요. I want to work and get married in Korea later.

= 나중에 한국에서 일도 하고 결혼도 하고 싶어요.

When listing past actions, situations, or states, -고 can be used with or without the past tense marker -았/었-.

• 어렸을 때 엠마는 성격이 밝았어요. 그리고 똑똑했어요.

→ 어렸을 때 엠마는 성격이 밝았고 똑똑했어요.
When she was young, Emma had a bright personality and was smart.

= 어렸을 때 엠마는 성격이 밝고 똑똑했어요.

When the meaning is negated before -고, it changes to -지 않고. In declarative and interrogative sentences, this form is -지 않고, while in imperative or propositive sentences, it becomes -지 말고.

• 밥을 먹지 않고 운동해요. I exercise without eating.   Declarative

• 숙제를 하지 않고 잤어요? Did you sleep without doing your homework?   Interrogative

• 늦게 자지 말고 일찍 일어나세요. Don't sleep late, wake up early.   Imperative

• 영화를 보지 말고 저녁을 먹읍시다. Let's have dinner instead of watching a movie.   Propositive

When -고 is attached to the negation 아니다 in "noun + 이다", it becomes 아니고 or 아니라.

• 로지 씨가 미국 사람이 아니고 학생도 아니에요. Rosie is not American, and she is not a student.

2 When sequencing

냄비에 물을 넣고 물을 끓이세요.
끓는 물에 라면을 넣고 스프도 넣으세요.

Put water in a pot, and boil the water.
Add the noodles to the boiling water, then add the
seasoning packet as well.

The ending -고 is used to indicate that an action or situation in one clause is causally connected to the action in the following clause. In this usage, -고 is combined only with verbs and implies that the action in the following clause occurs after the completion of the action in the preceding clause. The sequence of actions is essential; therefore, the clauses cannot be reversed.

- 운동하고 샤워해요. I exercise and take a shower. (= after exercising)
  ≠ 샤워하고 운동해요.

- 손을 씻고 밥을 먹어요. Wash your hands and eat. (= after washing)
  ≠ 밥을 먹고 손을 씻어요.

- 보통 수업이 끝나고 학생들이 집에 가요. Usually, students go home after class. (= after classes end)
  ≠ 학생들이 집에 가고 보통 수업이 끝나요.

When -고 is used to indicate a sequential connection, a tense marker cannot be placed before -고. Instead, the tense is indicated in the following clause.

- 매일 아침을 먹고 학교에 가요. I eat breakfast every day and go to school.　　Present

- 어제 수업이 끝나고 친구를 만났어요. I met my friend after class yesterday.　Past

- 다음 주말에 여자 친구하고 영화를 보고 이야기할 거예요.　　　　　　　Future
  Next weekend, I will watch a movie with my girlfriend and talk about it.

> **ⓘ Note**
> -고 can replace -고 나서 to emphasize the sequence of actions. -고 나서 is mainly used in spoken Korean, and a tense marker cannot come before -고 나서.
> - 먼저 숙제를 끝내고 친구를 만나세요. Finish your homework first and then meet your friends.
>   = 끝내고 나서

Quiz 40

TOPIK I | SCK 2

-아/어서 and [Sequential connection]

Kor. 41

저는 카페에 가서 (그 카페에서) 커피를 마셔요.

I go to a café and drink coffee (at the café).

제가 선물을 사서 (그 선물을) 친구에게 줬어요.

I bought a gift and gave it to my friend.

우리는 고기를 구워서 (그 고기를) 먹었어요.

We grilled meat and ate it.

1 -아/어서

The ending -아/어서 is a connective ending used to merge two sentences into one, indicating that the clauses are sequentially related.

식당에 가요. 그리고 음식을 먹어요. I go to a restaurant and eat some food (at the restaurant).

→ 식당에 가서 (그 식당에서) 음식을 먹어요.

The ending -아/어서 is only combined with verbs. If the verb stem ends in 하다, it changes to 해서. When the last vowel of the verb stem is ㅏ or ㅗ, -아서 is used, and for all other cases, -어서 is applied.

- 제가 친구한테 전화해서 (그 친구한테) 이야기해요. I call a friend and talk (to him).

- 저는 일찍 집에 와서 (그 집에서) 자요. I come home early and sleep (at home).

- 제 친구가 음식을 만들어서 (그 음식을) 먹어요. My friend made food and I ate (it).

2 Difference between -고 and -아/어서

vs.

친구를 만나고 영화를 봤어요.

I met a friend and (after meeting my friend) watched a movie.

친구를 만나서 영화를 봤어요.

I met a friend and (with that friend) watched a movie.

Unlike -고, which is used to list actions or states without necessarily implying a connection between them, -아/어서 is used when the action or place in the preceding clause is directly connected to the following clause.

- 도서관에 가고 공부해요.   Seperate actions: going to the library and studying elsewhere
  I go to the library and study (at a different place).

- 도서관에 가서 공부해요.   Connected actions: studying at the library after going there
  I go to the library and study (at the library).

3   Subject of -아/어서

The ending -아/어서 requires the same subject in both the preceding and following clauses.

- 제가 집에 와서 (제가) 전화할게요. (O) I will come home and and call you.

  제가 집에 와서 친구가 전화할게요. (×)

- 동생이 도서관에서 책을 빌려서 (동생이) 읽어요. (O)
  My younger brother borrowed a book from the library and he read it.

  동생이 도서관에서 책을 빌려서 제가 읽어요. (×)

This differs from -고, which can list actions performed by different subjects.

- 수업이 끝나고 제가 친구한테 전화할 거예요. After class ends, I will call my friend.

Omitting -아/어서 in commonly paired actions

In everyday speech, commonly paired actions are often expressed with -아/어서 between verbs. In these cases, the -아/어서 can be omitted in the verb combination.

- 저는 편의점에서 라면을 사서 먹어요. I buy and eat ramyeon at a convenience store.
                    = 사 먹어요.
- 제가 친구에게 김치를 만들어서 줬어요. I made and gave kimchi to my friend.
                    = 만들어 줬어요.

4   Tenses

The past tense marker -았/었- cannot be placed before -아/어서. Instead, the tense is indicated in the following clause.

- 보통 음식을 배달해요. 그리고 (그 음식을) 먹어요.   Present

  → 보통 음식을 배달해서 먹어요. I usually have food delivered and eat (that food).

- 어제 친구를 만났어요. 그리고 (친구하고 같이) 공원에 갔어요.   Past

  → 어제 친구를 만나서 공원에 갔어요. Yesterday, I met a friend and then we went to the park.

- 내일 시장에 갈 거예요. 그리고 (시장에서) 쇼핑할 거예요.   Future

  → 내일 시장에 가서 쇼핑할 거예요. Tomorrow, I will go to the market and shop.

Different meanings of the ending -아/어서

The ending -아/어서 is also used to indicate a reason, means, or method.

- 제가 핸드폰 배터리가 없어서 전화 못 했어요.   Reason

  I couldn't call because my cell phone battery was low.

- 친구는 걸어서 집에 가요. My friend walks home.   Means, Method

Grammar in Action

1 When expressing two actions in succession

보통 음식을 배달해서 (그 음식을) 먹어요.
I usually get food delivered and eat it.

The ending -아/어서 is used to express two connected actions in succession. The object of the action or the place where the action occurs is semantically connected to both the preceding and following clauses.

• A 수업 후에 뭐 해요? What do you do after class?

  B 수업 후에 친구를 만나서 (그 친구하고) 같이 공부해요.
    After class, I meet a friend and we study together (with that friend).

• A 지난 주말에 뭐 했어요? What did you do last weekend?

  B 고향에 가서 (고향에서) 부모님을 만났어요.
    I went to my hometown and met my parents (in my hometown).

2 When expressing continuous or simultaneous actions

친구가 6시에 일어나서 운동해요.
My friend wakes up at 6 and works out.

The ending -아/어서 is used to connect one action to another while maintaining the status or result of the previous action. Verbs such as 앉다 (to sit), 눕다 (to lie down), 전화하다 (to call), and 건너다 (to cross) are commonly combined with -아/어서 rather than -고 when describing continuous or simultaneous actions.

• 침대에 누워서 핸드폰을 해요. I use my cell phone while lying in bed.

• 의자에 앉아서 수업을 들으세요. Sit down and listen to the lesson.

• 저는 친구한테 전화해서 1시간 동안 얘기했어요. I called my friend and talked for an hour.

• 횡단보도를 건너서 오른쪽으로 가세요. Cross the crosswalk and go right.

Quiz 41

-거나 Or

Kor. 42

주말에 저는 집에서 쉬거나 게임해요.

On weekends, I rest at home or play games.

주말에 저는 친구를 만나거나 취미 활동을 해요.

On weekends, I meet friends or pursue my hobbies.

Grammar Essentials

1 -거나

The ending -거나 is a conjunctive ending used to indicate a choice between two or more actions or states. Both the preceding and following clauses describe possible actions or states.

방학 때 보통 여행을 <u>가거나</u> 아르바이트를 해요.

a choice between two actions

-거나 can be used with verbs and adjectives, regardless of whether the verb or adjective stem ends in a vowel or consonant.

- 보통 평일 저녁에 운동하거나 산책해요. I usually exercise or take a walk on weekday evenings.

- 집에 있을 때 음악을 듣거나 책을 읽어요. When I'm at home, I listen to music or read a book.

- 피곤하거나 머리가 아프면 이 약을 드세요. If you are tired or have a headache, take this medicine.

- 맵거나 짠 음식이 건강에 안 좋아요. Spicy or salty foods are not good for your health.

The subject of the preceding and following clauses with -거나 can be different.

- 내가 아프거나 다른 사람들에게 문제가 생기면, 이 번호로 연락하세요.
  If I am sick or other have problems, contact this number.

In Korean, when expressing a choice between two or more actions or states, verbs, and adjectives combine with the ending -거나, while a choice between two or more nouns uses the particle (이)나. If the preceding noun ends in a vowel, 나 is used; if it ends in a consonant, 이나 is added.

- 저녁 식사 후에 산책하거나 운동해요.   Verb + Verb
  After dinner, I either take a walk or exercise.

- 회사 근처 식당은 비싸거나 맛없어요.   Adjective + Adjective
  Restaurants near the office are either expensive or not tasty.

- 누구나 친구나 가족이 있어요.   Noun + Noun
  Everyone has either friends or family.

- 질문이 있으면 이메일이나 전화로 연락해 주세요.   Noun + Noun
  If you have any questions, please contact me by email or phone.

2 Conjugation

-거나					
보다	보거나	다르다	다르거나	맵다	맵거나
먹다	먹거나	걷다	걷거나	붓다	붓거나
아프다	아프거나	놀다	놀거나	그렇다	그렇거나

3 Negation

When negation markers such as -지 않다 or -지 못하다 are placed before -거나, they become -지 않거나 or -지 못하거나. Additionally, when 아니다 is placed before -거나, it becomes 아니거나.

- 매일 운동하지 않거나 걷지 않으면 살이 찔 거예요.
  You will gain weight if you do not exercise or walk daily.

- 저 가수가 유명하지 않거나 인기가 없을 거예요.
  That singer is either not famous or popular.

- 아마 마크 씨가 생선을 먹지 못하거나 좋아하지 않을 거예요. Mark probably can't eat or doesn't like fish.

- 아마 그것은 사실이 아니거나 잘못된 생각일 거예요. It's probably either not true or a misconception.

When forming imperative or propositive negations with -거나, -지 말거나 combines with the verb stem.

- 잠을 못 자요? 그러면 커피를 마시지 말거나 가벼운 운동을 해 보세요.
    (= 커피를 마시지 마세요. 또는)
  Can't sleep? Then don't drink coffee or try some light exercise.

- 너무 피곤해요? 밖에 나가지 말거나 집 근처에서만 산책합시다.
    (= 밖에 나가지 맙시다. 또는)
  Too tired? Let's not go out or take a walk near home.

4 Tenses

To express a choice between two or more past actions or states, -았/었- is not combined with -거나. Instead, the tense of the following clause (present, past, or future) may change, but the preceding clause with -거나 remains the same.

- 보통 친구들하고 놀거나 아르바이트해요.   Present
  I usually hang out with friends or work part-time.

- 학생 때 친구들하고 놀거나 아르바이트했어요.   Past
  When I was a student, I used to hang out with friends or work part-time.

- 앞으로 친구들하고 놀거나 아르바이트할 거예요.   Future
  I will hang out with friends or work part-time in the future.

To express one of two presumed past scenarios, -았/었- is combined with -거나 to indicate completion. However, -겠- cannot be combined with -거나.

- 아마 비밀번호를 잊어버렸거나 컴퓨터가 고장 났을 거예요.
  The password was probably forgotten, or the computer broke down.

- 아마 폴 씨가 아팠거나 바빴을 거예요. Paul was probably sick or busy.

- 다음 주에 친구하고 밥을 먹겠거나 커피를 마실 거예요. (✕)

  → 다음 주에 친구하고 밥을 먹거나 커피를 마실 거예요. (○)
    Next week I will eat or drink coffee with a friend.

Grammar in Action

1 When expressing a choice between actions or states

The ending -거나 is used to express a choice between two or more actions or states.

- A 내일 뭐 하고 싶어요? What do you want to do tomorrow?

  B 영화를 보거나 산책하고 싶어요. I want to watch a movie or go for a walk.

- A 언제 에어컨을 켜요? When do you turn on the air conditioner?

  B 날씨가 덥거나 습할 때 에어컨을 켜요. I turn on the air conditioner when it's hot or humid.

Typically, actions are connected with actions, and states with states when using -거나.

- 많이 걷거나 뛰면, 생활에 힘이 생겨요. If you walk a lot or run, you gain energy in life.

- 피곤하거나 힘이 없을 때 이 약을 드세요. Take this medicine when you are tired or lack energy.

2 When expressing indifference to the choice

먹거나 말거나 신경 쓰지 마세요.

Don't worry whether I eat it or not.

When the speaker does not care whether an action is performed or not, the structure -거나 -거나 is used to list multiple possible actions.

- A 질문이 있으면 어떻게 해요? What should I do if I have a question?

  B 이메일하거나 사무실에 오거나 뭐든지 괜찮아요. Emailing, coming to the office, or anything is fine.

- A 시간이 없는데 어떻게 운동해야 해요? I don't have time; how should I exercise?

  B 산책하거나 회사에 걸어가거나 계단으로 올라가거나 상관없어요. 몸을 많이 움직이세요.
  Taking a walk, walking to work, taking the stairs, it doesn't matter. Just move a lot.

When expressing that it does not matter whether an action is performed or not, the structure -거나 -지 않거나 is used. To emphasize indifference toward the performance of a specific action, the structure -거나 말거나 is used.

- 안경을 쓰거나 쓰지 않거나 상관없어요.
  It doesn't matter whether you wear glasses or not.

- 그 사람은 사람이 다치거나 말거나 관심이 없어요.
  That person doesn't care whether people get hurt or not.

Quiz 42

TOPIK I | SCK 2

-지만 but

Kor. 43

서울은 비가 오지만
부산은 비가 안 와요.
It's raining in Seoul, but not in Busan.

등산이 힘들지만 재미있어요. Hiking is tough, but fun.

제 친구가 열심히 공부했지만 결과가 좋지 않았어요.
My friend studied hard, but the results were not good.

Grammar Essentials

1 -지만

The ending -지만 is used to indicate a contrast between two clauses. It acknowledges the situation or state described in the preceding clause while introducing a different situation or state in the following clause, thus highlighting the contrast between them. When using -지만, the emphasis is placed more on the following clause than on the preceding clause, conveying both the contrast and emphasizing the meaning of the following clause.

> 음식이 <u>맛있어요</u>. <u>그렇지만</u> 음식이 정말 싸요.
>
> = 음식이 맛있지만 정말 싸요. The food is delicious, but it's really cheap.

The ending -지만 can be attached to verbs, adjectives, and "noun + 이다". For verbs and adjectives, -지만 is attached to the stem regardless of whether it ends in a vowel or a consonant. For "noun + 이다", use -지만 if the noun ends in a vowel; otherwise, use 이지만.

- 보통 아침을 먹지만 오늘은 아침을 안 먹었어요. I usually eat breakfast, but I didn't eat breakfast today.
- 오늘 날씨가 좋지만 집에서 쉬고 싶어요. The weather is nice today, but I want to rest at home.
- 저는 한국 사람이지만 한국어를 잘 못해요. I am Korean, but I am not good at Korean.

2 Conjugation

-지만					
오다	오지만	다르다	다르지만	쉽다	쉽지만
입다	입지만	듣다	듣지만	낫다	낫지만
바쁘다	바쁘지만	살다	살지만	그렇다	그렇지만

3 Emphasizing contrast with particles

When you want to emphasize the object of contrast while using the ending -지만, you can place the particle 은/는 after the noun that serves as the object of contrast.

- 저는 운동을 좋아하지만 제 친구는 운동을 싫어해요. I like exercising, but my friend hates exercising.
- 저는 고기는 먹을 수 있지만 해물은 먹을 수 없어요. I can eat meat, but I can't eat seafood.

The ending -지만, when used with the particle 도 in the following clause, compares two subjects or situations with similar qualities, highlighting the more important difference.

- 저는 수학을 좋아하지만 과학도 좋아해요. I like math, but I also like science.
- 제 친구는 영어를 잘하지만 일본어도 유창하게 잘해요.

  My friend is good at English, but is also fluent in Japanese.

4 Tenses

To express the past, the past tense marker -았/었- is added before -지만.

- 어제 가방을 샀지만 영수증을 안 받았어요. I bought a bag yesterday, but I didn't receive a receipt.
  (= 어제 가방을 샀어요. 그렇지만 영수증을 안 받았어요.)

- 부산에 가 봤지만 제주도에 안 가 봤어요. I have been to Busan, but I have not been to Jeju Island.
  (= 부산에 가 봤어요. 그렇지만 제주도에 안 가 봤어요.)

To convey speculation, -겠- is used before -지만.

- 기분이 나쁘겠지만 저도 어쩔 수 없어요. You must feel bad, but I can't help it.
  (= 기분이 나쁘겠어요. 그렇지만 저도 어쩔 수 없어요.)

- 제 얘기를 못 믿겠지만 이번 한 번만 믿어 주세요. You may not believe me, but please believe me just this once.
  (= 제 얘기를 못 믿겠어요. 그렇지만 이번 한 번만 믿어 주세요.)

5 Negation

To express negation, the negative markers 안 or -지 않다 can be placed before -지만. In the present tense, -지 않지만 is attached to the verb or adjective stem to indicate contrast. In the past tense, -았/었- combines with -지 않지만 to form -지 않았지만.

- 저는 고기를 먹지 않지만 생선을 먹어요. I don't eat meat, but I do eat fish.

- 날씨가 춥지 않지만 바람이 불어요. The weather is not cold, but it is windy.

- 제가 어제 친구를 만나지 않았지만 전화로 얘기했어요.
  I didn't meet my friend yesterday, but we talked on the phone.

- 저는 아직 배부르지 않았지만 음식을 그만 먹었어요. I wasn't full yet, but I stopped eating.

The negation for "noun + 이다" becomes 아니지만, while 아니다 is combined with -지만. When -았/었- is combined with 아니다 and -지만, it becomes 아니었지만.

- 그 사람은 가수가 아니지만 노래를 정말 잘해요. He is not a singer, but he sings really well.

- 청소가 제 일이 아니었지만 제가 청소했어요. Cleaning wasn't my job, but I cleaned it.

To imply speculation, -겠- can also be combined with -지 않거나 or 아니지만.

- 내일 날씨가 그렇게 춥지 않겠지만 옷을 따뜻하게 입고 가세요.
  The weather won't be that cold tomorrow, but dress warmly.

- 소문이 사실이 아니겠지만 우리가 소문을 확인해야 할 것 같아요.
  The rumor may not be true, but I think we should check it.

Grammar in Action

1 When expressing contrast between conflicting ideas

The ending -지만 is used when the content in the following clause contradicts the preceding clause, indicating a contrast. To emphasize the contrasting content, you can add the particle 은/는.

- 그 사람은 똑똑하지만 친절하지 않아요. That person is smart, but he is not kind.

- 제 친구는 중국어를 말할 수 있지만 한자를 읽을 수 없어요.
  My friend can speak Chinese, but he cannot read Chinese characters.

- A 집이 어때요? How is your house?

  B 월세가 비싸지만 깨끗해요. The monthly rent is expensive, but it's clean.

- A 요즘 바빠요? Are you busy these days?

  B 아니요, 지난주는 바빴지만 이번 주는 안 바빠요. No, I was busy last week, but I'm not busy this week.

2 When indicating an exception

The ending -지만 is used to indicate an exception that differs from what is generally accepted as a fact or truth. To emphasize the exception, you can use the particle 은/는 or 만.

- 보통 윤아가 학교에 일찍 오지만 오늘은 늦게 왔어요.
  Usually Yuna comes to school early, but today she came late.

- 모든 친구들이 이번 모임에 왔지만, 진수만 오지 않았어요.
  All my friends came to this meeting, but only Jinsu did not come

- 여름은 보통 덥지만 올해 여름은 덥지 않아요. Summer is usually hot, but this summer is not hot.

3 When indicating frequently used idiomatic expressions

The ending -지만 is often used in idiomatic expressions in colloquial speech.

- 죄송하지만, 펜 좀 빌려 주세요. Excuse me, please lend me a pen.

- 실례지만, 입구에 어떻게 가야 돼요? Excuse me, how do I get to the entrance?

- 미안하지만, 저를 도와줄 수 있어요? I'm sorry, but can you help me?

- 잘 모르겠지만, 미국에서 한국 음식이 아마 비쌀 거예요.
  I'm not sure, but Korean food is probably expensive in the US.

- 잘 아시겠지만, 서울은 주말에 길이 많이 막혀요.
  As you know, the roads in Seoul are very congested on weekends.

Quiz 43

219

진호하고 민수는 친한 친구지만 많이 달라요.
Jinho and Minsu are close friends, but they are very different.

진호는 요리를 잘하는데 민수는 요리를 못해요.
Jinho is good at cooking, but Minsu is not.

진호는 운동을 못하는데 민수는 운동을 잘해요.
Jinho is not good at sports, but Minsu excels at them.

집 근처 식당에 갔는데, 식당 음식이 정말 맛있었어요.
They went to a restaurant near their home, and the food was really delicious.

Grammar Essentials

1 -는데

The ending -는데 is used to introduce context or background information before stating the main point. It describes a situation or setting in the preceding clause, which is then contrasted with or expanded upon in the following clause.

집 근처 식당에 갔어요. 그런데 식당 음식이 정말 맛있었어요.

→ 식당에 갔는데, 식당 음식이 정말 맛있었어요.

Situation, Background   Main point to discuss

I went to a restaurant near my house, and the food was really delicious.

2 Conjugations

This ending can be attached to verbs, adjectives, and "noun + 이다", with conjugation varying as follows.

① Verbs: -는데

Regardless of whether the verb stem ends in a vowel or consonant, -는데 is used.

- 매일 지하철을 타는데 지하철이 정말 편해요. I take the subway every day, and it's really convenient.

- 보통 아침을 먹는데 오늘은 아침을 안 먹었어요. I usually have breakfast, but I didn't have it today.

- 친구와 자주 영화를 보는데 이번 주는 바빠서 영화 못 봐요.
  I usually watch movies with my friends, but I cannot watch movies this week because I'm busy.

② Adjectives: -(으)ㄴ데 or -는데

For adjectives, -(으)ㄴ데 is used based on the final sound of the stem. If the adjective stem ends in a vowel, -ㄴ데 is used, while -은데 is used if the stem ends in a consonant. However, for adjectives ending in 있다 or 없다, -는데 is used regardless of the final syllable.

- 지금 조금 피곤한데 내일 다시 일 시작합시다. I'm a bit tired now, let's start working again tomorrow.

- 오늘 날씨가 좋은데 같이 산책할까요? The weather is nice today, shall we go for a walk?

- 이 음식은 맛있는데 조금 맵네요. This food is delicious, but it's a bit spicy.

③ Nouns: 인데

Regardless of the noun's ending, 인데 is used.

- 유진 씨가 배우인데 이 영화에 나와요. Yujin is an actor, and he appears in this movie.

- 비빔밥이 한국 음식인데 외국인에게 조금 매울 수 있어요.
  Bibimbap is a Korean dish, but it might be a bit spicy for foreigners.

- 저 사람이 의사인데 아주 친절해요. That person is a doctor, and he is very kind.

3 Negation

To express negation, 안 or -지 않다 can be added before -(으)ㄴ/는데. The form varies depending on whether it combines with a verb or adjective.

1 Verbs: -지 않는데 is used.

- 보통 늦게 일어나지 않는데 오늘은 늦게 일어났어요.
  I usually don't wake up late, but today I woke up late.

- 보통 주말에 가게 문을 열지 않는데 이번 주말에 가게 문을 열었어요.
  Normally, we don't open the store on weekends, but this weekend we opened it.

2 Adjectives: -지 않은데 is used.

- 집세가 싸지 않은데 왜 이 집이 인기가 많아요? The rent is not cheap, why is this house so popular?

- 날씨가 좋지 않은데 다음에 등산 가는 게 어때요?
  The weather is not nice, how about going hiking next time?

3 Noun + 이다: The negation becomes 아닌데.

- 유진 씨는 가수가 아닌데 노래를 정말 잘해요. Yujin isn't a singer, but he sings really well.

- 폴 씨가 한국 사람이 아닌데 어떻게 한국어를 잘해요?
  Paul is not Korean, how can he speak Korean so well?

4 Tenses

1 Past: -았/었는데

To express context regarding a past event or state, the past tense marker -았/었- is combined with -는데 to form -았/었는데. This is used with verbs, adjectives, and "noun + 이다".

- 지난주에 제가 학교 앞 식당에 갔는데 음식이 정말 맛있었어요.
  I went to a restaurant in front of the school last week, and the food was really delicious.

- 제가 어제 구두를 신었는데 그 구두가 불편했어요. I wore shoes yesterday, but they were uncomfortable.

- 친구가 물건을 사지 않았는데 많이 구경했어요. My friend didn't buy anything but looked around a lot.

- 어렸을 때 저는 키가 작았는데 지금은 키가 커요. I was short when I was young, but now I am tall.

- 어제 휴가였는데 일이 많아서 일해야 했어요.
  It was a holiday yesterday, but I had to work due to the workload.

- 전에 학생이었는데 그때는 도서관에서 무료로 책을 빌릴 수 있었어요.
  I used to be a student, and back then, I could borrow books from the library for free.

2 Future and Speculation

To express context regarding a future event or state, use the following forms: -(으)ㄹ 건데, -(으)려고 하는데, or -(으)ㄹ 텐데.

▶ **-(으)ㄹ 건데**

Used with verbs to introduce context about a planned future event or action.

- 내년 축제를 5월에 할 건데 누가 담당하기로 했어요?
  We are planning to have the festival in May next year. Who is in charge?

- 우리 가족이 먹을 건데 건강에 좋은 음식을 준비해야죠.
  It's for our family to eat, so we need to prepare healthy food.

▶ **-(으)려고 하는데**

Used with verbs when the subject has an intention or plan for a future action.

- 수업을 신청하려고 하는데 어떻게 해야 해요? I plan to register for classes. How should I proceed?

- 마크 씨가 매운 음식을 먹으려고 하는데 친구들이 마크 씨를 말렸어요.
  Mark was going to eat spicy food, but his friends dissuaded him.

If the intention was in the past, -(으)려고 했는데 is used. This often indicates that the subject intended to perform an action but was unable to carry it out.

- 아까 말하려고 했는데 말 못 했어요. I was going to say something earlier, but I couldn't say it.

- 자료를 미리 찾으려고 했는데 전화가 와서 못 찾았어요.
  I intended to find the materials in advance, but I couldn't because I received a call.

▶ **-(으)ㄹ 텐데**

Used with verbs, adjectives, or "noun + 이다" to express the speaker's speculation about a future situation.

- 이 음식이 매울 텐데 다른 음식을 먹는 게 어때요?
  This food might be spicy. How about trying something else?

- 1시간 후에 식당 문을 닫을 텐데 빨리 식당에 갑시다.
  The restaurant will close in an hour, so let's go quickly.

- 저 사람이 학생일 텐데 아르바이트를 너무 많이 해요.
  That person is a student but works too many part-time jobs.

If expressing speculation about a situation that has already happened, -았/었- is added before -(으)ㄹ 텐데, forming -았/었을 텐데. This structure is used when the speaker is making a logical assumption or guess about the past.

- 어제 많이 아팠을 텐데, 지금은 괜찮아요? You must have been very sick yesterday. Are you okay now?

- 진수 씨는 학생 때 아르바이트 때문에 바빴을 텐데, 열심히 공부해서 장학금도 받았어요.
  Jinsu was busy with part-time jobs during his student days, but he studied hard and even received a scholarship.

- 선생님이 윤아 씨한테 벌써 말했을 텐데, 왜 윤아 씨가 이 사실을 모르고 있죠?
  The teacher must have already told Yuna about this; why doesn't she know?

- 오늘은 휴일이니까 식당이 문을 닫았을 텐데, 한번 식당에 전화해 보세요.
  Today is a holiday so the restaurant would be closed. Maybe try calling them.

Grammar in Action

1 When introducing the context as a statement

-(으)ㄴ/는데 is used to introduce the context, such as a situation, state, or emotion, before expressing the main point. Typically, there is a pause after -(으)ㄴ/는데 to differentiate the background information in the preceding clause from the main content in the following clause.

- 제주도에 갔는데 바다 경치가 정말 아름다웠어요.
  I went to Jeju Island, and the ocean scenery was really beautiful.

- 내일 공원에 가려고 하는데 같이 가고 싶은 사람을 찾고 있어요.
  I am planning to go to the park tomorrow, and am looking for someone to go with.

2 When expressing contrast

-(으)ㄴ/는데 is used to introduce a situation that contrasts with the main statement, emphasizing difference. The contrast can be made stronger by adding the particle 은/는 to the contrasting elements.

- 보통은 아침에 뉴스를 보는데, 오늘은 뉴스를 못 봤어요.
  I usually watch the news in the morning, but I couldn't watch it today.

- 어제는 날씨가 좋았는데, 오늘은 날씨가 안 좋아요. The weather was nice yesterday, but it is not good today.

3 When giving background before a question or request

-(으)ㄴ/는데 is used to provide context before a question, request, or suggestion. This structure helps the listener understand the situation before the speaker makes their main statement. The speaker softens their request by phrasing the preceding clause of -(으)ㄴ/는데 to introduce the context.

- 이번에 한국을 여행하려고 하는데, 어디가 제일 좋아요?   Question
  I am planning to travel to Korea. Where would you recommend going?

- 한국어 문법이 너무 어려운데, 저를 도와주세요.   Request
  Korean grammar is very difficult for me. Could you help me?

- 한국 음식을 먹고 싶은데, 우리 점심에 한국 음식을 먹어요!   Suggestion
  I want to eat Korean food, let's have Korean food for lunch!

-(으)ㄴ/는데 is also commonly used in idiomatic expressions before asking a question.

- 죄송한데요, 이 근처에 편의점이 있어요? Excuse me, is there a convenience store nearby?

- 이거 잘 모르겠는데, 이게 영어로 뭐예요? I don't quite understand this. What is this in English?

4 When only the background is introduced indirectly

-(으)ㄴ/는데 can be used in Korean as a polite expression. In spoken language, if only the preceding clause of -(으)ㄴ/는데 is used without the following clause, the sentence sounds softer and more indirect. Even if the following clause is omitted, the listener can usually guess the speaker's intent from the context.

- A 저한테 진수 씨 전화번호가 없는데요. (진수 씨 전화번호가 몇 번이에요?)
  I don't have Jinsu's phone number. (What number is Jinsu's phone number?)

  B 제가 가르쳐 드릴게요. I will let you know.

- A 제가 핸드폰을 집에 놓고 왔는데요. (핸드폰 좀 빌려 주세요.)
  I left my phone at home. (Could I use your phone?)

  B 그래요? 제 핸드폰 쓰세요. Really? Here, use my phone.

It is also possible to omit the following clause when responding to someone else's question, request, or suggestion.

- A 혹시 폴 씨 알아요? Do you know Paul?

  B 아니요, 저도 모르겠는데요. (그 사람이 누구예요?) No, I don't know either. (Who is Paul?)

- A 죄송한데요, 펜 좀 빌려 주세요. Sorry, could you lend me a pen?

  B 저도 없는데요. (다른 사람에게 빌리세요.) I don't have one either. (Try asking someone else for a pen.)

5 When expressing admiration

The ending -(으)ㄴ/는데 is used at the end of a sentence to express admiration for an action or state. When the intonation falls, it sounds like a declarative sentence, emphasizing admiration. Conversely, when the intonation rises, it sounds like a question, indicating that the speaker is expecting a response from the listener.

- A 노래 진짜 잘하는데? You really sing well, don't you?

  B 아니에요. 잘 못해요. No, I don't sing well.

- A 어, 진수 씨가 아직 안 왔는데요? Oh, Jinsu hasn't arrived yet, has he?

  B 맞아요. 5분 후에 올 거예요. Right, he will come in five minutes.

6 When requiring a response from the listener

-(으)ㄴ/는데 is used with a question mark to indicate that the speaker is waiting for a response from the listener. The intonation rises at the end of the sentence. This usage cannot be used in yes/no questions but is always used in WH-questions to require an answer.

- A 지금 등산 가요. I am going to hike now.

  B 어디로 등산 가는데요? Where are you going hiking?

- A 어제 내가 음식을 만들었어. I made some food yesterday.

  B 무슨 음식을 만들었는데? What kind of food did you make?

Quiz 44

-아/어서 because

어젯밤에 못 자서 너무 피곤해요.

I'm so tired because I couldn't sleep last night.

A 왜 회사에 못 가요? Why can't I go to work?

B 감기에 걸려서 못 가요. I can't go because I have a cold.

1 -아/어서

-아/어서 is a conjunctive ending that links a cause or reason to a resulting action or state.

> 날씨가 좋아요. 그래서 저는 산책하고 싶어요. The weather is nice. So I want to take a walk.
>
> → 날씨가 좋아서 저는 산책하고 싶어요. Because the weather is nice, I want to take a walk.

The ending -아/어서 is attached to the stem of a verb or adjective. If the stem ends in 하, -아/어서 changes to 해서. For verbs and adjectives whose stems end with the vowels ㅏ or ㅗ, -아서 is used. In all other cases, -어서 is applied.

- 바다를 좋아해서 바다에 자주 가요. (= 바다를 좋아해요. 그래서 바다에 자주 가요.)
  Because I like the sea, I often go to the sea.

- 요즘 너무 바빠서 친구를 못 만나요. (= 요즘 너무 바빠요. 그래서 친구를 못 만나요.)
  Because I've been too busy, I can't meet friends.

- 커피를 많이 마셔서 잠이 안 와요. (= 커피를 많이 마셔요. 그래서 잠이 안 와요.)
  Because I drink a lot of coffee, I can't sleep.

2 Conjugation

-아/어서			
하다	해서	다르다	*달라서
보다	봐서	걷다	*걸어서
읽다	읽어서	그렇다	*그래서
알다	알아서	맵다	*매워서
바쁘다	*바빠서	붓다	*부어서

3 Combination with "nouns + 이다"

When combined with "noun + 이다", the ending -아/어서 becomes (이)라서 or 여서/이어서. If the noun ends in a vowel, 라서 or 여서 is used. If the noun ends in a consonant, 이라서 or 이어서 is used.

- 동생이 운동선수라서 제가 운동에 관심이 있어요. My younger sibling is an athlete, so I am interested in sports.
  (= 운동선수여서)

- 제가 학생이라서 아침 일찍 학교에 가야 해요. I am a student, so I have to go to school early in the morning.
  (= 학생이어서)

4 Negation

To express negation with verbs or adjectives, place 안 or -지 않다 before -아/어서.

- 저는 게임을 <u>하지 않아서</u> 큰 모니터가 필요 없어요. I don't play games, so I don't need a big monitor.
  - (= 안 해서)

- 이 옷이 <u>비싸지 않아서</u> 많이 샀어요. This clothing isn't expensive, so I bought a lot.
  - (= 안 비싸서)

For nouns, 아니다 is combined with -아/어서 to form 아니라서 or 아니어서.

- 제가 한국 사람이 <u>아니라서</u> 한국 역사를 잘 몰라요. I am not Korean, so I don't know much about Korean history.
  - (= 아니어서)

5 Tenses

When expressing a cause or reason for a past event or state, -았/었- is not combined with -아/어서. Instead, the same form of -아/어서 is used, regardless of whether the cause or reason is in the present or past tense.

- 어제 많이 <u>공부했어요</u>. <u>그래서</u> 오늘 쉬고 싶어요.
  - → 어제 많이 <u>공부해서</u> 오늘 쉬고 싶어요. Because I studied a lot yesterday, I want to rest today.
    공부했어서 (X)

- 지난 주말에 여행 <u>갔어요</u>. <u>그래서</u> 집에 아무도 없었어요.
  - → 지난 주말에 여행 <u>가서</u> 집에 아무도 없었어요. The was no one at home because I traveled last weekend.
    갔어서 (✕)

- 저는 작년에 <u>학생이었어요</u>. <u>그래서</u> 일 안 했어요.
  - → 저는 작년에 <u>학생이라서</u> 일 했어요. Because I was a student last year, I worked.
    학생이었어서 (✕)

To express a future event or state as a cause or reason, nothing can be attached before -아/어서.

- 내일 우리 집에 친구가 <u>올 거예요</u>. <u>그래서</u> 오늘 청소해야 해요.
  - → 내일 우리 집에 친구가 <u>와서</u> 오늘 청소해야 해요.
    Because my friend is coming to our house tomorrow, I have to clean today.

- 이번 주말에 유나 씨가 <u>바쁠 거예요</u>. <u>그래서</u> 아마 시간이 없을 거예요.
  - → 이번 주말에 유나 씨가 <u>바빠서</u> 아마 시간이 없을 거예요.
    Yuna will be busy this weekend, so she probably won't have any time.

Grammar in Action

1 When stating a cause or reason

A 왜 음식을 안 먹었어요?
Why didn't you eat the food?

B 너무 매워서 안 먹었어요.
Because it was too spicy, I didn't eat it.

The ending -아/어서 is commonly used to explain the cause or reason for a result, often in response to the question "왜 (why)". In casual conversations, it is common to mention only the preceding clause, which provides the cause or reason, and omit the following clause that states the result.

- A 왜 한국어를 배워요? Why are you learning Korean?

  B 한국 가수를 좋아해서 한국어를 배워요. Because I like Korean singers.

- A 왜 회사를 그만뒀어요? Why did you quit your job?

  B 사업을 하고 싶어서요. Because I wanted to start a business.

2 When making excuses

-아/어서 is also used to make excuses for undesirable outcomes. It is one of the most commonly used endings to explain the cause or reason for a result, whether the outcome is positive or negative.

- A 왜 늦게 일어났어요? Why did you wake up late?

  B 어젯밤에 늦게 자서 늦게 일어났어요. Because I went to bed late last night, I woke up late.

- A 어제 왜 전화 안 했어요? Why didn't you call yesterday?

  B 미안해요. 어제 너무 바빠서 전화 못 했어요. Sorry, I was too busy yesterday, I couldn't call you.

3 When used as an idiomatic expression

-아/어서 is also used idiomatically to express feelings of gratitude, pleasure, or apology, along with the reason. When used this way, it cannot be replaced by other Korean grammar structures that express reason, such as -(으)니까 or -기 때문에.

- 항상 도와주셔서 감사합니다. Thank you for always helping.

- 안녕하세요. 만나서 반가워요. Hello, nice to meet you.

- 늦어서 미안해요. 많이 기다렸어요? Sorry I'm late. Have you been waiting long?

Quiz 45

-(으)니까 ..., so

Kor. 46

위험하니까 조심하세요. Be careful, it's dangerous.

매우니까 먹지 마세요. It's very spicy, so don't eat it.

Grammar Essentials

1 -(으)니까

The ending -(으)니까 is a conjunctive ending that links a clause indicating a reason with a clause expressing a result. It is always attached to the reason clause and cannot follow the result clause.

비가 와요. 그러니까 우산을 가져가세요.

→ 비가 오니까 우산을 가져가세요. It's raining, so take an umbrella.

The ending -(으)니까 is combined with verbs and adjectives to indicate cause or reason. If the stem ends in a vowel, -니까 is used, while -으니까 is used if the stem ends in a consonant.

- 배고프니까 먼저 밥을 먹고 싶어요. I'm hungry, so I want to eat first.

- 학생들이 공부하고 있으니까 조용히 해 주세요. The students are studying, so please be quiet.

- 제가 음식을 만드니까 이따가 같이 먹어요! I am making food, so let's eat together later!

When combined with nouns, (이)니까 is used to indicate cause or reason. If the noun ends in a vowel, 니까 is used, and if it ends in a consonant, 이니까 is applied.

- 오래된 자동차니까 천천히 운전하세요. It's an old car, so drive slowly.

- 유나 씨가 한국 사람이니까 한자를 알아요. Yuna is Korean, so she knows Chinese characters.

2 Conjugation

-(으)니까					
보다	보니까	다르다	다르니까	돕다	*도우니까
읽다	읽으니까	듣다	*들으니까	붓다	*부으니까
바쁘다	바쁘니까	멀다	*머니까	그렇다	*그러니까

3 Negation

To express negation for verbs and adjectives, place 안 or -지 않다 before -(으)니까.

- 사람들이 책을 읽지 않으니까 책 읽기 캠페인을 하면 어때요?
  Since people are not reading books, how about we run a reading campaign?

- 이번 주는 바쁘지 않으니까 아무 때나 연락하세요.
  I am not busy this week, so feel free to contact me anytime.

For nouns, 아니다 is combined with -(으)니까 to form 아니니까.

- 이제 학생이 아니니까 자기가 스스로 해야 해요.
  Now that you are no longer a student, you have to do things yourself.

4 Tenses

To express reasons for past actions or states, -았/었으니까 is used. This contrasts with -아/어서, which cannot combine with past tense markers.

- 어제 운동을 많이 했으니까 오늘은 쉬고 싶어요. Since I exercised a lot yesterday, I want to rest today.

- 지난주에 비가 왔으니까 축구 경기가 취소됐어요. Since it rained last week, the soccer game was canceled.

For nouns, if the noun ends in a vowel, use -였으니까; if it ends in a consonant, use -이었으니까.

- 10년 전 자동차가 빨간색이었으니까 이번에는 흰색 자동차를 샀어요.
  Since the car (I bought) ten years ago was red, I bought a white car this time.

To express reasons for scheduled future events or past actions and states, -(으)ㄹ 거니까 or -(으)ㄹ 테니까 can be used. -(으)ㄹ 거니까 is used for scheduled future events, while -(으)ㄹ 테니까 is used to express the speaker's intention or speculation about future events or conditions. It is important to note that for speculation, only -(으)ㄹ 테니까 is appropriate; -(으)ㄹ 거니까 is not used in this context.

- 비행기가 내일 9시에 출발할 거니까 8시까지 공항에 오세요.　Scheduled event
  = 출발할 테니까 (O)
  The plane is scheduled to depart at 9 AM tomorrow, so please arrive at the airport by 8 AM.

- 내가 다 준비할 테니까 너는 준비하지 말고 그냥 와.　Intention
  I will prepare everything, so just come without preparing anything.

- 소금을 많이 넣으면 짤 테니까 소금은 더 넣지 마세요.　Speculation
  ≠ 짤 거니까 (✕)
  If you add too much salt, it will be too salty, so don't add more salt.

The difference between -아/어서 and -(으)니까

Both -아/어서 and -(으)니까 express reasons or causes, but they differ in their usage:

▶ **Causality (Cause & Effect):**
-아/어서 is used when the preceding clause directly causes the following clause and cannot be used with past tense -았/었-. In contrast, -(으)니까 provides a reason and can be used with past tense -았/었-.

- 여행을 갔다 와서 돈이 없어요.　Cause of being out of money
  Because went on a trip, now I'm out of money.

- 지난번에 제주도에 갔다 왔으니까 이번에는 부산에 가요!　Reason for suggesting Busan
  I went to Jeju last time, so this time let's go to Busan!

▶ **Sentence Types:**
-아/어서 can be used when the following clause is a statement (declarative) or a question (interrogative). On the other hand, -(으)니까 can be used in any type of sentence, including commands and suggestions

- 건강에 좋아서 운동을 시작하세요. (✕)
  → 건강에 좋으니까 운동을 시작하세요. (O) Start exercising because it's good for your health.

- 오늘은 바빠서 내일 만나요! (✕)
  → 오늘은 바쁘니까 내일 만나요! (O) I'm busy today, so let's meet tomorrow.

Grammar in Action

1 When expressing personal reasons

-(으)니까 is used to express reasons based on personal judgment or decision-making. In this case, -(으)니까 can often be replaced with -아/어서, but there is a slight difference in nuance.

Unlike -아/어서, which focuses on the reason itself, -(으)니까 highlights the decision or judgment in the following clause.

- 저는 커피를 마시지 않으니까 차를 주문할게요. Since I don't drink coffee, I'll order tea.

- 제 친구는 알레르기가 있으니까 이 음식을 조심하는 게 좋겠어요.
  Since my friend has allergies, it would be wise to be cautious with this food.

- 시험이 내일이니까 오늘 더 공부해야 해요. Since the exam is tomorrow, I need to study more today.

2 When providing reasons for advice, requests, or suggestions

A 소리가 너무 크니까 소리를 줄여 주세요.
The sound is too loud, please turn it down.

B 죄송합니다. I'm sorry.

-(으)니까 is used when giving advice, making requests, giving warnings, or making suggestions to explain the reason for these actions.

For commands or suggestions, -(으)니까 is generally used instead of -아/어서. In written language, -(으)니까 can sometimes be shortened to -(으)니.

- A 건강이 안 좋아졌어요. 어떻게 해야 해요? My health has deteriorated. What should I do?

  B 가벼운 운동이 건강에 좋으니까 하루에 30분 걸으세요.
  Light exercise is good for your health, so try walking for 30 minutes a day.

- A 이번에 부산에 같이 여행 가요! Let's go on a trip to Busan together!

  B 지난번에 부산에 갔으니까 이번에는 제주도에 가는 게 어때요?
  Since we went to Busan last time, how about going to Jeju Island this time?

> **Note**
>
> In Korean, repeating reasoning expressions is generally avoided. Therefore, when expressing multiple reasons in one sentence, only one of these forms (-아/어서 or -(으)니까) should be used, not both.
>
> - 비가 오니까 운동할 수 없어서 일찍 집에 갔어요.
>   Since it's raining, I couldn't exercise and went home early.
>
> - 길이 미끄러워서 위험하니까 밖에 나가지 마세요.
>   Don't go outside because the road is slippery and dangerous.

Quiz 46

-기 때문에 becuase ...

Kor. 47

비가 많이 오고 있기 때문에 야구 경기가 취소되었습니다.

The baseball game was canceled because it is raining too much.

1 -기 때문에

-기 때문에 is used to connect a clause that provides a reason with a clause that presents a result. It attaches to the preceding clause to indicate the reason, followed by a subsequent clause that expresses the outcome. -기 때문에 has a meaning similar to -아/어서, which also indicates a reason, but -기 때문에 is more commonly used in formal situations or written Korean.

한국 친구가 있습니다. 그렇기 때문에 한국 생활에 쉽게 익숙해졌습니다.

→ 한국 친구가 있기 때문에 한국 생활에 쉽게 익숙해졌습니다.
    I easily got accustomed to life in Korea because I have a Korean friend.

-기 때문에 can be used with verbs, adjectives, and "noun + 이다". For verbs and adjectives, -기 때문에 is applied regardless of whether the stem ends in a vowel or consonant. When combined with "noun + 이다", it forms 이기 때문에. However, in spoken language, when the noun ends in a vowel, 이 is often omitted, resulting in 기 때문에.

- 오늘 바쁘기 때문에 시간이 없어요. I don't have time because I am busy today.

- 이게 인기가 많은 운동화기 때문에 다 팔렸어요. These sneakers sold out because they are very popular.

- 오늘 일요일이기 때문에 아마 식당이 안 할 거예요. Restaurants might be closed today because it is Sunday.

 Be careful!

"Noun + 이기 때문에" is used when the state or characteristic of a noun indicates the reason for a result. In contrast, "noun + 때문에" is used when the noun itself directly causes the outcome, often with a negative connotation.

- 남동생이 고등학생이기 때문에 매일 학교에 가요.
  Because my younger brother is a high school student, he goes to school everyday.

- 저 고등학생 때문에 싸움이 시작됐어요.
  The fight started because of that high school student.

-기 때문에 can be used in declarative and interrogative sentences but cannot be used in imperative sentences (commands or instructions) or propositive sentences (suggestions or proposals). To express a reason in imperative or propositive sentences, (으)니까 should be used instead.

- 수업이 일찍 끝났기 때문에 집에 일찍 갔어요. (O)   Declarative
  I went home early because the class ended early.

- 운동하지 않았기 때문에 건강이 나빠졌어요? (O)   Interrogative
  Did your health get worse because you did not exercise?

- 날씨가 춥기 때문에 코트를 가져가세요. (✕)   Imperative

- 오늘 다른 약속이 있기 때문에 다음에 다시 만나요! (✕)   Propositive
  Let's meet next time because I have another appointment today!

2 Conjugation

-기 때문에					
보다	보기 때문에	다르다	다르기 때문에	어렵다	어렵기 때문에
읽다	읽기 때문에	걷다	걷기 때문에	붓다	붓기 때문에
아프다	아프기 때문에	알다	알기 때문에	그렇다	그렇기 때문에

3 Negation

To express negation, 안 or -지 않다 is used before -기 때문에. The negation of "noun + 이다" is expressed as 아니기 때문에.

- 날씨가 안 좋기 때문에 산책을 안 하기로 했어요.
  I decided not to go for a walk because the weather is not good.

- 요즘 편지를 거의 쓰지 않기 때문에 우표를 사지 않아요.
  I don't buy stamps because I hardly write letters these days.

- 제가 학생이 아니기 때문에 학생 할인을 받을 수 없었습니다.
  I couldn't get a student discount because I am not a student.

4 Tense

To express a past event or state, the past tense marker -았/었- is added before -기 때문에, forming -았/었기 때문에. This contrasts with -아서/어서, which cannot be combined with -았/었-.

- 조금 전에 밥을 먹었기 때문에 지금 배 안 고파요.
  I am not hungry now because I ate a little while ago.

- 어제 날씨가 춥지 않았기 때문에 우리는 공원에서 산책했어요.
  We took a walk in the park yesterday because it was not cold.

When expressing the reason for a past event or state with a noun, use 였기 때문에 if the noun ends in a vowel, and 이었기 때문에 if it ends in a consonant.

- 이 노래는 엄마가 자주 불렀던 노래였기 때문에 어렸을 때부터 제가 많이 불렀어요.
  I have sung this song a lot since I was a child because my mother used to sing it often.

Tip

The difference between -기 때문에 and -(으)니까

Both -기 때문에 and -(으)니까 are used to express reasons, but they differ in sentence type usage. -기 때문에 can be used in declarative and interrogative sentences but cannot be used in imperative or propositive sentences. In contrast, -(으)니까 can be used in any sentence type, including imperative and propositive sentences.

- 이 책이 재미있기 때문에 한번 읽어 보세요. (×)
  → 이 책이 재미있으니까 한번 읽어 보세요. (○) This book is fun, so read it.
- 전에 이 영화를 봤기 때문에 다른 영화를 볼까요? (×)
  → 전에 이 영화를 봤으니까 다른 영화를 볼까요? (○)
    Shall we watch a different movie since I've seen this one before?

Grammar in Action

1 When giving reasons in formal situations

교통사고가 났기 때문에 길이 많이 막힙니다.

There is heavy traffic because there was a traffic accident.

-기 때문에 is often used to express reasons in formal situations, such as public presentations, lectures, news reports, and business contexts. It can also be used with 왜냐하면 to emphasize the reason.

- A 왜 회의가 취소되었습니까? Why was the meeting canceled?

  B 왜냐하면 갑자기 일이 생겼기 때문에 회의가 취소되었습니다.
  The meeting was canceled because something suddenly came up.

- A 왜 오늘 도서관이 문을 안 열었습니까? Why isn't the library open today?

  B 왜냐하면 오늘은 한국의 공휴일이기 때문입니다. It's because today is a Korean public holiday.

2 When giving reasons in written context

-기 때문에 is commonly used in formal written Korean, such as in news articles or books, where the -ㄴ/는다 style is often used.

- 한국 노래가 외국인에게 인기가 많기 때문에 한국 가수의 인기도 많아졌다.
  The popularity of Korean singers has increased because Korean songs are popular among foreigners.

- 사람들이 밤에 한강에 자주 간다. 왜냐하면 한강 야경이 예쁘기 때문이다.
  People often visit the Hangang River at night because the night view of the Hangang River is beautiful.

> **Tip**
>
> **The Difference Between -기 때문에 and -아/어서**
>
> Both -기 때문에 and -아서/어서 express reasons but differ in context and usage rules.
>
> -아서/어서 is used in both formal and informal situations, while -기 때문에 is mainly used in formal writing or structured language.
>
> - 날씨가 안 좋아서 비행기가 출발할 수 없어요.   Informal
> - 날씨가 안 좋기 때문에 비행기가 출발할 수 없습니다.   Formal
>   The plane can't take off because the weather is bad.
>
> -아서/어서 cannot be combined with -았/었-, while -기 때문에 can, forming -았/었기 때문에.
>
> - 핸드폰을 잃어버려서 전화할 수 없었어요.   Informal
> - 핸드폰을 잃어버렸기 때문에 전화할 수 없었습니다.   Formal
>   I couldn't call because I lost my cellphone.

Quiz 47

Lesson 47

-기 때문에

TOPIK I | SCK 2

-(으)ㄴ 후에 after

Kor. 48

제이크 씨가 운동한 후에 샤워해요. Jake takes a shower after exercising.

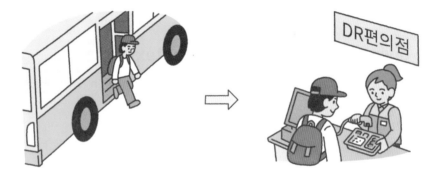

진수 씨가 버스에서 내린 후에 편의점에서 도시락을 사요.

Jinsu buys a lunch box at the convenience store after getting off the bus.

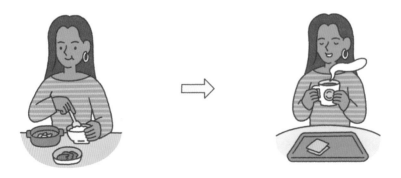

레이첼 씨가 점심을 먹은 후에 커피를 마셔요.

Rachel drinks coffee after eating lunch.

1 -(으)ㄴ 후에

-(으)ㄴ 후에 is used to indicate the temporal sequence of two events or actions. The earlier event is described in the preceding clause, followed by the later event in the following clause.

<u>운동한 후에</u> <u>샤워해요</u>. After exercising, I take a shower.
Earlier event   Later event

-(으)ㄴ 후에 is used with verbs. If the verb stem ends in a vowel, use -ㄴ 후에, and if the verb stem ends in a consonant, use -은 후에.

- 저는 운동을 한 후에 물을 마셨어요. I drank water after exercising.

- 보통 아이가 아침을 먹은 후에 학교에 가요. Usually, the child goes to school after having breakfast.

The expressions -(으)ㄴ 후에, -(으)ㄴ 다음에, and -(으)ㄴ 뒤에 can be used interchangeably without any difference in meaning, as they all indicate that one action takes place after another. However, their usage differs depending on the context: -(으)ㄴ 후에 is more commonly used in formal writing, while -(으)ㄴ 다음에 and -(으)ㄴ 뒤에 are frequently used in spoken Korean.

-(으)ㄴ 후에 is used with verbs.

- 보통 학생들이 대학교를 졸업한 후에 취직합니다. Usually students get a job after graduating from university.

- 호텔을 찾은 다음에 방을 예약해요. I reserve a room after finding a hotel.

- 책을 다 읽은 뒤에 친구한테 빌려주세요. Lend the book to a friend after you have finished reading it.

The subjects of the preceding and following clauses in -(으)ㄴ 후에 can be the same or different.

- 수업이 끝난 후에 학생들이 집에 가요. The students go home after class ends.

- 비가 온 후에 날씨가 추워졌어요. The weather got cold after it rained.

While -(으)ㄴ 후에, -(으)ㄴ 다음에, and -(으)ㄴ 뒤에 are all used with verbs, only 후에 and 뒤에 can be used with nouns; 다음에 cannot be used in this case.

- 식사한 후에 커피를 마셔요. (O) I drink coffee after I have a meal.
  = 식사한 뒤에 커피를 마셔요. (O)
  = 식사한 다음에 커피를 마셔요. (O)

- 식사 후에 커피를 마셔요. (O) I drink coffee after a meal.
  = 식사 뒤에 커피를 마셔요. (O)
  ≠ 식사 다음에 커피를 마셔요. (✕)

2 Conjugation

-(으)ㄴ 후에			
오다	온 후에	놀다	*논 후에
먹다	먹은 후에	돕다	*도운 후에
쓰다	쓴 후에	낫다	*나은 후에
듣다	*들은 후에	그렇다	*그런 후에

3 Combination with action verbs

-(으)ㄴ 후에 is generally used with action verbs and cannot be used with adjectives or state verbs such as 있다 or 없다. However, it can be combined with verbs that indicate the completion of a state, such as 생기다 (to occur).

- 사람들은 항상 문제가 있은 후에 문제에 대해 생각해요. (✕)
  - → 사람들은 항상 문제가 생긴 후에 문제에 대해 생각해요. (O)
    People always think about problems after they occur.

- 제 친구는 남자 친구가 없은 다음에 시간이 생길 거예요. (✕)
  - → 제 친구는 남자 친구하고 헤어진 다음에 시간이 생길 거예요. (O)
    My friend will have time after she breaks up with her boyfriend.

4 Negation

To express negation before -(으)ㄴ 후에, you can use 안, -지 않다, 못, or -지 못하다. However, in most cases, it sounds more natural to use -지 않고 or -지 못하고, as these forms better indicate a sequential connection between actions.

- 문제가 생기면 아무것도 만지지 않은 다음에 저한테 연락하세요.
  $$= 만지지 않고$$
  If a problem arises, do not touch anything and contact me.

- 공항에 늦게 도착해서 비행기를 타지 못한 다음에 그다음 비행기를 예약했어요.
  $$= 타지 못하고$$
  I arrived late at the airport and missed the plane, so I booked the next flight.

5 Tenses

Since -(으)ㄴ in -(으)ㄴ 후에 implies completion, it cannot be combined with past tense markers like -았/었-. Regardless of the tense, it is always expressed as -(으)ㄴ 후에.

- 보통 일이 끝난 후에 동료하고 같이 밥을 먹어요.   Present
  I usually eat with my colleagues after work is finished.

- 지난주에 일이 끝난 후에 동료하고 같이 밥을 먹었어요.   Past
  Last week, I ate with my colleagues after work was finished.

- 이따가 일이 끝난 후에 동료하고 같이 밥을 먹을 거예요.   Future
  Later, I will eat with my colleagues after work is finished.

Grammar in Action

1 When expressing the temporal order of events or actions

-(으)ㄴ 후에 is used to indicate the temporal sequence of events or actions. It is typically used in formal situations, whereas -(으)ㄴ 다음에 or -(으)ㄴ 뒤에 is used in informal contexts.

- A 언제 전화할 수 있습니까? When can you call?

  B 회의가 끝난 후에 전화하겠습니다. I'll call after the meeting ends.

- A 채소를 씻은 다음에 어떻게 해요? What do you do after washing the vegetables?

  B 여기에 넣으세요. Put them here.

2 When the following clause is omitted

In spoken language, when both speakers know the context, the following clause of -(으)ㄴ 다음에 is often omitted, especially when asking about a sequence of events after someone's explanation. In such cases, people say: "그다음에는? (And then?)". Although -(으)ㄴ 다음에, -(으)ㄴ 후에, and -(으)ㄴ 뒤에 are generally interchangeable when the following clause is included, only "그다음에는?" is used when it is omitted, not "그 후에는?" or "그 뒤에는?".

- A 언제 밥 먹으러 가요? When are we going to eat?

  B 회의 끝난 다음에요. After the meeting ends.

- A 보통 오후에 뭐 해요? What do you usually do in the afternoon?

  B 밥을 먹은 다음에 산책해요. I go for a walk after I eat.

  A 그다음에는요? (= 산책한 다음에는요?) And then?

  B 집에 가요. I go home.

3 When expressing time after an action

-(으)ㄴ 후에 can be used with a time noun to indicate how much time passes before the next action occurs. Since it requires a specific time reference, -(으)ㄴ 후에 cannot be used interchangeably with -(으)ㄴ 다음에.

- 물건을 주문한 5시간 후에 물건이 집에 도착했어요. The goods arrived at home 5 hours after I ordered them.

- 제 친구가 대학교를 졸업한 1년 후에 회사에 취직했어요.
  My friend got a job one year after graduating from university.

To indicate that the next action happens immediately after a previous one, you can use -(으)ㄴ 직후에. Adding 바로 (immediately) to the following clause further emphasizes this immediacy.

- 피곤해서 침대에 누운 직후에 바로 잠이 들었어요.
  I was so tired that I fell asleep immediately after lying down in bed.

Quiz 48

-기 전에 before

Kor. 49

음식을 먹기 전에 손을 씻어요. I wash my hands before eating food.

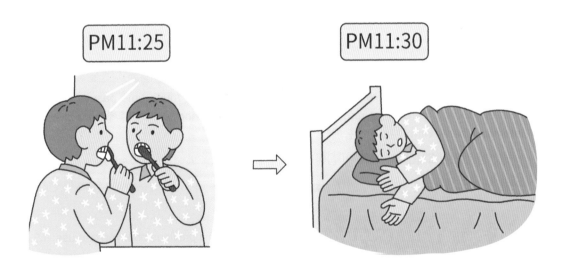

자기 전에 이를 닦아요. I brush my teeth before going to bed.

1   -기 전에

-기 전에 is used to express the temporal sequence of events, where the later event is mentioned first, and the earlier event follows. The clause before -기 전에 contains the later event, and the clause after -기 전에 contains the earlier event.

음식을 먹기 전에 손을 씻어요. Before eating, wash your hands.
Later event   Earlier event

-기 전에 is combined with verbs, regardless of whether the verb stem ends in either a vowel or a consonant.

- 저는 영화를 보기 전에 팝콘을 사요. I buy popcorn before watching a movie.

- 제 친구는 물건을 사기 전에 인터넷에서 정보를 찾아요.
  My friend looks for information online before buying a product.

- 옷을 입기 전에 사이즈를 확인해야 해요. You need to check the size before trying on clothes.

The subjects of the clauses before and after -기 전에 can be the same or different.

- 저는 회의를 시작하기 전에 회의 자료를 준비해요. I prepare meeting materials before starting the meeting.

- 비가 오기 전에 버스를 타세요. Catch the bus before it rains.

When combined with a verb, -기 전에 is used. However, when combined with a noun, 전에 is used after a noun.

- 식사하기 전에 손을 씻어요. Wash your hands before eating.

- 식사 전에 손을 씻어요. Wash your hands before the meal.

2   Conjugation

-기 전에			
보다	보기 전에	걷다	듣기 전에
읽다	읽기 전에	살다	살기 전에
쓰다	쓰기 전에	돕다	돕기 전에
누르다	누르기 전에	붓다	붓기 전에

3 Combination with action verbs

-기 전에 is typically combined with verbs and cannot be combined with adjectives. To use adjectives with -기 전에, they must first be converted into verbs.

- 날씨가 <u>춥기 전에</u> 겨울 옷을 준비해요. (✕)

  → 날씨가 추워지기 전에 겨울 옷을 준비해요. (O) I prepare winter clothes before it becomes cold.

- <u>모임이 있기 전에</u> 사람들한테 연락해야 해요. (✕)

  → 모임을 하기 전에 사람들한테 연락해야 해요. (O) You need to contact people before holding a meeting.

- <u>기회가 없기 전에</u> 빨리 신청하세요. (✕)

  → 기회를 놓치기 전에 빨리 신청하세요. (O) Apply quickly before missing the opportunity.

4 Tenses

Past tense markers like -았/었- cannot precede -기 전에 when expressing the temporal sequence of past events. -기 전에 remains the same regardless of tense, with the verb tense being determined by the following clause.

- 보통 이메일을 <u>보내기 전에</u> 확인해요.   Present

  (= 보내요. 그전에)

  I usually check emails before sending them.

- 지난주에 여행을 <u>떠나기 전에</u> 호텔을 예약했어요.   Past

  (= 떠났어요. 그전에)

  Last week, I booked a hotel before departing for the trip.

- 나중에 <u>후회하기 전에</u> 새로운 일에 도전할 거예요.   Future

  (= 후회할 거예요. 그전에)

  I will try something new before I regret it later.

1 When emphasizing the sequence of an action or situation

-기 전에 is used to emphasize that one action or situation occurs before another. You can further emphasize this sequence by using the adverb 바로 (just) before -기 전에.

- 비자를 신청하기 전에 신분증과 서류를 준비해 주세요.
  Please prepare your ID and documents before applying for a visa.

- 해가 지기 전에 산에서 내려오세요. Come down from the mountain before the sun sets.

- 집을 계약하기 전에 여러 집을 봐야 해요. You need to see several houses before signing a contract.

- 집에서 나오기 바로 전에 모든 불을 껐어요. I turned off all the lights just before leaving the house.

2 When expressing time before an action

In -기 전에, you can specify the amount of time before an action occurs by placing a time-related noun between -기 and 전에. You can also add the adverb 바로 ("right" or "just") before 전에 to emphasize that the action happens immediately beforehand. -기 바로 전에 and -기 직 전에 can be used interchangeably.

- 수업이 끝나기 10분 전에 한 학생이 교실에 들어왔어요.
  A student entered the classroom 10 minutes before class ended.

- 여행을 떠나기 일주일 전에 호텔을 예약해야 해요.
  You have to reserve a hotel a week before you go on a trip.

- 잠이 들기 바로 전에 전화가 왔어요. I received a phone call just before I fell asleep.
  = 잠이 들기 직전에 전화가 왔어요.

3 When emphasizing identity over role

-기 전에 is typically used with verbs to indicate the sequence of actions. However, it can also be used with "noun + 이다" to emphasize a person's identity or role before another situation.

- 저분은 회사의 사장이기 전에 한 아이의 엄마예요.
  Before being the company's president, she is a mother.

- 저 사람은 적군이기 전에 누군가의 가족이에요. That person is someone's family before he is an enemy.

Quiz 49

-(으)ㄹ 때 when

사진을 찍을 때 저는 웃었어요. 그런데 친구는 눈을 감았어요.

I smiled when the photo was taken, but my friend's eyes were closed.

1 -(으)ㄹ 때

-(으)ㄹ 때 is used to indicate a specific moment or duration of an action or state. In Korean, this form is always used in the preceding clause.

사진을 찍어요. 그때 친구가 웃어요.

= 사진을 찍을 때 친구가 웃어요. When I take photos, my friend smiles.
  Specific moment

-(으)ㄹ 때 combines with verbs, adjectives, and "noun + 이다".

For verbs and adjectives, use -ㄴ 때 if the stem ends in a vowel and -을 때 if it ends in a consonant.

- 저는 보통 아플 때 집에서 쉬어요. I usually rest at home when I'm sick.
- 친구를 만날 때 식당에서 밥 먹어요. When I meet friends, we eat at a restaurant.
- 스트레스가 많을 때 요가를 해 보세요. Try yoga when you are very stressed.
- 친구가 찾을 때 이 앱을 사용해요. My friend uses this app when looking for good restaurants.

For "noun + 이다", regardless of whether the noun ends in a vowel or consonant, 일 때 is always used. This structure is used when the preceding clause describes the state or identity of the subject.

- 제가 아이일 때 장난을 많이 쳤어요. When I was a young child, I played a lot of pranks.
- 제 친구가 대학생일 때 사업을 시작했어요. My friend started a business when he was a college student.

For specific times, like 휴가 (vacation), 크리스마스 (Christmas), 추석 (Chuseok), both 때 and the particle 에 can be used.

- 휴가 때 뭐 할 거예요? What are you going to do during the vacation?
  (= 휴가에 뭐 할 거예요?)

- 추석 때 고향에 갔다 왔어요. I went back to my hometown during Chuseok.
  (= 추석에 고향에 갔다 왔어요.)

- 크리스마스 때 가족을 만날 거예요. I'm going to see my family on Christmas.
  (= 크리스마스에 가족을 만날 거예요.)

However, for general times like 아침 (morning), 오후 (afternoon), 밤 (night), you must use the particle 에, not 때.

- 보통 아침 때 운동해요. (✗)
  → 보통 아침에 운동해요. (O) Usually, I exercise in the morning.

- 밤 때 집에서 크게 음악을 틀면 안 돼요. (✗)
  → 밤에 집에서 크게 음악을 틀면 안 돼요. (O) You shouldn't play loud music at home at night.

2 Conjugation

-(으)ㄹ 때					
싸다	쌀 때	다르다	다를 때	쉽다	*쉬울 때
먹다	먹을 때	듣다	*들을 때	낫다	*나을 때
바쁘다	바쁠 때	살다	*살 때	그렇다	*그럴 때

3 Using the subject particle

When the subjects of both the preceding and following clauses are the same, the subject in the preceding clause can take the particle 은/는. However, if the subjects are different, the subject in the preceding clause should take the particle 이/가.

- 친구는 피곤할 때 자요. My friend sleeps when tired.

  = 친구가 피곤할 때 자요.

- 친구는 저한테 연락할 때 저는 일하고 있어요. (✕)

  → 친구가 저한테 연락할 때 저는 일하고 있어요. (O) I'm working when my friend contacts me.

4 Negations

When -(으)ㄹ 때 combines with verbs or adjectives, negations like 안, -지 않다, 못, or -지 못하다 can be placed before -(으)ㄹ 때.

- 안 바쁠 때 제가 연락할게요. I will contact you when I'm not busy.

  = 바쁘지 않을 때 제가 연락할게요.

- 한국 사람의 말을 이해 못 할 때 저한테 물어보세요.
  Ask me when you don't understand what a Korean person says.

  = 한국 사람의 말을 이해하지 못할 때 저한테 물어보세요.

For nouns combined with "noun + 이다", the negation 아니다 becomes 아닐 때 when combined with -(으)ㄹ 때.

- 휴일이 아닐 때 저는 아침 일찍 일어나요. I wake up early when it's not a holiday.

5 Tenses

The tense in -(으)ㄹ 때 aligns with the tense of the following clause.

- 책을 읽을 때 안경을 써요.   `Present`   I wear glasses when I read a book.

- 어제 집에 있을 때 청소했어요.   `Past`   I cleaned when I was at home yesterday.

- 여행할 때 이 옷을 입을 거예요.   `Future`   I will wear these clothes when I travel.

To express that the action or state in the preceding clause was already completed and no longer ongoing, you can use -았/었을 때 to indicate past completion. If the following clause is also in the past, using -(으)ㄹ 때 in the preceding clause maintains the same tense as the following clause. However, -았/었을 때 emphasizes that the action or state in the preceding clause had already been completed beforehand.

- 전에 일할 때 매일 정장을 입었어요. I used to wear a suit every day when I worked before.

  = 전에 일했을 때 매일 정장을 입었어요.

- 지난주에 친구를 만날 때 재미있게 놀았어요. I had fun when I met my friend last week.

  = 지난주에 친구를 만났을 때 재미있게 놀았어요.

- 제 친구는 대학교에 다닐 때 아르바이트를 많이 했어요.
  My friend worked a lot of part-time jobs when she was in college.

  = 제 친구는 대학교에 다녔을 때 아르바이트를 많이 했어요.

6 Combination with particles

After -(으)ㄹ 때, particles such as 도, 만, 부터, 까지, or 마다 can be added.

- 다음에 여행 갈 때도 이 호텔을 예약하면 좋겠어요.
  I would also like to book this hotel next time I go on a trip.

- 저 사람은 식사할 때만 방에서 나와요. That person only comes out of the room when eating.

- 이 회사에서 일할 때부터 폴 씨하고 친하게 지냈어요.
  I have been close with Mr. Paul since I started working at this company.

- 친구가 집에 돌아올 때까지 파티 준비를 끝내야 해요.
  We have to finish preparing for the party by the time my friends get home.

- 친구들하고 만날 때마다 노래방에 가요. Whenever I meet with friends, we go to a noraebang.

Grammar in Action

1 When expressing the duration of an action or state

-(으)ㄹ 때 is used to express the duration for which an action or state continues.

- 제 친구는 스트레스를 받을 때 여행을 떠나요. My friend travels when she is stressed.
- 저는 운동할 때 음악을 듣는 것을 좋아해요. I like listening to music when I exercise.

When asking about the duration of an action or state, 언제 (when) is used for unspecified times.

- A 언제 행복해요? When are you happy?
  B 가족이 제 옆에 있을 때 행복해요. I'm happy when my family is with me.
  C 제가 하고 싶은 일을 할 때 행복해요. I'm happy when I'm doing what I like.

When asking what one does during an unspecified time, "뭐 해요? (What do you do?)" is used.

However, when inquiring about specific actions taken to solve a problem at a particular time, "어떻게 해요? (How do you handle it?)" is used.

- A 시간이 있을 때 보통 뭐 해요? What do you usually do when you have time?
  B 시간이 있을 때 핸드폰을 봐요. I look at my phone when I have time.
- A 에어컨이 고장 났을 때 어떻게 했어요? What did you do when the air conditioner broke down?
  B 에어컨이 고장 났을 때 서비스 센터에 연락했어요.
    I contacted the service center when the air conditioner broke down.

2 When expressing the moment when a specific action occurs

-(으)ㄹ 때 is used to express the moment a specific action occurs.

- 사진을 찍을 때 제가 눈을 감았어요. I closed my eyes when taking the picture.
- 제가 비를 맞을 때 친구가 우산을 줬어요. My friend gave me an umbrella when I was caught in the rain.
- 쓰레기를 버릴 때 분리 수거를 해야 해요. You should sort the trash when throwing it away.

Verbs that represent a brief moment are always written in a completed form, so -(으)ㄹ 때 cannot be used to express past events or incidents. Instead, -았/었을 때 must be used.

- 교통사고가 났을 때 많이 다쳤어요. I was badly injured when the traffic accident happened.
  ≠ 날 때 (✕)
- 그 여자를 처음 만났을 때 사랑에 빠졌어요. I fell in love when I first met her.
  ≠ 만날 때 (✕)
- 제 동생이 길을 잃어버렸을 때 걱정 많이 했어요. I was very worried when my brother got lost.
  ≠ 잃어버릴 때 (✕)

3 When indicating motion progress and motion completion

For motion verbs like 가다 (go), 오다 (come), the meanings of -(으)ㄹ 때 and -았/었을 때 differ.

- -(으)ㄹ 때 expresses the time during the motion.
- -았/었을 때 expresses the time when the motion was completed.

여행 갈 때 비행기를 탔어요.

I took a plane when I was going on a trip.

여행 갔을 때 우연히 친구를 만났어요.

I met a friend by chance when I traveled.

4 When expressing a certain period of life idiomatically

When expressing a specific period of life in an idiomatic way, -(으)ㄹ 때 is used as follows:

- 저는 어렸을 때 말이 별로 없었어요. When I was young, I didn't talk much.

- 제 동생이 고등학생 때 공부를 열심히 했어요. My younger brother studied hard in high school.
  (= 고등학생이었을 때 When my younger brother was a high school student)

- 대학생 때 미술에 관심이 있었어요. (When I was a college student,) I was interested in art at colleage.
  (= 대학생이었을 때)

Quiz 50

251

-(으)ㄴ 지 since

한국어 공부를 시작한 지 1년 됐어요.

It has been a year since I started studying Korean.

1 -(으)ㄴ 지

-(으)ㄴ 지 is used to indicate the duration of time an action or state has continued.

The preceding clause describes the ongoing event or state, and the following clause specifies the duration.

> 한국어 공부를 시작한 지 1년 됐어요. It has been a year since I started studying Korean.
>
> <u>Ongoing action or state</u>   <u>Duration</u>

-(으)ㄴ 지 is attached to a verb to indicate how long an action or state has continued. If the verb stem ends in a vowel, use -ㄴ 지, and if it ends in a consonant, use -은 지.

- 제 친구가 한국에 온 지 1년 됐어요. It has been a year since my friend came to Korea.

- 제가 이 책을 읽은 지 일주일 됐어요. It has been a week since I read this book.

To express the duration in the following clause, a time expression is typically used along with the verb 되다 (to become). Instead of 되다, you can also use verbs like 지나다 (to pass), 넘다 (to exceed), or 흐르다 (to flow) to describe the passage of time.

- 아침을 먹은 지 1시간 지났어요. It has been an hour since I had breakfast.

- 이 집에서 산 지 6개월 넘었어요. It has been over six months since I moved into this house.

- 고향을 떠난 지 10년이 흘렀어요. It's been ten years since I left my hometown.

To express an approximate duration, you can use 쯤 (about) after the time in informal speech and 정도 (approximately) in formal speech.

- 이 회사에서 일한 지 한 달쯤 됐어요. I've been working at this company for about a month.

- 그 친구를 알게 된 지 10년 정도 지났어요. It's been about 10 years since I got to know that friend.

> **✻ Be careful!**
>
> Sentences using -(으)ㄴ 지 can be rephrased using 동안 (for the duration).
> However, -(으)ㄴ 지 and 동안 cannot be used together.
> - 회사에 다닌 지 10년 동안 됐어요. (✗)
>   → 회사에 다닌 지 10년 됐어요. (O) I have worked at the company for 10 years.
>   = 회사에 10년 동안 다녔어요. (O)

2 Conjugation

	-(으)ㄴ 지		
보다	준 지	듣다	*들은 지
읽다	먹은 지	살다	*산 지
쓰다	쓴 지	돕다	*도운 지
부르다	부른 지	붓다	*부은 지

3 Negation

-(으)ㄴ 지 can be combined with negation markers such as 안, -지 않다, 못, or -지 못하다 to express the duration of a negative state.

- 밥을 안 먹은 지 하루 지났어요. It has been a day since I have not eaten.
  = 밥을 먹지 않은 지 하루 지났어요.

- 학교 친구를 못 만난 지 한참 됐어요. It has been quite a while since I have not met a school friend.
  = 학교 친구를 만나지 못한 지 한참 됐어요.

- 잠을 못 잔 지 꽤 됐어요. It's been a while since I couldn't sleep.
  = 잠을 자지 못한 지 꽤 됐어요.

4 Tense

Since -(으)ㄴ 지 already implies that the action was completed in the past, -았/었- should not be redundantly combined with it.

- 아침에 일어났는지 30분 됐어요. (✗)
  → 아침에 일어난 지 30분 됐어요. (O) It has been 30 minutes since I woke up this morning.

- 그 사람이 집에 갔는지 한참 지났어요. (✗)
  → 그 사람이 집에 간 지 한참 지났어요. (O) It's been a while since that person went home.

Moreover, -(으)ㄴ 지 expresses that something has continued up to the speaking moment, so 되다 is always expressed in the past tense.

- 민수 씨를 안 지 3년쯤 돼요. (✗)
  → 민수 씨를 안 지 3년쯤 됐어요. (O) It has been about three years since I have seen Minsu.

- 대학교를 졸업한 지 10년 넘어요. (✗)
  → 대학교를 졸업한 지 10년 넘었어요. (O) It's been over 10 years since I graduated from university.

Grammar in Action

1   When expressing the passage of time with -(으)ㄴ 지

-(으)ㄴ 지 is used to express how much time has passed since an action occurred or a state has persisted. A time expression is placed after -(으)ㄴ 지 to indicate the duration.

When asking about the duration, 얼마나 (how long) is used. In spoken language, the repetitive -(으)ㄴ 지 can be omitted in responses, leaving only the duration stated.

- A 헬스장에 다닌 지 얼마나 됐어요? How long have you been going to the gym?

  B <u>6개월</u> 됐어요. It's been six months.

- A 이 핸드폰을 산 지 얼마나 됐어요? How long have you had this cellphone?

  B <u>일주일</u> 됐어요. It's been a week.

2   When expressing psychological time

When no specific time durations are used in the following clause of -(으)ㄴ 지, psychological time can be expressed as follows:

▶ **Expressing a long time**

- 마크 씨가 한국에서 산 지 오래 됐어요. Mark has been living in Korea for a long time.

- 이 가수를 좋아한 지 한참 됐어요. I have liked this singer for quite some time.

- 운동을 시작한 지 꽤 됐어요. It's been quite a while since I started exercising.

▶ **Expressing a short time**

- 밥 먹은 지 얼마 안 됐어요. It hasn't been long since I ate.

- 집에 온 지 1시간도 안 됐어요. It's been less than an hour since I came home.

- 전화 받은 지 30분밖에 안 됐어요. It's only been 30 minutes since I answered the phone.

Quiz 51

TOPIK I | SCK 2

-(으)러 in order to

Kor. 52

진수가 배고파요.

Jinsu is hungry.

진수가 식당에 가요.

Jinsu is going to the restaurant.

진수가 배고파서 식당에 가요.

Jinsu is going to the restaurant because he is hungry.

진수가 식당에 가요.

Jinsu is going to the restaurant.

진수가 밥을 먹어요.

Jinsu is going to eat.

진수가 밥을 먹으러 식당에 가요.

Jinsu is going to the restaurant to eat.

1 -(으)러

The ending -(으)러 is a conjunctive ending that indicates the purpose of movement toward a destination. The purpose of movement is expressed in the preceding clause before -(으)러, and a motion verb such as 가다 (to go), 오다 (to come), or 다니다 (to attend) is used in the following clause.

저는 친구를 만나러 밖에 나가요. I go outside to meet a friend.
Purpose of movement   Action of movement

-(으)러 is used only with verbs indicating the purpose of an action. If the verb stem ends in a vowel, -러 is used, and if it ends in a consonant, -으러 is used.

- 마이클 씨가 한국어를 배우러 한국에 왔어요. Michael came to Korea to learn Korean.

- 뭐 하러 주민 센터에 가요? What for are you going to the community center?

- 밥을 먹으러 식당에 갑시다. Let's go to the restaurant to eat.

- 음악을 들으러 우리 집에 오세요. Come to our house to listen to music.

2 Conjugation

-(으)러			
보다	보러	듣다	*들으러
읽다	읽으러	살다	*살러
쓰다	쓰러	돕다	*도우러
부르다	부르러	낫다	*나으러

3 The subject of a sentence

-(으)러 requires that the subject of the preceding clause, which expresses the purpose of the action, and the subject of the following clause, which performs the action, be the same.

- 로지가 한국어를 배우러 마이클 씨가 학교에 가요. (✕)

  → 로지하고 마이클이 한국어를 배우러 학교에 가요. (O) Rosie and Michael go to school to learn Korean.

- 어제 가방을 잃어버렸어요. 그래서 친구들이 가방을 찾으러 제가 지하철역에 갔어요. (✕)

  → 제가 가방을 찾으러 친구들하고 지하철역에 갔어요. (O)

  I went to the subway station with my friends to look for my bag.

Lesson 52

-(으)러

4 Combination with verbs

The verbs that follow -(으)러 must be motion verbs such as 가다 (to go), 오다 (to come), and 다니다 (to attend). This also includes compound verbs like 나가다 (to go out), 나오다 (to come out), 들어가다 (to enter), and 들어오다 (to come in). Other action verbs that do not indicate movement cannot be used with -(으)러.

- 마이클 씨가 한국어를 배우러 학교에 가요. (O) Michael goes to school to learn Korean.

  마이클 씨가 한국 회사에서 일하러 <u>한국어를 배워요.</u> (✕)

- 저는 어제 친구를 만나러 밖에 나갔어요. (O) I went out yesterday to meet a friend.

  저는 어제 친구하고 얘기하러 <u>친구를 만났어요.</u> (✕)

Since -(으)러 expresses purpose related to action, only action verbs can be combined with it. State verbs or adjectives cannot be used before -(으)러.

- 예쁘러 미용실에 가요. (✕)

  → 예쁘게 머리를 자르러 미용실에 가요. (O) I go to the beauty salon to get a pretty haircut.

- 쉬고 <u>싶으러</u> 집에 갔어요. (✕)

  → 쉬러 집에 갔어요. (O) I went home to rest.

5 Negation

Since -(으)러 indicates the purpose of movement, it cannot be combined with negations like 안, -지 않다, 못, or -지 못하다.

- 저는 커피를 <u>안 마시러</u> 집에 가요. (✕)

  → 커피를 마시지 않고 밥을 먹으러 집에 가요. (O) I go home to eat without drinking coffee.

- 저는 고기를 <u>먹지 못하러</u> 다른 식당에 갔어요. (✕)

  → 고기를 먹지 못해서 채소를 먹으러 다른 식당에 갔어요. (O)
  I went to another restaurant to eat vegetables because I couldn't eat meat.

6 Tenses

The purpose expressed in the preceding clause of -(으)러 refers to an action that has not yet been realized, so past tense markers like -았/었- cannot be combined before -(으)러.

- 영화를 <u>봤으러</u> 영화관에 갔어요. (✕)

  → 영화를 보러 영화관에 갔어요. (O) I went to the cinema to watch a movie.

The tense is applied to the verb following -(으)러. The ending -(으)러 remains the same whether the sentence is in the past, present, or future.

- 보통 저녁마다 운동하러 공원에 <u>가요.</u> Present I usually go to the park to exercise.

- 지난주에 가방을 사러 공항 면세점에 <u>갔다 왔어요.</u> Past
  Last week, I went to the airport duty-free shop to buy a bag.

- 내일 저는 음식을 만들러 친구 집에 <u>갈 거예요.</u> Future Tomorrow, I will go to my friend's house to cook.

258

1 When expressing the purpose of movement

When inquiring about the purpose of movement, use 왜 (why) similarly to how you would ask about reasons or causes. To express purpose, answer with -(으)러, and to express causes or reasons, use -아/어서. If the question specifically targets the purpose, use 뭐 하러.

- A 왜 카페에 가요? Why are you going to the cafe?

  B 일하러 가요. I am going to work.

- A 뭐 하러 공원에 가요? What are you going to the park for?

  B 운동하러 가요. I am going to exercise.

 Be careful!

왜 can ask about both reasons and purposes.

- A 왜 한국에 왔어요?

  = 뭐 하러 한국에 왔어요? (O) Why did you come to Korea?

  B 한국어를 배우러 한국에 왔어요. I came to Korea to learn Korean.

뭐 하러 is used only for purposes.

- A 왜 한국에 왔어요? Why did you come to Korea?

  ≠ 뭐 하러 한국에 왔어요? (✕)

  B 한국 노래를 좋아해서 한국에 왔어요. I came to Korea because I like Korean music.

The sentence types that can use -(으)러 include not only declarative and interrogative sentences but also imperative and propositive sentences.

- 보통 운동하러 공원에 가요. Declarative I usually go to the park to exercise.

- 어제 친구를 만나러 어디에 갔어요? Interrogative Where did you go yesterday to meet your friend?

- 가족을 만나러 고향에 가 보세요. Imperative Go to your hometown to meet your family.

- 영화 보러 오랜만에 영화관에 갑시다! Propositive Let's go to the cinema to watch a movie after a long time!

 Note

Particle for destination in motion verbs with -(으)러

When using -(으)러 with motion verbs like 가다 (to go) or 오다 (to come), the destination is indicated by the particle 에. The placement of the destination and the particle 에 is flexible and can appear either before or after -(으)러 in the sentence.

- 친구를 만나러 한강 공원에 가요.

  = 한강 공원에 친구를 만나러 가요. I go to Hangang Park to meet a friend.

Quiz 52

Lesson 52 -(으)러

늘게 일어났어요.

I woke up late.

택시를 탔어요.

I took a taxi.

늘게 일어나서 택시를 탔어요.

I woke up late and took a taxi.

택시를 탔어요.

I took a taxi.

회사에 빨리 가요.

I'm going to work quickly.

회사에 빨리 가려고 택시를 타요.

I take a taxi to get to work quickly.

Grammar Essentials

1 -(으)려고

The ending -(으)려고 is a conjunctive ending that indicates the subject's intention to perform an action. The preceding clause expresses the intention, while the following clause describes the action taken to fulfill that intention.

저는 맛집을 찾으려고 검색해요. I am searching to find a good restaurant.

Purpose of the action   Action to achieve the purpose

Since the intention expressed by -(으)려고 is realized through an action, it only combines with verbs. If the verb stem ends in a vowel, -려고 is used, and if the verb stem ends in a consonant, -으려고 is used.

- 저는 한국 회사에서 일하려고 한국어를 배워요. I am learning Korean to work at a Korean company.

- 동생이 비빔밥을 만들려고 채소를 샀어요. My younger sibling bought vegetables to make bibimbap.

- 에이미 씨는 저녁을 먹으려고 친구를 만나요. Amy is meeting a friend to have dinner.

2 Conjugation

-(으)려고			
주다	주려고	듣다	*들으려고
읽다	읽으려고	살다	*살려고
쓰다	쓰려고	돕다	*도우려고
부르다	부르려고	붓다	*부으려고

3 Subjects of a sentence

The subjects of the preceding clause and the following clause of -(으)려고 are the same when they are animate, such as people or animals. However, if the subjects are inanimate, they can be either the same or different.

- 내일 아침에 진수는 일찍 일어나려고 (진수가) 알람 시계를 맞췄어요.   Animate subject
  To wake up early tomorrow morning, Jinsu set the alarm clock.

- 강아지는 나를 맞이하려고 (강아지가) 항상 문 앞에서 기다려요.   Animate subject
  The puppy always waits at the door to greet me.

- 배가 출발하려고 (배가) 기적 소리를 냈어요.   Inanimate subject
  The ship sounded its horn as it is about to depart.

- 비가 오려고 하늘에 구름이 꼈어요.   Inanimate subject
  Clouds gathered in the sky as it was about to rain.

4 Combination with verbs

Since -(으)려고 expresses intention, it only combines with verbs. Adjectives cannot be used with -(으)려고. However, unlike -(으)러, state verbs like 있다 can precede -(으)려고.

- 예쁘려고 화장했어요. (✗)

  예쁘게 보이려고 화장했어요. (O) I put on makeup to appear pretty.

- 편하려고 엘리베이터를 탔어요. (✗)

  → 편하게 가려고 엘리베이터를 탔어요. (O) I took the elevator to be comfortable.

- 주말에 집에만 있으려고 음식을 많이 샀어요. I bought a lot of food to stay home on the weekend.

- 예뻐지려고 화장품과 옷에 신경을 쓰고 있어요.
  I am paying attention to cosmetics and clothes to look pretty.

5 Negation

Since -(으)려고 expresses intention, it can combine with negations like 안 or -지 않다, but not with 못 or -지 못하다. However, these negations can be used after -(으)려고.

- 공부할 때 자지 않으려고 저는 커피를 마셔요. (O) I drink coffee to stay awake while studying.

- 피아노를 못 치려고 피아노 수업에 안 갔어요. (✗)

  → 피아노를 안 치려고 피아노 수업에 안 갔어요. (O) I didn't go to piano lessons so as not to play the piano.

- 폴 씨는 휴가 때 집에서 쉬려고 친구를 안 만나요. (O)
  Paul doesn't meet friends during vacation in order to rest at home.

- 회사에서 보고서를 끝내려고 모임에 못 갔어요. (O)
  I couldn't go to the gathering to finish the report at work.

6 Tenses

The intention expressed by -(으)려고 is yet to be realized, so past tense markers -았/었- cannot be used before -(으)려고.

- 보통 학생한테 줬으려고 책을 준비했어요. (✗)

  보통 학생한테 주려고 책을 준비했어요. (O) I prepared the book to give to the regular student.

The tense is applied to the verb following -(으)려고. The sentence can be in the present, past, or future tense, but -(으)려고 itself remains unchanged.

- 보통 한국어 듣기를 연습하려고 한국 드라마를 많이 봐요. `Present`
  I often watch Korean dramas to practice Korean listening.

- 학생한테 주려고 어제 책을 준비했어요. `Past`
  I prepared the book yesterday to give to the student.

- 이번 휴가 때 여행 가려고 내일 비행기 표를 살 거예요. `Future`
  I am going to buy a plane ticket tomorrow to go on vacation.

Grammar in Action

1 When indicating the intention of a specific action

The ending -(으)려고 is used to express the intention behind a specific action. It can be used in declarative and interrogative sentences, but not in imperative or propositive sentences.

- 보통 운동하려고 운동 기구를 샀어요. (O)　Declarative　I bought exercise equipment to exercise.

- 어제 음식을 만들려고 장을 봤어요? (O)　Interrogative　Did you go shopping to make food yesterday?

- 고향에 가려고 비행기표를 사세요. (✗)　Imperative　Buy a plane ticket to go home.

- 파티를 준비하려고 같이 쇼핑합시다! (✗)　Propositive　Let's shop together to prepare for the party!

When asking about the intention behind an action, 왜 (why) can be used. To specifically inquire about the purpose, 뭐 하려고 (what for) can be used.

- A 왜 아무 말도 안 해요? Why aren't you saying anything?

  B 친구 비밀을 지키려고 아무 말도 안 해요. I'm not saying anything to keep my friend's secret.

- A 뭐 하려고 아침 일찍 공원에 가요? What are you going to do so early in the park in the morning?

  B 운동하려고 아침 일찍 공원에 가요. I go to the park early in the morning to exercise.

2 When omitting the following clause of -(으)려고

When answering a question about intention, the following clause can be omitted if it is understood by the participants.

- A 왜 밖에 안 나가요? Why don't you go outside?

  B 청소 좀 하려고요. (밖에 안 나가요.) (I'm staying in) to do some cleaning.

- A 왜 일찍 일어났어? Why did you wake up early?

  B 배고파서 뭐 좀 먹으려고. (일찍 일어났어.)
  (I woke up early) because I was hungry and wanted to eat something.

Be careful!

In colloquial speech, -려고 is sometimes pronounced as [ㄹ려고].
However, in writing, it should always follow the standard orthography as -(으)려고.

- 머리가 아파서 병원에 가려고요. My head hurts, so I'm going to the hospital.
  [갈려고요]

The difference between -(으)려고 and -(으)러

▶ **Combination with verbs**

-(으)려고 and -(으)러 may seem similar in meaning, but they have different grammatical functions. -(으)려고 expresses the subject's intention to perform an action and can be used with any action verb, while -(으)러 indicates the purpose of movement toward a destination and is limited to motion verbs.

- 저는 나중에 가수가 되러 노래를 연습하고 있어요. (×)

  저는 나중에 가수가 되려고 노래를 연습하고 있어요. (O)
  I am practicing to sing to become a singer later.

Motion verbs can be used with -(으)려고, but using -(으)려고 emphasizes the intention of movement, while -(으)러 emphasizes the purpose

- 내일 친구하고 놀러 친구 집에 갈 거예요. (O)   Purpose
  I'm going to my friend's house tomorrow to hang out.

  내일 친구하고 놀려고 친구 집에 갈 거예요. (O)   Intention
  I'm going to my friend's house tomorrow to hang out.

▶ **Subject of the sentence**

-(으)러 indicates the purpose of movement, so the subjects of both clauses must be the same. In contrast, -(으)려고 expresses the subject's intention for a situation to occur, allowing the subjects of the two clauses to be either the same or different.

- 민수는 가족과 같이 시간을 보내러 (민수는) 일찍 집에 갔어요. (O)
  Minsu went home early to spend time with his family.

- 민수는 가족과 같이 시간을 보내려고 (민수는) 회의를 취소했어요. (O)
  Minsu canceled the meeting to spend time with his family.

- 콘서트가 시작되러 우리는 콘서트장에 갔어요. (×)
  We went to the concert hall as the concert was about to start.

- 콘서트가 시작되려고 조명이 꺼졌어요. (O)
  The lights went out as the concert was about to start.

▶ **Combination with negation**

-(으)려고 can be combined with negations such as 안 or -지 않다, allowing the expression of intentional avoidance of actions. On the other hand, -(으)러 cannot be combined with negation because it strictly indicates the purpose of movement, which cannot logically convey a negative intention in this structure.

- 진수는 실수하지 않으려고 문제를 다시 한번 확인했어요. (O)
  Jinsu checked the problem again not to make a mistake.

- 진수는 늦지 않으러 일찍 갔어요. (×)
  → 진수는 늦지 않으려고 일찍 갔어요. (O) Jinsu went early not to be late.

▶ **Type of sentences**

-(으)려고, which shows the subject's intention, is used only in statements and questions, and cannot be used in commands or suggestions. In contrast, -(으)러, indicating the purpose of movement, can be freely used in commands and suggestions to prompt or advise others.

- 책을 빌리려고 도서관에 가세요. (×)

  책을 빌리러 도서관에 가세요. (O) Go to the library to borrow a book.

- 친구 생일을 축하하려고 생일 파티에 갑시다. (×)

  친구 생일을 축하하러 생일 파티에 갑시다. (O)
  Let's go to the birthday party to celebrate our friend's birthday.

3 When trying to do something with intention

-(으)려고 is used with the verb 하다 in the following clause to indicate trying or planning to do something.

- 요즘 건강에 관심이 있어서 달리기 동호회에 가입하려고 해요.
  I'm interested in health these days, so I'm planning to join a running club.

- 전에는 모든 것을 완벽하게 하려고 했어요. I used to try to do everything perfectly.

- 그 사람은 다시 시작하려고 할 거예요. He will try to start again.

4 When expressing doubt and asking a question

-(으)려고 is used when the speaker expresses doubt and asks about the intention of an action. To emphasize disagreement or disbelief, intonation can be raised at the end of the sentence.

- 이런 일로 친한 친구하고 싸우려고?
  Are you going to fight with your close friend over something like this?

- 그렇게 큰 돈을 쓰려고? Are you going to spend that much money?

Quiz 53

Kor. 54

돈이 생기면 멋진 자동차를 사고 싶어요.

If I get some money, I want to buy a nice car.

집에 도착하면 문자 주세요. Please text me when you get home.

Grammar Essentials

1 -(으)면

The ending -(으)면 is a conjunctive ending that indicates conditions or assumptions. It connects two clauses: the preceding clause of -(으)면 states a condition or assumption, and the following clause describes the result.

한국 음악을 좋아해요. 그러면 이 콘서트에 가 보세요.

→ 한국 음악을 좋아하면 이 콘서트에 가 보세요. If you like Korean music, you should try going to this concert.
   Conditional clause   Result clause

-(으)면 is attached to verbs, adjectives, and "noun + 이다" to express conditional statements. For verbs and adjectives, use -면 if the stem ends in a vowel and -으면 if it ends in a consonant.

- 비가 오면 운동하지 마세요. If it rains, do not exercise.
- 책을 읽으면 밤에 야식을 먹을 거예요. If you read a book, you will eat a late-night snack.
- 너무 많이 추우면 사람들이 밖에 나가지 않아요. If it's very cold, people won't go outside.

For "noun + 이다", use 면 if the noun ends in a vowel and 이면 if it ends in a consonant.

- 남자면 왼쪽으로 가세요. If it's a man, go left.
- 학생이면 박물관에 무료로 들어갈 수 있어요. If it's a student, you can enter the museum for free.

2 Conjugation

-(으)면					
보다	보면	다르다	다르면	맵다	*매우면
먹다	먹으면	걷다	*걸으면	낫다	*나으면
바쁘다	바쁘면	살다	*살면	그렇다	*그러면

3 Negation

When using -(으)면 with verbs or adjectives, negations such as 안, -지 않다, 못, or -지 못하다 can be added before -(으)면. For "noun + 이다", the negation is formed by 아니다, which combines with -(으)면 to become 아니면.

- 이번 주에 안 바쁘면 저를 도와줄 수 있어요? If you are not busy this week, can you help me?
- 아이들이 저녁을 먹지 않으면 야식을 먹을 거예요. If the children do not eat dinner, they will have a snack later.
- 외국인이 한국어 발음을 못 하면 한국 사람들과 얘기할 수 없어요.
  If a foreigner cannot pronounce Korean, they cannot talk with Koreans.
- 그 얘기가 사실이 아니면 큰 문제가 생길 거예요. If that story is not true, it will cause a big problem.

Lesson 54

1 When presenting uncertain hypothetical conditions

열심히 공부하면 다음에는 좋은 성적을
받을 수 있을 거야.

If you study hard, you can get good grades next time.

The ending -(으)면 is used to present uncertain hypothetical situations as conditions in the preceding clause. The clause following -(으)면 describes the result if the condition is met.

The structure "-(으)면… -(으)ㄹ 것이다" is often used in such cases to emphasize uncertainty. Additionally, adverbs like 만약 or 만일 can be added to further highlight the hypothetical nature of the statement.

- 내가 노래를 잘하면 가수가 될 거예요. If I sing well, I will become a singer.
- 만약 사람들이 없으면 공연을 취소할 거예요. If there are no people, the performance will be canceled.
- 만일 친구가 시험에 떨어지면 정말 속상할 거예요. If my friend fails the test, I will be really upset.

 Be careful!

When the subjects of the preceding and following clauses of -(으)면 are different, the subject in the -(으)면 clause must take the particle 이/가, not 은/는.

- 여동생은 대학교에 입학하면 아버지가 좋아할 거예요. (✕)
  → 여동생이 대학교에 입학하면 아버지가 좋아할 거예요. (○)
    If my younger sister gets into university, my father will be happy.

When -(으)면 is used to express an uncertain hypothetical situation in the past, adding the past tense marker -았/었- forms -았/었으면, which indicates a hypothetical situation that is contrary to a past fact.

- 어제 날씨가 안 좋았으면 집에 있었을 거예요. 그런데 어제 날씨가 좋아서 산책했어요.
  If the weather had been bad yesterday, I would have stayed at home. However, the weather was good, so I went for a walk.
- 제가 미리 말했으면 친구가 화 안 났을 거예요. 하지만 제가 미리 말 안 해서 친구가 화났어요.
  If I had told my friend earlier, they wouldn't have been angry. However, I didn't tell them in advance, so they got angry.
- 시험이 쉬웠으면 일찍 끝났을 거예요. 하지만 시험이 어려워서 늦게 끝났어요.
  If the exam had been easy, it would have ended early. However, the exam was difficult, so it ended late.

Note

Since -았/었으면 posits a situation contrary to past facts as a hypothetical scenario, it is also used to express a wish or regret about something that has not occurred in reality.

To someone who is sick
- 빨리 나았으면 해요. I hope you recover quickly.

In a situation where a war seems likely
- 전쟁이 일어나지 않았으면 좋겠어요. I wish a war would not occur.

2 When expressing results that follow specific conditions

저는 아이스크림을 먹으면 배탈이 나요.
When I eat a lot of ice cream, I get an upset stomach.

The ending -(으)면 is used to express the condition under which a predictable event or habitual situation occurs. The preceding clause states the condition, while the following clause shows the result that is inevitably linked to the condition.

- 음식이 완성되면 음식을 먹어 보세요. Try the food when it's ready.

- 제 친구는 매운 음식을 먹으면 땀이 나요. My friend sweats when he eats spicy food.

- 겨울에 눈이 많이 오면 수업이 취소돼요. When it snows a lot in the winter, classes are canceled.

- 숙제를 끝내면 핸드폰 해도 돼. When you finish your homework, you can use your smartphone.

 Note

The difference between -(으)면 and -(으)ㄹ 때

In Korean, "when" can be translated as either -(으)ㄹ 때 or -(으)면. The ending -(으)ㄹ 때 emphasizes the moment or the duration of a specific action, while -(으)면 highlights the specific conditions necessary for an event or situation to occur.

- 한국 사람들이 인사할 때 "안녕하세요"라고 말해요. Koreans say "Hello" when greeting.
- 친구하고 얘기할 때 영어로 말해요. I speak English when talking with my friend.
- 집에 도착하면 전화해. Call me when you get home.
- 봄이 오면 벚꽃이 아름답게 피어요. When spring comes, the cherry blossoms bloom beautifully.

When -았/었- is added before -(으)면, forming -았/었으면, it indicates that the condition involves events or situations that have already been completed.

- 청소를 다 했으면 쉬세요. Rest after you've finished cleaning.

- 수업이 끝났으면 같이 놀러 가요! Let's go out after class ends!

The difference between -(으)면 and -았/었으면 lies in whether the condition has been fulfilled at the moment of speaking. -(으)면 implies that the condition has not yet been met, such as when the coffee has not been finished yet. In contrast, -았/었으면 indicates that the condition has already been completed, meaning the coffee has already been finished.

- 커피를 다 마시면 집에 갑시다. Let's go home when we finish the coffee.

- 커피를 다 마셨으면 집에 갑시다. Let's go home if we have finished the coffee.

Quiz 54

-아/어도 even if

Kor. 55

저는 비가 조금만 와도 우산을 써요.

I use an umbrella even when it rains a little.

그런데 폴 씨는 비가 와도 우산을 안 써요.

But, Paul does not use an umbrella even when it rains.

Grammar Essentials

1 -아/어도

The ending -아/어도 is used to indicate that a certain situation or action occurs or continues regardless of another action or state. The preceding clause describes an action or state, while the following clause presents a situation that happens irrespective of the preceding clause. To emphasize the meaning of -아/어도, the adverb 아무리 (no matter how) can be added to the preceding clause.

폴 씨는 몸이 안 <u>좋아요</u>. <u>그래도</u> 매일 운동해요.

➡ 폴 씨는 몸이 안 좋아도 매일 운동해요. Even if Paul is not feeling well, he exercises every day.

-아/어도 combines with verbs, adjectives, and "noun + 이다" to express the meaning of "even if" or "even though". For verbs and adjectives, -아/어도 is added based on the verb or adjective stem: if the verb or adjective ends in 하다, 하 combines with -어도 to form -해도. If the last vowel of the stem is ㅏ or ㅗ, -아도 is added, and for all other verbs and adjectives, -어도 is used.

- 하나만 주문해도 배달 돼요. Even if you order just one, it will be delivered.

- 날씨가 따뜻해도 바람이 불어요. Even if the weather is warm, the wind blows.

- 집에 가도 집에 음식이 없어요. Even if I go home, there is no food at home.

- 존 씨는 키가 작아도 운동을 잘해요. Even though John is short, he is good at sports.

- 이 책을 읽어도 이해 못 해요. Even if I read this book, I don't understand it.

- 아무리 음식이 맛없어도 다 먹어야 해요. Even if the food doesn't taste good, you have to eat it all.

For "noun + 이다", 라도 or 여도 is added if the noun ends in a vowel, and 이라도 or 이어도 is added if it ends in a consonant.

- 그 사람이 의사라도 모든 병을 고칠 수 없어요.
  Even if that person is a doctor, he can't cure every illness.
  (= 그 사람이 의사여도 모든 병을 고칠 수 없어요.)

- 내일이 휴일이라도 식당 문을 열 거예요. Even if tomorrow is a holiday, the restaurant will be open.
  (= 내일이 휴일이어도 식당 문을 열 거예요.)

Lesson 55

-아/어도

271

2 Conjugation

-아/어도					
보다	봐도	다르다	달라도	맵다	*매워도
먹다	먹어도	걷다	*걸어도	붓다	*부어도
아프다	아파도	놀다	살아도	그렇다	*그래도

3 Negation

Before -아/어도, negations such as 안, -지 않다, 못, -지 못하다 can be combined.

- 전화하지 않지 않아도 친구들하고 연락할 수 있어요. Even if I don't call, I can contact my friends.

- 공부가 쉽지 않아도 저는 공부를 포기하지 않을 거예요. Even if studying isn't easy, I won't give up studying.

- 저는 음식을 잘 만들지 못해도 음식 맛을 잘 알아요. Even if I can't cook well, I know the taste of food.

For "noun + 이다", 아니다 becomes 아니라도 or 아니어도.

- 이건 전문가가 아니라도 알 수 있어요. Even if you're not an expert, you can know this.
  (= 이건 전문가가 아니어도 알 수 있어요.)

4 Tenses

The tense of the clause preceding -아/어도 should match the tense of the following clause. While the following clause can be in the present, past, or future tense, -아/어도 itself remains unchanged.

- 많이 자도 피곤해요.   Present   Even if I sleep a lot, I'm still tired.

- 많이 자도 피곤했어요.   Past   Even if I slept a lot, I was still tired.

- 많이 자도 피곤할 거예요.   Future   Even if I sleep a lot, I will still be tired.

-겠- can also be combined before -아/어도.

- 지금은 그 사람을 못 믿겠어도 조금만 기다려 보세요. Even if you can't trust that person now, just wait a little.

When assuming that a situation that did not actually occur had happened, -았/었- can be added before -아/어도 to form -았/었어도. -았/었어도 is commonly used in combination with -았/었을 거예요 to indicate hypothetical past situations.

- 제가 하지 않았어도 다른 사람이 했을 거예요. Even if I hadn't done it, someone else would have.

- 그 사람은 안 바빴어도 안 왔을 거예요. Even if that person wasn't busy, he wouldn't have come.

1 When an outcome remains unchanged regardless of actions or states

-아/어도 is used to express unchanging outcomes regardless of the actions taken or states experienced. These outcomes can be either positive or negative. To emphasize the clause before -아/어도, the adverb 아무리 (no matter how) can be used.

- A 음식이 매운데 괜찮을까요? Will you be okay if the food is spicy?

  B 아무리 음식이 매워도 먹을 거예요. 저는 매운 음식을 좋아해요.
  No matter how spicy the food is, I'll eat it. I like spicy food.

- A 요즘 공부가 어때요? How is studying going these days?

  B 너무 어려워서 공부해도 소용없어요. It's so hard that studying is useless.

Using opposing verbs or adjectives with -아/어도 repeatedly can emphasize an unchanging result.

- 전화해도 안 해도 그 사람은 상관없을 거예요. Whether you call or not, that person won't care.

- 돈이 있어도 없어도 행복할 수 있어요. Whether you have money or not, you can be happy.

2 When emphasizing the meaning of -아/어도

To emphasize the preceding clause before -아/어도, you can use -아/어도 repeatedly.

- 음식이 정말 많아서 음식을 먹어도 먹어도 끝이 없어요.
  There is so much food that, even if you eat and eat, there is no end.

- 집이 커도 커도 이렇게 클 수 없어요. The house is so big, it's unbelievably large no matter how big.

- 너무 지저분해서 청소를 해도 해도 더 청소해야 해요.
  It's so messy that, even if you clean and clean, you still have to clean more.

Quiz 55

-(으)면서 while

Kor. 56

진수는 샤워하면서 노래를 불러요.

Jinsu is singing while taking a shower.

수민은 음악을 들으면서 공부해요.

Sumin is studying while listening to music.

1 -(으)면서

The ending -(으)면서 is used to indicate that two actions are happening simultaneously or that two states coexist. The subject of the clauses before and after -(으)면서 must be the same.

<blockquote>
진수 씨는 <u>샤워해요</u>. 그러면서 노래를 불러요.

→ 진수 씨는 샤워하면서 노래를 불러요. Jinsu sings while taking a shower.
</blockquote>

-(으)면서 is attached to verbs, adjectives, and "noun + 이다". For verbs or adjectives, -면서 is added based on the final sound of the stem: use -면서 if the stem ends in a vowel and -으면서 if it ends in a consonant.

- 저는 낮에 일하면서 밤에 공부하고 있어요. I work during the day while studying at night.

- 이 자동차가 조용하면서 빨라요. This car is quiet yet fast.

- 매일 1시간씩 걸으면서 음악을 들어요. I listen to music while walking for an hour every day.

- 이 영화가 재미있으면서 감동적이에요. This movie is interesting yet moving.

For "noun + 이다", 이면서 is used regardless of whether the noun ends in a vowel or a consonant. In colloquial speech, 이 is often omitted, becoming 면서 when the noun ends in a vowel.

- 그 사람은 의사이면서 작가예요. That person is a doctor while also being a writer.

- 이 사람은 홍콩 사람이면서 영국 국적도 갖고 있어요.
  This person is from Hong Kong and also is of British nationality.

- 그 사람은 대학원생이면서 학부생에게 강의를 해요.
  The person is a graduate student while also lecturing to undergraduate students.

2 Conjugation

-(으)면서			
보다	보면서	살다	*살면서
먹다	먹으면서	돕다	*도우면서
바쁘다	바쁘면서	붓다	*부으면서
듣다	*들으면서	그렇다	*그러면서

3 Negation

-(으)면서 can be used with negative expressions such as 안, -지 않다, 못, -지 못하다.

- 그 사람은 아무것도 하지 않으면서 불평만 말해요. He does nothing yet complains all the time.

- 저는 다른 사람을 방해 안 하면서 혼자 살고 있어요. I live alone without disturbing others.

- 그 사람은 잘 알지도 못하면서 아는 척해요. He pretends to know even though he doesn't know well.

- 이 방은 작지 않으면서 깨끗해서 마음에 들어요. This room is not small and is clean, which I like.

- 이렇게 검은색 옷을 입으면 답답하지 않으면서 멋있어요.
  Wearing black clothes like this is stylish without being oppressive.

For "noun + 이다", the negation 아니다 becomes 아니면서.

- 진수는 학생이 아니면서 학생처럼 무거운 가방을 가지고 다녀요.
  Jinsu is not a student, yet he carries a heavy bag.

4 Tenses

The tense of -(으)면서 must match the tense of the following clause. It is used when two actions occur simultaneously in the past or when two states coexist.

- 어제 핸드폰을 봤으면서 밥을 먹었어요. (✗)

  → 어제 핸드폰을 보면서 밥을 먹었어요. (O) I ate while watching my phone.

Regardless of whether the following clause is in the present, past, or future tense, -(으)면서 remains unchanged.

- 보통 영화를 보면서 팝콘을 먹어요. I usually eat popcorn while watching a movie. `Present`

- 비빔밥이 매우면서 맛있었어요. The bibimbap was spicy yet delicious. `Past`

- 내일 책을 읽으면서 집에 있을 거예요. Tomorrow, I will stay at home while reading a book. `Future`

5 -(으)면서 = -(으)며

-(으)면서 and -(으)며 are interchangeable, but -(으)며 is more formal or literary and is commonly used in written language and official documents. When attaching these endings, use -며 if the verb or adjective stem ends in a vowel, and -으며 if it ends in a consonant.

- 그 사람은 항상 웃으면서 말해요. `Informal` = 그 사람은 항상 웃으며 말한다. `Literary`
  He always talks while smiling.   He always talks while smiling.

- 그 사람은 친절하면서 냉정해요. `Informal` = 그 사람은 친절하며 냉정합니다. `Formal`
  He is kind yet cold.   He is kind and cold.

Grammar in Action

1 When two actions happen simultaneously or over a period

-(으)면서 is used when two actions happen at the same time or when two repetitive actions occur over a period. It is typically combined with verbs.

- A 지금 뭐 해요? What are you doing now?

  B 핸드폰을 보면서 밥을 먹어요. I'm eating while looking at my phone.

- A 요즘 어떻게 지내요? How have you been lately?

  B 대학교에 다니면서 아르바이트하고 있어요. I've been attending university while working part-time.

2 When two characteristics coexist

한국어 수업이 어려우면서 재미있어요.

Korean classes are difficult yet fun.

-(으)면서 is also used when two characteristics coexist, which can be similar or contrasting. To express contrasting characteristics, the particle 도 can be added after -(으)면서 to form -(으)면서도. This form is commonly used with adjectives or "noun + 이다".

- 선생님이 친절하면서 엄격해요. The teacher is kind yet strict.

- 이 음식은 건강에 좋으면서 맛있습니다. This food is good for your health while also being delicious.

- 저는 1인 기업가예요. 그래서 우리 가게의 사장이면서 직원이에요.
  I am a solo entrepreneur. So, I am both the owner and an employee of our store.

3 When an action leads to a distinctive change

-(으)면서 is used to express a distinctive change that occurs as a result of an action. It is combined with verbs, and the following clause describes the change.

- 규칙적으로 음식을 먹으면서 건강이 좋아졌어요. My health has improved by eating regularly.

- 운동을 시작하면서 생활에 힘이 나는 것 같아요. I feel energized since I started exercising.

- 도시의 치안이 나빠지면서 이 도시에서 살기 어려워졌어요.
  The safety of the city has deteriorated, making it difficult to live here.

Quiz 56

277

Kor. 57

책을 읽다가 잠이 들었어요.

I fell asleep while reading.

주차하다가 사고가 났어요.

There was an accident while parking.

Grammar Essentials

1 -다가

The ending -다가 is used when an action or state is unexpectedly interrupted and transitions into another action or situation, or when a different situation arises.

<u>집에 가다가</u> 길에서 <u>친구를 우연히 만났어요</u>. I ran into my friend on my way home.

an ongoing action   unexpected situation

The ending -다가 can be attached to verbs, adjectives, and "noun + 이다". For verbs and adjectives, -다가 is used regardless of whether the stem ends in a vowel or a consonant. For nouns, attach -다가 if the noun ends in a vowel and -이다가 if it ends in a consonant.

- 저는 회사에서 일하다가 여자 친구를 만났어요.
  I was working at the company and then met my girlfriend.

- 친구가 수업을 듣다가 화장실에 갔어요. I was listening to the class and then went to the bathroom.

- 아침에는 머리가 아프다가 오후에는 머리가 안 아파요.
  In the morning, my head hurt, and then in the afternoon, it didn't hurt.

- 조금 전까지 3번이 정답이다가 4번이 정답으로 바뀌었어요.
  A little while ago, number 3 was the correct answer, but it changed to number 4.

> **ⓘ Note**
>
> **The difference between -(으)면서 and -다가**
>
> Both -다가 and -(으)면서 require the subjects of the preceding and following clauses to be the same. However, -(으)면서 indicates that the actions of the preceding and following clauses occur simultaneously, whereas -다가 shows that the action of the preceding clause was unintentionally interrupted and transitioned to the action of the following clause.
>
> - 영화를 보면서 울었어요. Expresses simultaneous watching and crying
>   I cried while watching a movie.
> - 영화를 보다가 울었어요. Expresses crying during the movie
>   I was watching a movie and then cried.

2 Conjugation

-다가					
바쁘다	바쁘다가	부르다	부르다가	굽다	굽다가
먹다	먹다가	듣다	듣다가	붓다	붓다가
쓰다	쓰다가	살다	살다가	그렇다	*그러다가

3 Subjects of a sentence

The subjects of the preceding and following clauses of -다가 must be the same. -다가 cannot be used if the subjects of the preceding and following clauses are different.

- 친구가 샤워하다가 (친구가) 전화를 받았어요. (O)
  My friend was showering and then (my friend) received a call.

- 친구가 샤워하다가 전화가 왔어요. (✗)
  = 친구가 샤워하는 동안에 전화가 왔어요. (O)
  I received an incoming call while my friend was showering.

4 Negation

Negations like 안, -지 않다, 못, or -지 못하다 can precede -다가. For nouns, the negation 아니다 becomes 아니다가.

- 민호 씨가 일 안 하다가 상사한테 혼나고 있어요.
  Minho is getting scolded by his boss because he wasn't working.

- 그 남자는 여자에게 고백하지 못하다가 그 여자를 놓쳤어요.
  That man failed to confess to the woman and ended up losing her.

- 이전부터 그 사실을 알고 있었는데, 어제까지 문제가 아니다가 오늘 문제가 됐어요.
  I knew that fact before, and until yesterday it was not a problem, but today it became one.

5 Tenses

The tense indicated by -다가 is the same as the tense of the following clause. -다가 is used regardless of whether the tense of the following clause is present, past, or future.

- 보통 아침에 회사에 가다가 편의점에서 아침을 사요.
  I usually buy breakfast at a convenience store while going to the office in the morning.   Present

- 어제 제가 친구 얘기를 듣다가 갑자기 화가 났어요.
  Yesterday, I suddenly got angry while listening to my friend's story.   Past

- 앞으로 사장님과 일하다가 놀라게 될 거예요.
  In the future, you will be surprised while working with the boss.   Future

-다가 can be preceded by -았/었- to express that the action or state of the preceding clause was completed before transitioning into the action or state of the following clause.

- 저는 문제를 확인하려고 불을 켰다가 껐어요.
  I turned on the light to check the problem and then turned it off.

- 제 친구는 5년 동안 비정규직이었다가 드디어 정규직이 됐어요.
  My friend had been a temporary employee for five years and finally became a permanent employee.

Grammar in Action

1 When one action interrupts another

The ending -다가 is used when one action or state is interrupted or when an unexpected or unintended situation arises during an ongoing action.

- 지하철을 타고 가다가 길에서 옛날 친구를 만났어요.
  I ran into an old friend in the street while riding the subway.

- 길을 걷다가 예쁜 여자를 보고 사랑에 빠졌어요.
  I fell in love after seeing a beautiful woman while walking.

- 청소하다가 중요한 서류를 찾았어요. I found important documents while cleaning.

- 버스를 타고 가다가 우산을 잃어버렸어요. I lost my umbrella while taking the bus.

- 친구가 쇼핑하다가 지갑을 잃어버렸어요. My friend lost my wallet while shopping.

2 When an action or state transitions to another

오전에 날씨가 흐리다가 오후에 맑겠습니다.

The weather will be cloudy in the morning and then clear up in the afternoon.

The ending -다가 is also used when an action or state transitions into another action or state. Adding -다가 말다 to a verb stem indicates that an action was in progress but then stopped before completion. In colloquial speech, 가 is often omitted, resulting in -다 말다 being more commonly used.

- 학교에 다니다가 휴학하고 아르바이트하고 있어요.
  I was attending school and then took a break to work part-time.

- 교실이 시끄럽다가 선생님이 교실에 오니까 다시 조용해졌어요.
  The classroom was noisy until the teacher came in, then it quieted down.

- 영화를 보다가 잠이 들었어요. I fell asleep while watching a movie.

- 처음에는 한국어 공부가 어렵다가 점점 쉬워졌어요.
  At first, studying Korean was difficult, but then it gradually became easier.

- 어제 그림을 그리다 말았어요. (= 어제 그림을 그리다가 그만뒀어요.)
  I was drawing a picture yesterday but then I stopped.

3 When transitioning to another action after completion

-았/었다가 (a combination of the completed meaning -았/었- with -다가) is used to express the transition from one action to another immediately after the first action has been completed. The subjects of both the preceding and following clauses of -았/었다가 are the same.

- 동료가 사무실에 들어갔다가 다시 나왔어요. A coworker went into the office and then came back out.

- 커피를 마셨다가 너무 뜨거워서 바로 물을 마셨어요.
  I drank coffee, but it was too hot, so I drank water right away.

- A 이번에 어디로 여행 갈 거예요? Where are you going on a trip this time?

  B 부산에 갔다가 제주도에 갈 거예요. I'm going to Busan and then Jeju Island.

4 When indicating action in progress and action completion

공원에 가다가 친구를 만났어요.
I met a friend while going to the park.

공원에 갔다가 친구를 만났어요.
I went to the park and met a friend.

The usage of motion verbs like 가다 (to go) and 오다 (to come) shows a clear difference in meaning between the progression of a movement and its completion. -다가 used with a motion verb indicates that the movement is ongoing, whereas -았/었다가 used with a motion verb indicates that the movement has been completed.

- 식당에 가다가 (길에서) 유명한 배우를 만났어요. I met a famous actor on the way to the restaurant.

- 식당에 갔다가 (식당에서) 유명한 배우를 만났어요. I met a famous actor at the restaurant.

This difference in meaning between -다가 and -았/었다가 can also be seen with verbs other than motion verbs:

- 친구에게 얘기하다가 그만뒀어요. I was talking to my friend and then I stopped.

- 친구에게 얘기했다가 후회했어요. I regretted it after I had talked to my friend.

5 When an action causes an unexpected result

요리하다가 손을 다쳤어요.
I hurt my hand while cooking.

The ending -다가 is used to indicate that the process of an action serves as the cause or basis for a situation. Specifically, -다가 is employed in the following clause when the outcome, whether negative or positive, is unintended and unforeseen by the subject of the sentence. This usage helps explain the circumstances under which these unexpected results occurred. To inquire about the process, phrases like "어떻게 하다가? (how it happened that?)" or the abbreviation "어쩌다가? (how on earth?)" are used.

- 횡단보도를 건너다가 교통사고가 났어요.
  There was a traffic accident while I was crossing the pedestrian crosswalk.

- A 어쩌다가 옷이 찢어졌어요? How did your clothes get torn?

  B 작은 옷을 입다가 옷이 찢어졌어요. They tore while I was trying on a tight outfit.

- A 어떻게 하다가 결혼하게 됐어요? How did you end up getting married?

  B 유럽을 여행하다가 아내를 만나서 결혼하게 됐어요.
    I met my wife while traveling in Europe and we got married.

6 When indicating actions or states repeatedly

Using -다가 repeatedly with verbs or adjectives that indicate opposite states can express that certain actions or states occur alternately. It's often structured as -다가 -다가 하다, but 가 in -다가 can also be omitted to form -다 -다 하다.

- 요즘 이상해요. 기분이 좋다가 나쁘다가 해요.
  It's strange these days. I feel good and bad.

- 그 영화는 재미있고 감동적인 영화라서 울다가 웃다가 했어요.
  That movie is fun and touching, so I was crying and laughing.

- 유키 씨는 한국 사람하고 결혼해서 한국하고 일본을 왔다 갔다 해요.
  Yuki often travels back and forth between Korea and Japan because she married a Korean.

- 불을 껐다 켰다 하지 마세요. 고장 날 수 있어요.
  Don't turn the light on and off; it might break.

Quiz 57

TOPIK I | SCK 2

-는 동안에 while, during

Kor. 58

선생님이 칠판에 쓰는 동안에 학생들이 핸드폰을 보고 있어요.

Students are looking at their phones while the teacher is writing on the board.

친구가 음식을 만드는 동안에 제가 청소를 했어요.

I cleaned up while my friend was cooking.

Grammar Essentials

1 -는 동안에

The expression -는 동안에 is used to indicate that the action or state in the following clause occurs at the same time as the action or state in the preceding clause. It emphasizes that two actions or states happen simultaneously.

우리가 여행하는 동안에 제 친구가 우리 개를 돌봐줬어요.

an ongoing action | simultaneous co-occurring action

While we were traveling, my friend took care of our dog.

-는 동안에 attaches to verb stems, regardless of whether the verb stem ends in a vowel or consonant.

- 보통 책을 읽는 동안에 음악을 들어요. I usually listen to music while reading a book.

- 친구가 운전하는 동안에 제가 옆자리에서 길을 찾았어요. I navigated while my friend was driving.

- 제가 집에 없는 동안에 택배가 집에 왔어요. A package arrived at my house while I was away.

- 보통 가게 직원이 일하는 동안에 핸드폰을 보지 않아요.
  I usually don't look at my phone while the store staff is working.

-는 동안에 is attached to verbs to indicate the duration of an action, while 동안 is added to nouns to refer to the specific time period indicated by the noun.

- 저는 쉬는 동안 이메일을 보지 않을 거예요. I won't check emails while I am resting.

- 저는 휴가 동안 한국을 여행하고 싶어요. I want to travel around Korea during my vacation.

> **ⓘ Note**
>
> **The difference between -는 동안에 and -(으)면서**
>
> Both -는 동안에 and -(으)면서 express that two actions or states occur simultaneously. The key difference is that -(으)면서 requires the subjects of both actions or states to be the same, while -는 동안에 can be used regardless of whether the subjects are the same or different.
>
> - 여자가 전화하면서 텔레비전을 봐요. (O) = 여자가 전화하는 동안에 텔레비전을 봐요. (O)
>   The woman watches television while making a phone call.
>
> - 여자가 전화하는 동안에 남자가 텔레비전을 봐요. (O) ≠ 여자가 전화하면서 남자가 텔레비전을 봐요. (✗)
>   The woman is on the phone while the man watches television.

2 Conjugation

-는 동안에			
하다	하는 동안에	걷다	걷는 동안에
찾다	찾는 동안에	살다	*사는 동안에
쓰다	쓰는 동안에	굽다	굽는 동안에
부르다	부르는 동안에	낫다	낫는 동안에

3 Subjects of a sentence

The subjects of the preceding and following clauses of -는 동안에 can be the same or different.

- 제가 자는 동안에 꿈을 꾸지 않아요. I don't dream while I am sleeping.
- 제가 자는 동안에 친구가 아침을 준비했어요. My friend prepared breakfast while I was sleeping.
- 그 사람을 사랑하는 동안에 저는 정말 행복했어요. I was really happy while I was in love with that person.

4 Negation

Negations such as 안, -지 않다, 못, or -지 못하다 can precede -는 동안에. To emphasize the duration of the preceding clause, the particle 도 can be added.

- 내가 글을 안 쓰는 동안에 사람들이 예전에 쓴 글을 읽어 줬어요.
  People read my old writings while I wasn't writing.
- 우리가 아무 생각을 하지 않는 동안에도 뇌는 계속 일을 해요.
  Our brain continues to work even when we aren't thinking about anything.
- 너를 만나지 못하는 동안에도 너를 많이 보고 싶었어. I missed you even while I couldn't meet you.

5 Tenses

The tense of the clause preceding -는 동안에 must match the tense of the following clause. -는 동안에 is used regardless of whether the following clause is in the present, past, or future tense.

- 저는 운전하는 동안에 핸드폰을 보지 않아요. I don't look at my phone while driving.   `Present`
- 제가 밥을 먹는 동안에 친구가 얘기했어요. My friend talked while I was eating.   `Past`
- 동생이 시험을 보는 동안에 제가 밖에서 동생을 기다릴 거예요.   `Future`
  I will wait outside while my brother takes the exam.

To indicate that the preceding clause occurred before the succeeding clause, -고 나서 can be used instead of -는 동안에. This shows that the first action has already been completed before the second action begins.

- 아기가 잠든 동안에 엄마가 책을 읽었어요. A mother read a book while the baby was asleep.
- 동생이 회사에 간 동안에 제가 집에서 청소해요. I clean the house while my brother is at work.
- 친구가 여행을 떠난 동안에 많은 일이 일어났어요. A lot happened while my friend was away on a trip.

Grammar in Action

1 When expressing two simultaneous actions

제가 전화하는 동안에 고양이가 밖에 나갔어요.
My cat went outside while I was on the phone.

-는 동안에 is used when two actions occur simultaneously. It is particularly used to emphasize that one action continues for the entire duration of another action.

• 아이가 숙제를 하는 동안에 저는 저녁을 준비했어요. I prepared dinner while my child was doing homework.

• 저는 비가 내리는 동안에 창문을 청소했어요. I cleaned the windows while it was raining.

• 회사에서 일하는 동안에 계속 의자에 앉아 있어요. I continuously sit in a chair while working at the office.

2 When emphasizing the duration of a situation or state

-는 동안에 is also used to emphasize the duration during which a certain situation or state continues. The particle 도 can be added after -는 동안에 to further emphasize the entire duration of the situation.

• 제 친구가 병원에 있는 동안에 제가 매일 병원에 방문했어요.
  I visited my friend in the hospital every day while he was there.

• 영화가 상영되는 동안에 팝콘을 다 먹었어요. I finished all the popcorn during the movie.

• 회사 발표가 진행되는 동안에도 제 동료가 핸드폰을 보고 있어요.
  My colleague is looking at her phone even while the company presentation is going on.

To ask about the duration of the action in the preceding clause, use 언제 (when).

• A 언제 두 사람이 사귀게 됐어요? When did the two of you start dating?

  B 같이 헬스장을 다니는 동안에 가까워지면서 사귀게 됐어요.
    We got closer while going to the gym together and started dating.

To inquire about the action in the following clause, use 뭐 (what).

• A 한국에 사는 동안에 뭐 하고 싶어요? What do you want to do while living in Korea?

  B 한국에 사는 동안에 한국 여기저기를 여행하고 싶어요.
    I want to travel around Korea while I am living here.

Quiz 58

PART

4

Derivational Endings and Speech Styles

Adnominal endings
-은/는/을

Kor. 59

5:41 / 11:46

사람들에게 인기가 많은 사람이 민수 씨예요.

왼쪽에 모자를 쓴 사람이 유진 씨예요.

오른쪽에 웃고 있는 사람이 저예요.

The person who is popular with people is Minsu.
The person who is wearing a hat on the left is Yujin.
The person who is smiling on the right is me.

1 Adnominal endings

In Korean, adnominal words, phrases, and clauses always precede the noun they modify. When modifying a noun, adnominal words, phrases, and clauses must be accompanied by an adnominal ending. These endings, when combined with an adnominal modifier, function like adjectives, describing the noun or providing additional information about it.

▶ **Adnominal word:**

저는 <u>작은</u> 가방을 사고 싶어요. I want to buy a small bag.
adnominal ending

▶ **Adnominal phrase:**

우리는 아주 <u>비싼</u> 음식을 먹었어요. We ate very expensive food.
adnominal ending

▶ **Adnominal clause:**

<u>모자를 쓴</u> 사람이 유진 씨예요. The person who is wearing the hat is Yujin.
adnominal ending

The form of the adnominal ending varies depending on whether it combines with a verb, adjective, and "noun + 이다", as well as the tenses (present, past, or future).

- 저분이 한국어를 <u>가르치는</u> 선생님이에요.　　　　Verb | Present
  That person is a teacher who teaches Korean.

- 이번 휴가 때 <u>바다 경치로 유명한</u> 곳에 여행 가고 싶어요.　　Adjective | Present
  I want to travel to a place famous for its sea view this vacation.

- 어제 <u>친구하고 본</u> 영화 제목이 뭐예요?　　　　Verb | Past
  What is the title of the movie I watched with a friend yesterday?

- 지금 <u>제가 먹을</u> 음식을 고르고 있어요.　　　　Verb | Future
  I am choosing the food I will eat now.

Tip

Adnominal clauses in Korean vs. Relative clauses in English

In English, relative clauses modify nouns using relative pronouns like who, when, where, etc. However, in Korean, adnominal clauses do not use relative pronouns; instead, they require an adnominal ending.

- 저는 <u>비가 오는</u> 날씨를 좋아해요. I like th e weather <u>when it rains</u>.
  adnominal endings　　　　　　　　　relative pronoun

2 The adnominal ending for present tense

The adnominal ending used for present tense indicates that the action or state described in the modifying clause occurs repeatedly or continuously, as in habitual actions.

친구가 자주 먹는 음식은 한국 음식이에요. The food that my friend often eats is Korean food.

1 Forms

The form of the present tense adnominal ending depends on whether it attaches to a verb, adjective, and "noun + 이다". For verbs, -는 is added regardless of whether the verb stem ends in a vowel or consonant. For adjectives, -ㄴ is added if the stem ends in a vowel, and -은 is added if it ends in a consonant. However, adjectives that include -있다/-없다 (e.g., 많다, 작다, 없다) also use -는. For "noun + 이다", 인 is added regardless of whether the noun ends in a vowel or consonant.

Verbs	• 매일 제가 보는 프로그램은 뉴스예요. The program that I watch every day is the news. • 민수 씨가 찾는 물건이 여기에 없어요. The item that Minsu is looking for is not here.
Adjectives	• 머리가 아픈 사람은 집에 가서 쉬세요. People who have headaches should go home and rest. • 역사에 관심이 많은 사람이 박물관에 자주 가요. People who are interested in history often go to the museum. • 여권이 없는 학생은 다른 신분증이 필요해요. Students who do not have a passport need another form of ID.
Noun + 이다	• 직업이 간호사인 지혜 씨는 지금 아프리카에서 일하고 있어요. Jihye, whose job is a nurse, is currently working in Africa. • 취미가 운동인 준하 씨는 매일 한강 공원에서 뛰고 있어요. Joonha, whose hobby is exercise, runs in Hangang Park every day.

2 Conjugation

	Verb + -는		Adjective + -(으)ㄴ
보다	보는	싸다	싼
먹다	먹는	작다	작은
쓰다	쓰는	아프다	아픈
부르다	부르는	다르다	다른
듣다	듣는	그렇다	*그런
살다	*사는	길다	*긴
돕다	돕는	춥다	*추운
붓다	붓는	낫다	*나은

3 Matching tenses with the present adnominal ending

The present adnominal ending -는 indicates that the action in the modifying clause occurs simultaneously with the main clause. For example, in "진수가 친구한테 말하는 (which Jinsu was telling his friend)", -는 shows that the action happened at the same time as the main clause, even if the main clause is in the past tense.

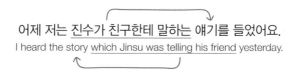

어제 저는 진수가 친구한테 말하는 얘기를 들었어요.
I heard the story which Jinsu was telling his friend yesterday.

4 Negation with present adnominal endings

Negations such as 안, -지 않다, 못, or -지 못하다 can be used before present tense adnominal endings. The negation form depends on whether it is attached to a verb, adjective, or "noun + 이다":

The negation form in present adnominal endings depends on the word type: for verbs, -지 않는 or -지 못하는 is used; for adjectives, -지 않은 is used; and for "noun + 이다", the negation form is 아닌.

Verbs	• 제가 먹지 않는 음식은 회예요. The food that I do not eat is raw fish. • 한국 노래를 부르지 못하는 사람은 다른 노래를 불러도 돼요. People who cannot sing Korean songs can sing other songs.
Adjectives	• 집이 여기에서 멀지 않은 사람은 같이 만나요! People whose homes are not far from here, let's meet together!
Noun + 이다	• 학생이 아닌 사람은 오른쪽에 줄 서 주세요. People who are not students, please line up on the right.

3 Adnominal ending for past tense

The adnominal ending for past tense indicates that the action or state in the modifying clause occurred before the time of speaking.

지난주에 먹은 음식의 이름이 뭐예요? What is the name of the food that you ate last week?

❶ Forms

The past tense adnominal ending varies depending on whether it attaches to a verb, adjective, and "noun + 이다". For verbs, -ㄴ is added if the stem ends in a vowel, and -은 if it ends in a consonant. For adjectives, -았/었던 is added. For "noun + 이다", 였던 is added if the noun ends in a vowel and 이었던 if it ends in a consonant.

Verbs	• 어제 제가 말한 얘기는 비밀로 해 주세요. Please keep the story which I told yesterday a secret. • 학생 때 많이 들은 음악은 힙합이에요. The music that I listened to a lot during my student days was hip hop.
Adjectives	• 어제 길이 복잡했던 이유는 축제 때문이에요. The reason the road was crowded yesterday is because of the festival. • 작년에 등산할 때 피곤했던 기억이 나요. I remember that I was tired when hiking last year.
Noun + 이다	• 작년까지 변호사였던 친구가 일을 그만뒀어요. My friend, who was a lawyer until last year, quit his job. • 작년까지 고등학생이었던 동생이 올해 대학생이 됐어요. My younger sibling, who was a high school student until last year, became a university student this year.

2 Conjugation

	Verb + -(으)ㄴ		Adjective + -았/었던
보다	본	싸다	쌌던
먹다	먹은	작다	작았던
쓰다	쓴	아프다	아팠던
부르다	부른	다르다	*달랐던
듣다	*들은	길다	길었던
살다	*산	춥다	*추웠던
돕다	*도운	낫다	*나았던
붓다	*부은	그렇다	*그랬던

3 Negation with past adnominal endings

Negations such as 안, -지 않다, 못, or -지 못하다 can precede past tense adnominal endings, with forms varying by word type. For verbs, -지 않은 or -지 못한 is used. For adjectives, -지 않았던 is used. For "noun + 이다", the form 아니었던 is used. Negations such as 안, -지 않다, 못, or -지 못하다 can precede past tense adnominal endings, with forms varying by word type. For verbs, -지 않은 or -지 못한 is used. For adjectives, -지 않았던 is used. For "noun + 이다", the form 아니었던 is used.

Verbs	• 지난주에 먹지 않은 음식을 먹고 싶어요. I want to eat the food that I didn't eat last week. • 작년에 한국에 오지 못한 이유가 뭐예요? What is the reason you couldn't come to Korea last year?
Adjectives	• 지난주에 바쁘지 않았던 사람이 이번 주에 바빠요. The person who wasn't busy last week is busy this week.
Noun + 이다	• 사실이 아니었던 이야기를 하고 있어요. They are talking about something that wasn't true.

🕮 Note

Past tense adnominal ending -았/었던

The past tense adnominal ending -았/었던, mainly used with adjectives and "noun + 이다", can also be used with verbs. While -(으)ㄴ indicates the completion of an action, -았/었던 refers to recollection of a past event. In most cases, -(으)ㄴ can be replaced by -았/었던 when recalling past events from memory, but -았/었던 cannot describe actions completed just before speaking.

• 어제 진수가 말한 얘기 들었어? Did you hear what Jinsu said yesterday?
        = 말했던 얘기

• 시험 문제를 끝까지 다 한 사람은 시험지를 내세요.
        ≠ 했던 사람
  Those who have completed all the exam questions, please submit your papers.

4 Adnominal ending for future tense

The adnominal ending for future tense indicates that the action or state in the modifying clause has not yet occurred or is being speculated about from the speaker's current perspective.

다음 주에 모임에 올 사람들에게 장소를 알려야 해요.
We need to inform the people who will come to the gathering next week about the location.

1 Forms

The future tense adnominal ending varies depending on whether it attaches to a verb, adjective, and "noun + 이다". For verbs and adjectives, -ㄹ is added if the stem ends in a vowel and -을 if it ends in a consonant. For "noun + 이다", 일 is added regardless of whether the noun ends in a vowel or consonant.

Verbs	• 아직 제가 미국에 갈 기회가 없었어요. I haven't had the opportunity that will allow me to go to the US yet. • 다음 주에 먹을 음식을 사러 가요. Let's go buy the food that we will eat next week.
Adjectives	• 나중에 키가 클 사람은 지금 알 수 있어요. You can tell now the person that will be tall later. • 아마 사람이 많을 곳에 안 가고 싶어요. I don't want to go to a place that will probably be crowded.
Noun + 이다	• 가벼운 증상이지만 암일 위험이 있어요. There's a risk that it will be cancer, even though the symptoms are mild. • 저 사람이 범인일 가능성이 있어요. There's a possibility that that person will be the culprit.

2 Idiomatic expressions with adnominal endings for the future

When the noun being modified refers to something that has not yet happened, such as an opportunity, promise, or possibility, the adnominal ending is always -(으)ㄹ.

- 그 사람과 인사할 <u>기회</u>가 없었어요. I haven't had the opportunity to greet that person.

- 그 사람과 다음에 다시 만날 <u>약속</u>을 했어요. I made a promise to meet that person again next time.

- 요즘 할 <u>일</u>이 많아요. I have a lot of work to do these days.

- 보고서를 준비할 <u>시간</u>이 없어요. I don't have time to prepare the report.

- 다음 주에 식당을 예약할 <u>계획</u>이에요. I am planning to reserve a restaurant next week.

3 Conjugation

Verb + -(으)ㄹ		Adjective + -(으)ㄹ	
보다	볼	싸다	쌀
먹다	먹을	작다	작을
쓰다	쓸	아프다	아플
부르다	부를	다르다	다를
듣다	*들을	길다	*길
살다	*살	춥다	*추울
돕다	*도울	낫다	*나을
붓다	*부을	그렇다	*그럴

4 Negation with future tense adnominal endings

Negations such as 안, -지 않다, 못, and -지 못하다 can be used before future tense adnominal endings, depending on the word type. For verbs, -지 않을 or -지 못할 is used. For adjectives, -지 않을 is used. For "noun + 이다", the negation form 아닐 is used.

Verbs	• <u>앞으로 하지 않을</u> 일 때문에 스트레스 받지 마세요. Don't stress over things <u>that you won't do in the future</u>. • 발표를 열심히 준비했지만 내일 <u>발표하지 못할</u> 가능성도 있어요. I worked hard on the presentation, but there is a possibility <u>that I won't be able to present it tomorrow</u>.
Adjectives	• 아마 <u>바쁘지 않을</u> 사람만 올 거예요. Only people <u>who probably won't be busy</u> will come.
Noun + 이다	• 그 얘기는 <u>사실이 아닐</u> 확률이 높아요. There is a high probability <u>that the story is not true</u>.

1 When modifying nouns to provide more detail

An adnominal clause is used before a noun to describe it or provide more detailed information. When asking about the characteristics of a noun, 어떤 (what kind of) is used in the question.

- A 진수 씨가 어떤 사람이에요? What kind of person is Jinsu?

  B 다른 사람의 말을 잘 들어주는 사람이에요. He is a person who listens well to others.

- A 어떤 옷을 사고 싶어요? What kind of clothes do you want to buy?

  B 한국에서 만든 옷을 사고 싶어요. I want to buy clothes that are made in Korea.

An adnominal clause is also used to ask a question while providing a detailed explanation.

- A 저기 청바지를 입은 사람이 누구예요? Who is the person that is wearing jeans over there?

  B 마이클 씨예요. It's Michael.

- A 한국 전통 음식으로 유명한 장소가 어디예요? Where is the place that is famous for Korean traditional food?

  B 전라도예요. It's Jeolla Province.

- A 모든 가족이 모일 시간이 언제예요? What is the time when all the family will gather?

  B 설날이나 추석이에요. It's during the Lunar New Year or Chuseok.

When combining two or more adnominal clauses in a sentence to describe a noun, use the endings -고 or -지만 to connect the clauses, and use the adnominal ending only once.

- 저는 음식이 맛있고 가격이 싼 식당에 매일 가요.
  I go to a restaurant where the food is delicious and the prices are cheap every day.

- 지하철역에서 가깝지만 사람들이 너무 많지 않은 식당을 찾고 있어요.
  I'm looking for a restaurant that is close to the subway station but not too crowded.

Tip

Subject particle in adnominal clauses

In an adnominal clause, only the subject particle 이/가 can be used after the subject; the particle 은/는 cannot be used.

- 어제 저는 본 영화가 재미있었어요. (✕)

  → 어제 제가 본 영화가 재미있었어요. (○) The movie I watched yesterday was interesting.

- 어제 친구는 먹은 음식이 맛있었어요. (✕)

  → 어제 친구가 먹은 음식이 맛있었어요. (○) The food my friend ate yesterday was delicious.

2 When using adnominal endings with 것 to function as nouns

In Korean, combining the adnominal ending with the pronoun 것 functions similarly to gerunds (-ing) in English. This structure can act as a noun, serving as the subject, object, or complement in a sentence. The form of the adnominal ending varies depending on the type of word (verb, adjective) and the tense (present, past, or future).

- 저는 음식을 만드는 것을 좋아해요. I like cooking food.

- 규칙적으로 걷는 것이 건강에 좋아요. Walking regularly is good for your health.

- 매일 아침 피곤한 것이 반복되면 쉬어야 해요. If you repeatedly feel tired every morning, you need to rest.

- 운동할 때 머리가 짧은 것이 편해요. Having short hair is convenient when exercising.

- 회의에서 들은 것을 말해 주세요. Please tell me what you heard in the meeting.

- 진수가 집에 있던 것을 가져왔어요. Jinsu brought the thing that was at home.

In informal or colloquial speech, -는 것이 can be contracted to -는 게, and -는 것을 can be contracted to -는 걸 or -는 거.

- 주말에 공원을 산책하는 게 어때요? How about taking a walk in the park on the weekend?
  - (= 산책하는 것이)

- 숙제가 많은 게 싫어요. I don't like having a lot of homework.
  (= 숙제가 많은 것이)

- 한국 음식을 먹는 게 익숙해요. I'm used to eating Korean food.
  (= 한국 음식을 먹는 것이)

- 혼자 영화를 보는 거 좋아해요. I like watching movies alone.
  (= 혼자 영화를 보는 것을)

- 누구나 기다리는 걸 배워야 해요. Everyone has to learn to wait.
  - (= 기다리는 것을)

- 음식을 먹을 때 저는 보통 건강에 좋은 거 먹어요. When I eat food, I usually eat healthy things.
  (=건강에 좋은 것을)

Quiz 59

TOPIK II ｜ SCK 2

Adverbial ending -게

Kor. 60

유나 씨는 음식을 맛있게 만들어요.

Yuna makes food deliciously.

유나 씨는 다음 날 일찍 일어나게 알람을 맞춰요.

Yuna sets an alarm to wake up early the next day.

1 Adverbial ending -게

In Korean, adverbs, adverbial phrases, and adverbial clauses are placed before adjectives, verbs, and verb phrases to modify them. The adverbial ending -게 attaches to adjective or verb stems to form adverbial phrases or clauses, as shown in the examples below. It can be used regardless of whether the stem ends in a vowel or a consonant.

- 핵심만 <u>간단하게</u> 말해 주세요. Please speak <u>simply</u> about the main point.

- <u>다른 사람들이 들을 수 있게</u> 천천히 말해 주세요. Please speak slowly <u>so that others can hear.</u>

In Korean, the position of adverbs, adverbial phrases, or clauses within a sentence is relatively flexible. As long as the predicate is positioned at the end of the sentence, the placement of the subject and adverb or the object and adverb can be freely adjusted.

- 친구가 가방을 <u>싸게</u> 샀어요. My friend bought the bag cheaply.

  = 친구가 <u>싸게</u> 가방을 샀어요.

- <u>문제를 빨리 해결하게</u> 제가 친구를 도와줬어요. I helped my friend quickly solve the problem.

  = 제가 <u>문제를 빨리 해결하게</u> 친구를 도와줬어요.

2 Negation

The adverbial ending -게 can be preceded by negations such as 안, -지 않다, 못, or -지 못하다. These negations combine with verb stems to form -지 않게 or -지 못하게. Similarly, when combined with adjective stems, they express a state or characteristic that is lacking, insufficient, or does not meet expectations.

- <u>부모님이 걱정 안 하게</u> 부모님께 자주 연락해요. I frequently contact my parents so they won't worry.

- <u>문제가 생기지 않게</u> 미리 준비했어요. I prepared in advance so that no problems would arise.

- 우리 팀이 며칠 동안 노력했지만 보고서가 <u>완벽하지 못하게</u> 보였어요.
  Our team worked hard for several days, but the report still seemed imperfect.

3 Tense

The adverbial ending -게 follows the tense of the main verb. The tense of the adverbial phrase must match the tense of the following clause.

- <u>감기에 걸리지 않게</u> 매일 비타민을 먹어요.   Present
  I take vitamins every day so that I don't catch a cold.

- 비가 많이 오지 않았지만 <u>옷이 젖지 않게</u> 우산을 썼어요.   Past
  It didn't rain much, but I used an umbrella so my clothes wouldn't get wet.

- <u>일찍 퇴근할 수 있게</u> 빨리 자료를 완성할 거예요.   Future
  I will quickly finish the materials so I can leave work early.

Grammar in Action

1 When expressing the manner or degree of an action or state

The adverbial ending -게 is attached to the stem of an adjective to form an adverb, expressing the manner or degree of an action or state. When asking about the manner or degree of an action or state, 어떻게 (how) is used to form the question.

- 두 사람이 결혼해서 행복하게 지내면 좋겠어요. I hope the two people live happily after getting married.

- 이 문제를 간단하게 생각해 보세요. Try thinking about this problem simply.

- A 과자를 어떻게 만들까요? How should we make the cookies?

  B 너무 작지 않게 만들어 주세요. Please make them not too small.

2 When expressing the purpose of an action

The adverbial ending -게 is attached to the stem of a verb to express the purpose of an action. The purpose is presented in the preceding clause before -게, while the action that fulfills the purpose appears in the following clause.

- 시험을 잘 보게 저는 열심히 공부했어요. I studied hard so that I could do well on the exam.

- 우리는 화면이 잘 보이게 앞줄에 앉았어요. We sat in the front row so that we could see the screen well.

- 학생들이 잘 이해할 수 있게 선생님이 한국어 문법을 설명했어요.
  The teacher explained Korean grammar so that the students could understand it well.

- 도서관에서 다른 사람에게 방해되지 않게 우리는 조용히 말했어요.
  We spoke quietly in the library so that we wouldn't disturb others.

When asking about the purpose of an action, 왜 (why) is used to form the question. To ask more directly about the specific purpose of an action, 뭐 하게 (for what purpose) can be used.

- A 왜 메모하고 있어요? Why are you taking notes?

  B 전화번호를 잊어버리지 않게 메모하고 있어요. I'm taking notes so that I don't forget the phone number.

- A 왜 음식을 덜 맵게 만들었어요? Why did you make the food less spicy?

  B 외국 친구들도 잘 먹을 수 있게 음식을 덜 맵게 만들었어요.
  I made the food less spicy so that my foreign friends could eat it well.

- A 이 옷을 뭐 하게 샀어요? What did you buy these clothes for?

  B 조카에게 선물하게 이 옷을 샀어요. I bought these clothes to give them as a gift to my nephew.

-게 as an auxiliary conjunctive ending

-게 can also function as an auxiliary conjunctive ending. When used with the auxiliary verb 하다, it expresses a causative meaning (making someone do something). When used with the auxiliary verb 되다, it conveys a passive meaning (a situation occurring as a result of other circumstances).

저 사람은 매일 저를 짜증나게 해요.
That person annoys me every day.

1. -게 하다: Expressing causation of an action or state

-게 하다 is used when the subject of the sentence influences someone or something, causing them to perform a certain action or enter a specific state. It combines with verb stems or adjective stems and can often be replaced with -게 만들다 (to make something happen). When forming questions, 어떻게 (how) is used.

- 제 아이는 저를 매일 웃게 해요. My child makes me smile every day.
- 제가 스쿼트를 20번 끝낼 때까지 친구가 저를 쉬지 못하게 했어요.
  My friend didn't let me rest until I finished 20 squats.
- 그 소식이 우리를 안심하게 만들었어요. The news made us feel reassured.
- A 친구가 다이어트 때문에 고민이에요. 어떻게 해야 해요?
  My friend is worried about dieting. What should I do?

  B 친구가 밤에 음식을 먹지 못하게 해야 해요. You should make sure your friend doesn't eat at night.

2. -게 되다: Expressing the result of reaching a situation or state

-게 되다 is used to express that the subject of the sentence reaches a certain situation or state without intentional effort, often due to external circumstances. It combines with verb stems or adjective stems. When forming questions, 어떻게 (how) is used.

- 프로젝트가 연기돼서 시간이 생기게 됐어요. The project was delayed, so I ended up with some free time.
- 친구 덕분에 좋은 책을 읽게 됐어요. Thanks to my friend, I got to read a good book.
- 새로운 친구를 사귀면서 성격이 활발하게 됐어요. I became outgoing after making a new friend.
- 스트레스를 받다가 여행을 다녀온 다음에 마음이 편안하게 됐어요.
  I was stressed, but after going on a trip, I became relaxed.

Quiz 60

Nominalizing endings -기 and -(으)ㅁ

Kor. 61

A 취미가 뭐예요?

B 제 취미는 사진 찍기예요.

A What is your hobby?
B My hobby is taking pictures.

A 이 카메라가 어때요?

B 카메라가 사진 찍기 좋아요.

A How is this camera?
B The camera is good for taking pictures.

생활에서 핸드폰이 중요함을 잘 알고 있어요.

I am well aware of the importance of mobile phones in daily life.

식당에 핸드폰을 놓고 왔음을 알았어요.

I realized I left my mobile phone at the restaurant.

1 Nominalizing ending -기

The nominalizing ending -기 attaches to the stems of verbs, adjectives, and "noun + 이다" to convert them into nouns. It is primarily used to nominalize general actions or states. By using -기 to nominalize these forms, they can function as subjects, objects, or predicates within a sentence.

빨리 걷기가 쉽지 않아요. Walking fast is not easy.

1 Forms

The nominalizing ending -기 attaches to the stems of verbs, adjectives, and "noun + 이다" regardless of whether they end in a vowel or consonant. Since -기 turns the stem into a noun, various particles can freely attach to the resulting noun.

- 이 부츠를 신기가 불편해요. Wearing these boots is uncomfortable.
- 우리 모두가 건강하기를 바라고 있어요. We all hope to be healthy.
- 건강 습관은 계단으로 걷기부터 시작해 보세요. Start your healthy habits by climbing the stairs.
- 그 사람이 나쁜 사람이 아니기를 기도했어요. I prayed that the person wasn't a bad person.

2 Combination with -았/었-

To nominalize a past action or state, the nominalizing ending -기 generally does not combine with the past tense markers -았/었-.

- 어제 밥을 먹었기가 힘들었어요. (✗)
  → 어제 밥을 먹기가 힘들었어요. (O) It was difficult to eat yesterday.

However, when expressing a desire or expectation that an action or state has been completed, particularly with verbs like 기대하다 (to expect) or 바라다 (to hope), the past tense markers -았/었- can be attached before -기.

- 동생이 이번 면접을 잘 봤기를 기대하고 있어요. I am hoping that my younger sibling did well in the interview.
- 친구 회사가 목표를 이루었기를 바랍니다. I hope my friend's company achieved its goals.

> **Note**
>
> The nominalizing ending -기 and the nominalizing suffix -기 both exist. The nominalizing ending -기 attaches to stems to create noun phrases or clauses, nominalizing actions or states.
>
> In contrast, the nominalizing suffix -기 attaches to stems to create nouns that denote general concepts of activities or actions. For example, the nominalizing suffix -기 changes verbs into nouns. (e.g., 말하다 → 말하기, 듣다 → 듣기, 걷다 → 걷기)
>
> - 나는 말하기가 듣기보다 어려운 것 같아. I think speaking is harder than listening. `suffix`
> - 많은 사람들 앞에서 말하기가 쉽지 않아요. Speaking in front of many people is not easy. `nominalizer`

2 Nominalizing ending -(으)ㅁ

The nominalizing ending -(으)ㅁ attaches to the stems of verbs, adjectives, and "noun + 이다" to transform them into nouns. This nominalizing ending is typically used to indicate that an action or state has been completed. By using -(으)ㅁ to nominalize verbs, adjectives, and "noun + 이다", these forms can function as subjects, objects, or predicates in a sentence.

- <u>혼자 아기를 돌봄</u>이 쉽지 않아요. Taking care of a baby alone is not easy.

  Subject

- <u>가족이 소중함</u>을 잊지 마세요. Don't forget the preciousness of family.

  Object

1 Forms

The nominalizing ending -(으)ㅁ attaches as -ㅁ if the verb or adjective stem ends in a vowel and as -음 if it ends in a consonant. In the case of "noun + 이다", -ㅁ is attached regardless of whether the noun ends in a vowel or a consonant. Since -(으)ㅁ turns the stem into a noun, various particles can freely attach to the resulting noun.

- 이 영화를 보고 <u>내가 행복함</u>을 알았어요. I realized my happiness after watching this movie.

- 항상 <u>부모님이 너를 위해 기도하고 있음</u>도 기억해.
  Remember that your parents are always praying for you, too.

- <u>우리가 아직 학생임</u>을 그 사람한테 말했어? Did you tell that person that we are still students?

- <u>그 말이 거짓말이 아님</u>이 분명해요. It's obvious that those words are not lies.

2 Conjugation

-(으)ㅁ					
보다	봄	부르다	부름	쉽다	*쉬움
읽다	읽음	듣다	*들음	붓다	*부음
바쁘다	바쁨	만들다	만듦	그렇다	*그럼

3 Combination with -았/었-

To nominalize a past action or state, the nominalizer -(으)ㅁ combines with the past tense markers -았/었-.

- 제가 다른 사람의 신발을 잘못 <u>신었음</u>을 나중에 알았어요.
  I later realized <u>that I had worn someone else's shoes by mistake</u>.

- 그 말 때문에 유나 씨가 상처 <u>받았음</u>이 분명해요.
  It is clear <u>that Yuna was hurt by those words</u>.

Grammar in Action

1 When describing future actions or abstract concepts

The nominalizing ending -기 is used to describe future actions when attached to verb stems. It is often used when writing down resolutions or plans. Additionally, -기 can be attached to adjective stems to express abstract concepts or general facts.

올해에는 꼭 ⋯ Must do this year

☑ 아침에 일찍 일어나기 Get up early in the morning

☑ 매일 30분 운동하기 Exercise for 30 minutes every day

☑ 한국어로 말하기 Speak in Korean

☑ 건강한 음식을 먹기 Eat healthy food

☑ 항상 건강하기 Always stay healthy

2 When expressing constructions using -기 with adjectives

The nominalizing ending -기 is used with adjectives such as 쉽다/어렵다, 편하다/불편하다, and 좋다/나쁘다 to form expressions like -기 쉽다/어렵다, -기 편하다/불편하다, and -기 좋다/나쁘다. In these constructions, -기 typically combines with verbs to describe the ease, convenience, or quality of performing a specific action. The particle 가 or 에 may follow -기 but can also be omitted. Additionally, an adverb may be inserted between -기 and the adjective.

- 이 부츠를 신기 불편해요. Wearing these boots is uncomfortable.

- 이 음식을 만들기가 쉬워요. 그래서 혼자 만들 수 있어요.
  It is easy to make this food. So, I can make it alone.

- 이 옷은 지퍼가 있어서 입기에 편해요. These clothes have a zipper, so they are easy to wear.

- 학생 때 아침 일찍 일어나기 진짜 싫었어요.
  When I was a student, I really hated getting up early in the morning.

3 When clarifying the source of statements

The nominalizing ending -기 is used with particles 에 or 로 to indicate the source of a statement from one's own observation, judgment, or something heard from others. It is used idiomatically.

- 내가 보기에 이 일은 혼자 할 수 없어요. In my opinion, this work cannot be done alone.

- 제가 느끼기에 아침보다 저녁에 머리가 더 아픈 것 같아요.
  I feel that my head hurts more in the evening than in the morning.

- 제가 듣기로는 한국 사람들이 노래를 정말 잘해요.
  From what I've heard, Koreans are really good at singing.

- 제가 알기로는 한국 사람들이 아파트를 좋아해요. As far as I know, Koreans like apartments.

4 When describing additional actions or states with -기도 하다

The grammatical pattern -기도 하다 is used by attaching it to the stem of a verb, adjective, and "noun + 이다" to describe additional actions or states.

- 보통 식당에서 저녁을 먹어요. <u>가끔 집에서 배달해서 먹기도 해요</u>.
  <u>I usually eat dinner at a restaurant. <u>Sometimes, I also have it delivered to my home</u>.</u>

- 전에는 헬스장에서 운동했어요. <u>가끔 집에서 운동하기도 했어요</u>.
  I used to work out at the gym. <u>Sometimes, I also worked out at home</u>.

- 동생이 정말 귀여워요. 하지만 <u>때로 귀찮기도 해요</u>.
  My younger sister is really cute. But <u>sometimes she is also annoying</u>.

- 어제 몸이 안 좋았어요. <u>머리가 아프기도 했어요</u>. I wasn't feeling well yesterday. <u>My head also hurt</u>.

- 저는 선생님이에요. 그리고 <u>한 아이의 엄마이기도 해요</u>. I'm a teacher. And, <u>also the mother of a child</u>.

5 When describing exclusive actions or states with -기만 하다

The grammatical pattern -기만 하다 is used by attaching -기만 하다 to the stem of a verb, adjective, and "noun + 이다" to describe actions or states that are exclusively done.

- 제 친구는 <u>옷을 사기만 하고</u> 입지 않아요. My friend <u>only buys clothes</u> and doesn't wear them.

- 동생이 이유를 말하지 않고 <u>울기만 해요</u>. My younger sibling <u>only cries</u> without explaining why.

- 너무 피곤해서 주말에 <u>자기만 했어요</u>. I was so tired that I <u>only slept</u> over the weekend.

- 제 친구는 <u>책이 많기만 해요</u>. 그런데 책을 안 읽어요.
  My friend <u>only has many books</u>. But he doesn't read them.

- 어제 간 식당은 <u>음식이 비싸기만 했어요</u>. The restaurant I went to yesterday <u>had expensive food</u>.

6 When using -기 with verbs like 바라다/기대하다/원하다

The nominalizing ending -기 is used with verbs like 바라다 (to hope), 기대하다 (to expect), and 원하다 (to want) to express the speaker's hopes or expectations for something that has not yet been realized. Verb or adjective stems are combined with -기. The particle 를 can be attached after -기 or omitted. When the desired or expected content refers to a completed action or state, the past tense markers -았/었- can be attached before -기.

- <u>언제나 행복하기</u> 바랍니다. I hope <u>you are always happy</u>.

- 그 사람은 <u>이번 경기에서 우리 팀이 꼭 이기기</u>를 기대하고 있어요. He is expecting <u>our team to win this game</u>.

- <u>이번 시험에 합격하기</u>를 원해요. I want <u>to pass this exam</u>.

- <u>친구가 고향에 안전하게 도착했기</u>를 바라고 있어요. I hope <u>my friend arrived safely in her hometown</u>.

7 When expressing completed actions or states

The nominalizing ending -(으)ㅁ turns verbs, adjectives, and "noun + 이다" into nouns that indicate completed actions or states, functioning as subjects or objects in a sentence. It often appears with cognition-related expressions to show the recognition of certain facts. When recognizing a completed action or state, the past tense markers -았/었- are attached before -(으)ㅁ.

- <u>모든 일에 항상 감사함</u>이 제일 중요해. <u>Being grateful for everything</u> is the most important.

- 저는 직원에게 디자인보다 <u>품질이 중요함</u>을 강조했어요.
  I emphasized to the staff <u>that quality is more important than design</u>.

- 사고가 난 후 3일이 지나서 <u>민수 상태가 좋지 않음</u>이 알려졌어요.
  It was known <u>that Minsu's condition was not good</u> three days after the accident.

- 제 친구는 <u>자신이 대학 교수임</u>을 자랑스럽게 생각하고 있어요.
  My friend is proud <u>to be a university professor</u>.

- 제 친구가 이 문제를 <u>해결했음</u>을 알게 되었어요.
  I found out <u>that my friend solved this problem</u>.

- <u>보고서가 제출되었음</u>을 확인했습니다.
  I confirmed <u>that the report was submitted</u>.

8 When conveying completed facts or states concisely

The nominalizing ending -(으)ㅁ is used to convey completed facts or states clearly and concisely. It is commonly used in notices, memos, presentation materials, meeting minutes, and reports.

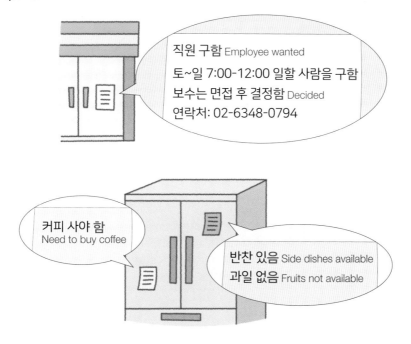

Quiz 61

반말 Informal casual speech

Kor. 62

A 음식 배달 뭐 시킬까? What should we order for food delivery?

B 난 치킨. I want chicken.

C 난 떡볶이 먹고 싶어. I want to eat tteokbokki.

Grammar Essentials

1 반말 Informal casual speech

In Korean, speech styles change depending on whether the situation is formal or informal, and whether the listener is of higher or lower status than the speaker. Among Korean speech styles, 반말 (informal casual speech) is used in informal situations where the listener is very close to the speaker, making it unnecessary to use formalities or honorifics. For example, 반말 is commonly used with peers, younger family members, or close friends.

The form of 반말 is derived from the informal polite form -아/어요 by omitting the politeness marker 요. It is created by attaching -아/어 to the stem of a verb or adjective.

- 요즘 운동하고 있어요. These days, I'm working out.

- 한국 음식이 맛있어요. Korean food is delicious.

- 여기에서 기다릴게요. I will wait here.

- 집에서 쉬고 싶어요. I want to rest at home.

To express negation in 반말, 안, -지 않다, 못, or -지 못하다 can be combined with verbs or adjectives. In 반말, affirmative responses use 응 or 어 instead of 네, and negative responses use 아니 instead of 아니요.

Affirmative	Negative
A 오늘 시간 있어? Do you have time today?	A 어제 전화했어? Did you call yesterday?
B 어, 시간 있어. Yeah, I have time.	B 아니, 전화 안 했어. No, I didn't call.

2 Noun + 이다

The verb 이다 is attached to nouns as (이)야 in 반말. If the noun ends in a vowel, 야 is attached; if it ends in a consonant, 이야 is attached. The negation of the noun is expressed as 아니야.

- 저 사람이 유명한 배우야. That person is a famous actor.

- 마크 취미가 운동이야. Mark's hobby is exercising.

- 이 사람은 학생이 아니야. This person is not a student.

 Be careful!

아니 is a negative response, while 아니야 is the negation of a noun.

- A 제임스가 미국 사람이야? Is James American?
  B 아니, 미국 사람이 아니야. 캐나다 사람이야. No, he's not American. He's Canadian.

3 Tense

In 반말, past events or states are expressed by omitting the politeness marker 요 from the past tense -았/었어요 form. The future tense -(으)ㄹ 거예요 becomes -(으)ㄹ 거야 in 반말. Since 거 in -(으)ㄹ 거야 is a noun, the ending 예요 changes to 야, forming -(으)ㄹ 거야.

- 어제 너무 바빴어요. I was very busy yesterday.
- 지난주에 친구를 안 만났어요. I didn't meet my friend last week.
- 내일 영화를 볼 거야. I will watch a movie tomorrow.
- 그 사람이 다음에 한국 음식을 먹을 거야. That person will eat Korean food next time.

4 Pronouns

In 반말, the first person pronoun 저 is replaced with 나, and the second person pronoun 당신 or the honorific marker 씨 after a name is replaced with 너. Various particles can also be attached to 나 and 너, creating different variations.

▶ **First-person singular pronouns**

Humble	Casual	Examples
저는	나는	나는 집에 있을 거야. I will be at home.
저를	나를	나를 만나고 싶어? Do you want to meet me?
저한테	나한테	나한테 전화했어? Did you call me?
저하고	나하고	나하고 같이 갔어. I went with you.
저도	나도	나도 그렇게 생각해. I think so too.
저만	나만	나만 자전거가 없어. Only I don't have a bicycle.
저의 (= 제)	나의 (= 내)	이게 내 책이야. This is my book.
제가	내가	내가 연락할게. I will contact you.

▶ **Second-person singular pronouns**

Humble	Casual	Examples
당신은	너는	너는 오늘 뭐 할 거야? What are you going to do today?
당신을	너를	나는 너를 좋아해. I like you.
당신한테	너한테	너한테 이메일을 보냈어. I sent you an email.
당신하고	너하고	너하고 여행 가고 싶어. I want to go on a trip with you.
당신도	너도	너도 그렇게 생각해? Do you think so too?
당신만	너만	너만 숙제 안 냈어. Only you didn't turn in the homework.
당신의	너의 (= 네)	이 사람이 네 동생이야? Is this person your younger sibling?
당신이	네가	네가 제일 예뻐. You are the prettiest.

> **🔈 Note**
>
> The first-person pronoun 내 and the second-person pronoun 네 are spelled differently but have similar pronunciations. To avoid confusion in spoken language, 네 (you) is sometimes pronounced as 니.
>
> - 니가 제일 예뻐. You are the prettiest.
>   = 네가
> - 이 자동차가 네 거야. This car is yours.
>   = 니

312

▶ First-person plural pronouns

Humble	Casual	Examples
저희는	우리는	우리는 친구야. We are friends.
저희를	우리를	우리를 기다리고 있어? Are you waiting for us?
저희가	우리가	우리가 준비할게. We will prepare it.

▶ Second-person plural pronouns

Honorific	Casual	Examples
여러분은	너희는	너희는 뭐 할 거야? What are you doing?
여러분을	너희를	너희를 보고 싶었어. I missed you.
여러분이	너희가	너희가 최고야. You are the best.

▶ Third-person singular pronouns

Original	Contraction	Examples
이 사람	얘 (= 이 아이)	얘가 누구야? Who is this?
그 사람	걔 (= 그 아이)	걔는 오늘 안 올 거야. He won't come today.
저 사람	쟤 (= 저 아이)	쟤가 내 여자 친구야. She is my girlfriend.

▶ Third-person plural pronouns

Original	Contraction	Examples
이 사람들	얘들 (= 이 아이들)	얘들이 내 친구들이야. These are my friends.
그 사람들	걔들 (= 그 아이들)	걔들한테 내가 얘기할게. I will tell them.
저 사람들	쟤들 (= 저 아이들)	쟤들이 너를 만나고 싶어해. They want to meet you.

▶ Contracted pronouns with particles

Pronoun	Original	Contraction	Example
First-person singular	나는	난	난 안 할 거야. I won't do it.
	나를	날	날 봐. 그리고 웃어. Look at me. And smile.
Second-person singular	너는	넌	넌 언제 여행 갈 거야? When are you going on a trip?
	너를	널	널 기다렸어. I was waiting for you.
Third-person singular	걔는	걘	걘 우리랑 달라. He's different from us.
	걔를	걜	걜 지켜보고 있어. I'm watching him.

5 Particles used in 반말

In 반말, the following particles are frequently used:

Normal	Casual	Example
에게 to	한테	동생한테 보여주려고 해. I intend to show it to my younger sibling.
에게서 from	한테서 (= 한테)	친구한테서 연락 왔어. I got a message from a friend.
하고 with	랑	너랑 같이 산책하고 싶어 I want to take a walk with you.
	이랑	얘들이랑 같이 점심 먹고 있어. I'm eating lunch with these kids.
하고 and	랑	친구랑 내가 같이 준비했어. My friend and I prepared it together.
	이랑	음식이랑 음료수를 샀어. I bought food and drinks.

6 Sentence types

1 Declarative and interrogative sentences

In 반말, declarative and interrogative sentences are formed by omitting the politeness marker 요 from the informal polite form -아/어요.

- A 왜 연락 안 했어? Why didn't you contact me?

  B 미안해. 너무 바빠서 연락 못 했어. Sorry, I was too busy to contact you.

- A 네 이름이 뭐야? What's your name?

  B 내 이름은 민수야. My name is Minsu.

2 Imperative sentences

The informal polite imperative form -(으)세요 includes the honorific marker -(으)시-. In 반말, both the honorific -(으)시- and the politeness marker 요 are omitted, leaving only -아/어. The negative imperative form changes from -지 마세요 to -지 마.

- 이거 받아. 생일 선물이야. Take this. It's a birthday present.

- 여기에서 기다려. 곧 돌아올게. Wait here. I'll be back soon.

- 걱정하지 마. 내가 도와줄게. Don't worry. I'll help you.

When making requests, -아/어 주세요 becomes -아/어 줘 in 반말 by omitting the honorific -(으)시- and the politeness marker 요. When giving advice or recommendations, -아/어 보세요 becomes -아/어 봐 in 반말.

- 다음 달에 여행 갈 거야. 좋은 곳을 추천해 줘. I'm going on a trip next month. Recommend a good place.

- 이 책 읽어 봐. 진짜 재미있어. Read this book. It's really interesting.

3 Propositive sentences

In 반말, the propositive form is created by attaching -자 to the verb stem, regardless of whether the stem ends in a vowel or consonant. The negative form changes from -지 맙시다 to -지 말자.

- 힘들지만 우리 웃자. 좋은 날이 올 거야. It's tough, but let's smile. Good days will come.

- 너무 슬퍼하지 말자. 지나간 일은 잊어버리자. Let's not be too sad. Let's forget the past.

Additionally, suggestion forms like -(으)ㄹ까요, -(으)ㄹ래요, and -는 게 어때요 are used in 반말 by omitting the politeness marker 요.

- A 오늘 영화 볼까? Shall we watch a movie today?

  B 좋아. Sure.

- A 점심 같이 먹을래? Do you want to have lunch together?

  B 그러자. Let's do that.

- A 이번 주 토요일에 만나는 게 어때? How about meeting this Saturday?

  B 이번 주 토요일 말고 일요일에 보자. Let's meet on Sunday instead of this Saturday.

7 Addressing and referring to people

In 반말, when calling someone by name, a particle is attached after the name. If the name ends in a vowel, 야 is attached; if it ends in a consonant, 아 is attached. However, for non-Korean names, it is more natural not to attach a particle.

- 민수야, 오늘 뭐 해? Minsu, what are you doing today?

- 지윤아, 어디 가? Jiyun, where are you going?

- 마이클, 나 좀 도와줘. Michael, help me out.

When an adult calls a child whose name they do not know, or when peers call each other instead of using names, the interjection 야 is used. However, 야 is typically used among close friends, so using 야 without a pre-existing sense of intimacy can sound rude.

- 야, 너 이리 와 봐. Hey, come here.   Calling a young child

- 야, 조금만 천천히 가. Hey, slow down a bit.   Calling a close peer friend

In 반말, the third person can be referred to by their name. If the name ends in a consonant, 이 is inserted between the name and the particle for easier pronunciation.

- 인성이가 진수한테 말했어. Inseong told Jinsu.

- 준하가 민정이를 좋아해. Junha likes Minjeong.

Grammar in Action

1 When speaking to close family, friends, or children

A 이거 먹을래? Do you want to eat this?
B 네, 주세요. Yes, please.

반말 is commonly used by older family members when speaking to younger family members or peers in close relationships. For example, parents use it with their children, and older siblings use it with younger siblings. Additionally, school peers often use 반말 with each other.

- A 우리 뭐 할래? What do you want to do?   Father speaking to child

  B 아빠, 공원에 놀러 가요! Dad, let's go to the park!

- A 나 먼저 갈게. 주말 잘 보내. I'll go first. Have a nice weekend.   Speaking to a school friend

  B 너도 주말 잘 보내. 잘 가. You too. Take care.

Even if the other person is younger or of lower status, 반말 should not be used with adults unless there is a close relationship, especially when meeting for the first time. For example, using 반말 with a young-looking store clerk you are meeting for the first time is inappropriate. Instead, Koreans use the informal polite form -아/어요 when speaking to strangers who appear younger.

- A 이거 얼마야? (✗) → 얼마예요? (O) How much is this?   To a store clerk

  B 20,000원이에요. It's 20,000 won.

Koreans often ask about age or title upon first meeting to ensure they use the appropriate speech style based on the formality of the situation (formal or informal) and the hierarchical relationship (age or status). When meeting an adult for the first time in an informal setting and intending to continue the relationship, it is polite to ask if you can use 반말. Additionally, if a senior intentionally avoids using 반말 with a junior, it may be interpreted as a sign of wanting to maintain some distance.

When an adult meets a child under ten for the first time and wishes to speak gently and foster closeness, using 반말 is appropriate.

- A 안녕! 너 몇 살이야? Hi! How old are you?

  B 7살이에요. I'm seven.

2 When messaging friends on social media or via text

유나
오늘 어디에서 봐? Where should we meet today?

남산 어때? How about Namsan?

유나
산 싫어. ㅠㅠ I don't like mountains. ㅠㅠ

그럼, 어디 갈래? Then, where do you want to go?

유나
한강 어때? How about the Hangang River?

좋아. ^^ Sounds good. ^^

유나
2시 괜찮아? Is 2 PM okay?

좋아. 그때 봐. Great. See you then.

반말 is commonly used when messaging friends you already speak casually with on social media or via text. Koreans often use emoticons in their messages, such as ^^ to express happiness and ㅠㅠ to show sadness or discomfort.

- A 내가 도와줄게. I'll help you.

  B 고마워 ^^ Thanks. ^^

- A 같이 놀래? Do you want to hang out?

  B 미안해. 몸이 안 좋아. ㅠㅠ Sorry, I'm not feeling well. ㅠㅠ

Quiz 62

격식체 Formal polite speech -(스)ㅂ니다

Kor. 63

A 안녕하십니까? 김진수입니다.

B 처음 뵙겠습니다.

A Hello. This is Jinsu Kim.
B Nice to meet you.

이상으로 뉴스를 마치겠습니다. 시청해 주셔서 감사합니다.

This concludes the news. Thank you for watching.

1 Formal polite speech -(스)ㅂ니다

In Korean, verb and adjective endings change based on the formality of the situation and the level of respect required for the conversation partner. Formal polite speech is commonly used in official and professional settings to show respect. For instance, it is often used when speaking to colleagues at work, assisting customers at airports or department stores, and in other service-oriented interactions. Additionally, formal polite speech is standard in public speeches, official proceedings, and news broadcasts.

In the formal polite form, -ㅂ니다 or -습니다 is added to the stem of a verb, adjective, and "noun + 이다". For verbs or adjectives, add -ㅂ니다 if the stem ends in a vowel and -습니다 if it ends in a consonant. For "nouns + 이다", 입니다 is used regardless of whether the noun ends in a vowel or consonant.

- 회의가 10시에 시작합니다. The meeting starts at 10 o'clock.

- 회의를 시작하기 전에 자료를 읽습니다. I read the material before starting the meeting.

- 오전에 회의 준비 때문에 바쁩니다. I am busy preparing for a meeting in the morning.

- 요즘 회사에 일이 많습니다. There is a lot of work at the company these days.

- 이것이 제 서류입니다. This is my document.

- 이곳이 제가 자주 가는 식당입니다. This place is a restaurant I often go to.

2 Negation

To express negation in formal polite speech, 안, -지 않다, 못, and -지 못하다 can be used with verbs or adjectives. Since formal polite speech is more formal, -지 않다 and -지 못하다 are generally preferred over 안 or 못.

- 오늘 날씨가 좋지 않습니다. The weather is not good today.

- 저는 생선을 먹지 못합니다. I can't eat fish.

For negating "noun + 이다", the form 아닙니다 is used.

- 저는 이 회사 직원이 아닙니다. I am not an employee of this company.

3 Tenses

In formal polite speech, past events or states are expressed by adding -았습니다 or -었습니다 to verbs, adjectives, and "noun + 이다".

For verbs and adjectives, if the verb stem includes 하다, it combines with -였습니다 to form 했습니다. When the stem ends in ㅏ or ㅗ, -았습니다 is attached, and -었습니다 is used in all other cases. To form the negative, -지 않았습니다 is added to the verb or adjective stem.

- 조금 전에 회의가 끝났습니다. The meeting ended a little while ago.

- 지난주에 프로젝트 때문에 바빴습니다. I was busy with a project last week.

- 지난주에 피곤해서 일하지 않았습니다. I didn't work last week because I was tired.

For "noun + 이다", 였습니다 is used if the noun ends in a vowel, and 이었습니다 is added if it ends in a consonant. The negative form is expressed using 아니었습니다.

- 어렸을 때 취미가 요리였습니다. When I was young, my hobby was cooking.

- 저는 10년 전에 학생이었습니다. I was a student 10 years ago.

- 이것은 우리 팀의 잘못이 아니었습니다. This wasn't our team's fault.

To express a future event or make a speculation in formal polite speech, you can use -겠습니다 or -(으)ㄹ 것입니다. In spoken language, -(으)ㄹ 것입니다 is often shortened to -(으)ㄹ 겁니다.

- 최선을 다해서 열심히 하겠습니다.　　　　　will
  I will do my best and work hard.

- 다음 주에 새 프로젝트를 시작할 것입니다.　　　schedule
  I will start a new project next week.

- 이 건물에 엘리베이터가 생기면 편하겠습니다.　　speculation
  It would be convenient if there was an elevator in this building.

4 Conjugation

	-(스)ㅂ니다	-았/었습니다	-겠습니다 / -(으)ㄹ 것입니다
크다	큽니다	컸습니다	크겠습니다 / 클 것입니다
찾다	찾습니다	찾았습니다	찾겠습니다 / 찾을 것입니다
바쁘다	바쁩니다	바빴습니다	바쁘겠습니다 / 바쁠 것입니다
다르다	다릅니다	*달랐습니다	다르겠습니다 / 다를 것입니다
듣다	듣습니다	*들었습니다	듣겠습니다 / *들을 것입니다
살다	*삽니다	살았습니다	살겠습니다 / *살 것입니다
춥다	춥습니다	*추웠습니다	춥겠습니다 / *추울 것입니다
짓다	짓습니다	*지었습니다	짓겠습니다 / *지을 것입니다
그렇다	그렇습니다	*그랬습니다	그렇겠습니다 / *그럴 것입니다
이다	서류입니다	서류였습니다	서류이겠습니다 / 서류일 것입니다
이다	직업입니다	직업이었습니다	직업이겠습니다 / 직업일 것입니다

5 Sentence types

1 Declarative and interrogative sentences

Declarative and interrogative sentences in formal polite speech use distinct endings. To form a declarative sentence, -ㅂ니다 is added if the verb or adjective stem ends in a vowel, and -습니다 is added if it ends in a consonant. For interrogative sentences, -ㅂ니까 or -습니까 is used depending on the stem ending.

- A 한국어 공부가 끝나면 무엇을 하고 **싶습니까?** What do you want to do after studying Korean?

  B 한국 회사에 취직하고 **싶습니다.** I want to get a job at a Korean company.

- A 어제 뉴스를 **봤습니까?** Did you watch the news yesterday?

  B 아니요, 뉴스를 보지 **못했습니다.** No, I didn't see the news.

- A 무슨 색을 **고르겠습니까?** What color would you choose?

  B 저는 파란색을 **고르겠습니다.** I will choose blue.

2 Imperative sentences

To form imperative sentences, -(으)십시오 is added to the verb stem. If the verb stem ends in a vowel, -십시오 is used, whereas if it ends in a consonant, -으십시오 is attached. For negation, -지 마십시오 is used regardless of the verb stem ending.

- 더 자세한 사항은 사무실에 **문의하십시오.** Please, contact the office for further details.

- 9시에 출발합니다. **늦지 마십시오.** We leave at 9 o'clock. Don't be late.

Common verbs such as 먹다 (to eat), 마시다 (to drink), 있다 (to stay), 자다 (to sleep), and 말하다 (to speak) take on special forms when combined with the honorific -(으)시-. These verbs change to 잡수시다, 드시다, 계시다, 주무시다, and 말씀하시다, respectively.

Since the formal imperative -(으)십시오 also includes the honorific -(으)시-, these verbs should be used in their special forms in formal polite commands.

- 식기 전에 음식을 **드십시오.** 먹다 Eat food before it cools down.

- 여기 잠깐 **계십시오.** 있다 Please stay here for a moment.

- 안녕히 **주무십시오.** 자다 Good night.

3 Propositive sentences

Propositive sentences in formal polite speech are formed by adding -(으)ㅂ시다 to the verb stem. If the stem ends in a vowel, -ㅂ시다 is added, while -읍시다 is used when the stem ends in a consonant. To express a negative proposition, -지 맙시다 is used regardless of the stem ending.

- 내일 다시 만나서 **얘기합시다.** Let's meet again tomorrow and talk.

- 서로 상처받는 말을 하지 **맙시다.** Let's not say things that hurt each other.

1   When speaking in formal business settings

A 보고서 받으셨습니까?
Have you received the report?

B 받았습니다. 수고하셨습니다.
Yes, I have. Thank you for your effort.

Formal polite speech is commonly used in formal and official settings, especially in professional environments, such as when speaking with colleagues at work. The formal polite speech form -(스)ㅂ니다 conveys respect for the listener, making it the standard form of communication among colleagues of the same rank. If the conversation partner is older or holds a higher position, the subject honorific -(으)시- should be used when referring to them as the subject of a sentence and as an object honorific when referring to them as the object.

- A 오늘 회의가 몇 시에 시작합니까? What time does the meeting start today?
  B 오전 10시에 시작합니다. It starts at 10 am.

- A 부장님, 언제 출장 가십니까? Manager, when are you going on a business trip?
  B 다음 주에 출장 갑니다. I'm going on a business trip next week.

- A 고객님, 잠깐 기다리셔도 되겠습니까? Customer, can you wait a moment?
  B 네, 천천히 하십시오, 여기에서 기다리겠습니다. Yes, please take your time. I will wait here.

The subject honorific -(으)시- should not be used when there is no need to elevate the subject of the sentence. However, if the subject refers to a part of the respected person's body or mood, -(으)시- can be used.

- A 부장님, 서류가 어디에 있으십니까? (✗) → 있습니까? (O) Manager, where are the documents?
  B 두 번째 서랍 안에 있습니다. They're in the second drawer.

- A 부장님, 오늘 몸이 어떠십니까? (O) Manager, how are you feeling today?
  B 오늘 괜찮습니다. I'm feeling okay today.

The propositive sentence ending -(으)ㅂ시다 is used when the speaker suggests an action without inquiring about the listener's intention. However, in formal contexts, when the listener is older or holds a higher status than the speaker, it is considered inappropriate for the speaker to propose an action without considering the listener's intent. Therefore, in real-life situations, when addressing someone older or of higher status, it is more common to use -(으)시죠 instead of -(으)ㅂ시다.

- 식당을 예약했습니다. 식사 먼저 하시죠. I made a reservation at a restaurant. Let's eat first.

2 When giving a formal speech or presentation in public

지금부터 발표를 시작하겠습니다.
I will start the presentation now.

Formal polite speech is used when making formal speeches or presentations in front of the public. News announcers and TV hosts also use formal polite speech when addressing viewers. Announcements at airports, subways, train stations, and other public places, which address an unspecified number of people, also use formal polite speech. It is best to avoid using abbreviations (e.g., 좀, 근데) commonly found in conversational speech when speaking formally.

- 이것으로 제 발표를 마치겠습니다. 끝까지 들어 주셔서 감사합니다.
  This concludes my presentation. Thank you for listening until the end.

- 기차는 10시에 출발합니다. 탑승자는 출발 10분 전까지 탑승해 주시기 바랍니다.
  The train leaves at 10 o'clock. Passengers are requested to board at least 10 minutes prior to departure.

When making a formal request to an unspecified audience, it is generally preferred to use -(으)시기 바랍니다 rather than -(으)세요. Additionally, -아/어 주시기 바랍니다 is preferred over -아/어 주세요.

- 2층에 서류를 제출하시기 바랍니다. (= 제출하세요.)
  Please submit documents on the 2nd floor.

- 질문이 있으시면 언제든지 이메일이나 전화로 문의해 주시기 바랍니다. (= 문의해 주세요.)
  If you have any questions, please contact us by email or phone at any time.

Quiz 63

존댓말 Honorifics

Kor. 64

어머니께서 음식을 잘 만드세요.
저도 음식을 잘 만들어요.

My mother cooks well. I also cook well.

저는 크리스마스 때 할머니께 선물을 드렸어요.
동생한테도 선물을 줬어요.

I gave my grandmother a present at Christmas.
I also gave my younger sibling a present.

A 할아버지, 어떻게 지내세요?

B 그럼, 잘 지내. 너는 어떻게 지내?

A 저도 잘 지내요.

A Grandpa, how are you?
B Yes, I'm doing well. How are you?
A I'm doing well too.

1 존댓말 Honorifics

In Korean, 존댓말 (honorifics) are used to show respect when referring to someone older or of higher status than oneself. The honorific system in Korean is divided into three main types:

- Subject honorifics: Show respect to the subject of the sentence.
- Object honorifics: Show respect to the object of the sentence.
- Addressee honorifics: Show respect to the listener.

2 Subject honorifics

이 사람이 제 동생이에요. This is my younger brother.
동생이 책을 좋아해요. My brother likes books.
그래서 매일 책을 읽어요. So, he reads every day.
동생이 정말 귀여워요. He is really cute.

이분이 제 할아버지세요. This is my grandfather.
할아버지께서 책을 좋아하세요. My grandfather likes books.
그래서 매일 책을 읽으세요. So, he reads every day.
할아버지께서 정말 대단하세요. He is really great.

Subject honorifics are used to show respect to the subject of a sentence by attaching -(으)시- to the stem of a verb, adjective, or "noun + 이다". Honorifics are unnecessary when the subject is of equal or lower status, such as a younger sibling. However, they must be used if the subject is an elder or someone of higher status, such as a grandparent. Additionally, when using -(으)시-, the subject particle 이/가 can be replaced with 께서, and 은/는 with 께서 는 to further emphasize respect.

- 할아버지께서 매일 운동하세요. Grandfather exercises everyday.   `Honorific`

  동생이 매일 운동해요. My younger brother exercises every day.   `Non-honorific`

- 어머니께서는 항상 밝은 색 옷을 입으세요. Mother always wears bright-colored clothes.   `Honorific`

  언니는 항상 밝은 색 옷을 입어요. My older sister always wears bright-colored clothes.   `Non-honorific`

When adding subject honorifics, attach -세요 if the verb or adjective stem ends in a vowel, and -으세요 if it ends in a consonant. For "noun + 이다", use 세요 when the noun ends in a vowel and 이세요 when it ends in a consonant.

- 아버지께서 항상 바쁘세요. Father is always busy.

- 할머니께서 많이 웃으세요. Grandmother laughs a lot.

- 어머니께서 의사세요. Mother is a doctor.

- 아버지께서는 선생님이세요. Father is a teacher.

If the subject of a sentence is not a person who should be respected but a part of that person's body, you may use the subject honorific -(으)시-, but you must use 이/가 instead of the particle 께서.

- 아버지 손께서 크세요. (✗)
  → 아버지 손이 크세요. (O) Father's hands are big.

- 어머니 목소리께서 크세요. (✗)
  → 어머니 목소리가 예쁘세요. (O) Mother's voice is beautiful.

If the subject of a sentence is not a person who should be treated with respect but rather that person's possession (e.g., a car, bag, etc.), the subject honorific -(으)시- should not be used.

- 아버지 자동차가 멋있으세요. (✗)
  → 아버지 자동차가 멋있어요. (O) Father's car is cool.

- 어머니 가방이 비싸세요. (✗)
  → 어머니 가방이 비싸요. (O) Mother's bag is expensive.

The informal polite present tense ending -(으)세요 is created by combining the subject honorific -(으)시- with the informal present tense ending -아/어요. Although this form looks identical to the imperative ending -(으)세요, their meanings are different.

- 할아버지께서 매일 운동하세요. Grandfather exercises every day.   Subject honorific
- 건강을 위해 매일 운동하세요. Exercise every day for your health.   Imperative

1 Special verbs

Certain verbs frequently used in daily life, such as 먹다 (to eat), 마시다 (to drink), 있다 (to exist), 자다 (to sleep), and 말하다 (to speak), have special honorific forms when combined with the subject honorific -(으)시-.

Normal	Honorific	Examples
먹다	잡수시다 드시다	• 할아버지께서 아침을 잡수세요. (O) Grandfather eats breakfast. 할아버지께서 아침을 먹으세요 (×) • 선생님께서 점심을 드세요. (O) The teacher has lunch.
마시다	드시다	• 할머니께서 차를 드세요. (O) Grandmother drinks tea. 할머니께서 차를 마시세요 (×)
있다	계시다 Existence 있으시다 Possession	• 아버지께서 방에 계세요. (O) Father is in the room. • 어머니께서 친구가 많이 있으세요. (O) Mother has many friends.
자다	주무시다	• 지금 아버지께서 주무세요. (O) Father is sleeping now. 지금 아버지께서 자세요 (×)
말하다	말씀하시다	• 사장님께서 말씀하세요. (O) The boss is speaking. 사장님께서 말하세요 (×)

Note

The verb 먹다 changes to 드시다 or 잡수시다 depending on the subject. 드시다 is a general honorific used to show respect, while 잡수시다 conveys a higher level of respect and is primarily used for elderly individuals, such as grandparents.

2 Special nouns

Certain commonly used nouns in daily life, such as 집 (house), 밥 (meal/rice), 사람 (person), 말 (speech/words), and 생신 (birthday), also have distinct honorific forms when used with subject honorifics.

Normal	Honorific	Examples
집	댁	할머니께서 댁에 가세요. Grandmother goes home.
밥	진지	할아버지께서 진지를 드세요. Grandfather eats a meal.
사람	분	아버지의 친구 분이 병원에서 일하세요. Father's friend works at a hospital.
말	말씀	어머니 말씀이 맞아요. Mother's words are correct.
생일	생신	내일 어머니 생신이세요. Tomorrow is mother's birthday.

3 Negation

Negation in Korean can be expressed in several ways. You can add 안 or 못 before a verb or adjective. Alternatively, use -지 않다 or -지 못하다 with the verb or adjective stem. For "noun + 이다", use 아니다 to indicate negation.

- 어머니께서 기분이 안 좋으세요. Mother is not in a good mood.

- 아버지께서 지금 일하지 않으세요. Father is not working right now.

- 할아버지께서 컴퓨터를 못 하세요. Grandfather cannot use the computer.

- 할머니께서 뛰지 못하세요. Grandmother cannot run.

- 아버지께서 경찰이 아니세요. Father is not a police officer.

The verb 있다 has two meanings, and its honorific form changes depending on the context. When 있다 expresses existence (being in a certain place), use the honorific form 계시다. When it expresses possession (having something or being in a relationship with someone/something), use 있으시다. To express negation, use 안 계시다 for existence and 없으시다 for possession.

- 할아버지께서 집에 계세요. 그런데 할머니께서 집에 안 계세요.
  Grandfather is at home. But grandmother is not at home.

- 할머니께서 노트북이 있으세요. 그런데 할아버지께서 노트북이 없으세요.
  Grandmother has a laptop. But grandfather does not have a laptop.

The honorific form of grammatical patterns using 있다 changes based on its meaning. When expressing the progressive form -고 있다, it becomes -고 계시다 in honorific speech. When expressing ability or possibility -(으)ㄹ 수 있다, it changes to -(으)ㄹ 수 있으시다 in honorific speech.

- 할머니께서 요즘 외국어를 공부하고 계세요. Grandmother is studying a foreign language these days.

- 지금 아버지께서 뉴스를 안 보고 계세요. Father is not watching the news right now.

- 어머니께서 한국 노래를 부를 수 있으세요. Mother can sing Korean songs.

- 할아버지께서 한자를 읽을 수 없으세요. Grandfather cannot read Chinese characters.

4 Tenses

To express tense in subject honorifics in polite informal speech, add the tense marker after -(으)시-.

- Present tense: -(으)세요 (formed by combining -(으)시- with -아/어요)
- Past tense: -(으)셨어요 (formed by combining -(으)시- with -았/었어요)
- Future tense: -(으)실 거예요 (formed by combining -(으)시- with -(으)ㄹ 거예요)

▶ For past tense

- 어제 할아버지께서 집에 계셨어요. Grandfather was at home yesterday.
- 어제 할머니께서 책을 찾으셨어요. Grandmother found the book yesterday.
- 어제 아버지께서 피곤하셨어요. Father was tired yesterday.
- 어제 어머니께서 괜찮으셨어요. Mother was okay yesterday.
- 어머니께서 전에 간호사셨어요. Mother was a nurse before.
- 아버지께서 전에 선생님이셨어요. Father was a teacher before.

▶ For future tense

- 내일 할아버지께서 집에서 쉬실 거예요. Grandfather will rest at home tomorrow.
- 내일 할머니께서 선물을 받으실 거예요. Grandmother will receive a gift tomorrow.
- 내일 아버지께서 피곤하실 거예요. Father will be tired tomorrow.
- 아마 어머니께서 괜찮으실 거예요. Mother will probably be okay.
- 진수 어머니께서 아마 의사실 거예요. Jinsu's mother will probably be a doctor.
- 진수 아버지께서 아마 선생님이실 거예요. Jinsu's father will probably be a teacher.

5 Conjugation

	Present -(으)세요	Past -(으)셨어요	Future / Speculation -(으)실 거예요
크다	크세요	크셨어요	크실 거예요
찾다	찾으세요	찾으셨어요	찾으실 거예요
바쁘다	바쁘세요	바쁘셨어요	바쁘실 거예요
다르다	다르세요	다르셨어요	다르실 거예요
듣다	*들으세요	*들으셨어요	*들으실 거예요
살다	*사세요	*사셨셨어요	*사실 거예요
춥다	*추우세요	*추우셨어요	*추우실 거예요
짓다	*지으세요	*지으셨어요	*지으실 거예요
그렇다	*그러세요	*그러셨어요	*그러실 거예요
이다	교수세요	교수셨어요	교수실 거예요
이다	경찰이세요	경찰이셨어요	경찰이실 거예요

3 Object honorifics

제가 친구에게 전화번호를 물어봐요.

I ask my friend for his phone number.

제가 할머니께 전화번호를 여쭤봐요.

I ask my grandmother for her phone number.

Object honorifics in modern Korean are used to show respect to the object of a sentence. Certain verbs change to reflect this respect. For example, the verbs 주다 (to give), 만나다 (to meet), 묻다 (to ask), and 데리다 (to accompany) are replaced with 드리다 (to give respectfully), 뵙다 (to meet respectfully), 여쭙다 (to ask respectfully), and 모시다 (to accompany respectfully) when the object is someone deserving of respect.

Additionally, when using object honorifics, the particles 에게 or 한테 are replaced with 께. However, the particle 을/를 remains unchanged.

Normal	Honorific	Examples
주다 (to give)	드리다	• 저는 설날 때 어머니께 용돈을 드려요. I give my mother money on New Year's Day.
만나다, 보다 (to meet, to see)	뵙다, 뵈다	• 친구가 아버지를 뵈러 갔어요. My friend went to see my father. • 저는 사장님을 뵙고 왔어요. I met the boss and came back.
묻다 (to ask)	여쭙다	• 제가 선생님께 여쭤볼게요. I will ask the teacher.
데리다 (to accompany)	모시다	• 저는 부모님을 모시고 공항에 갔어요. I took my parents to the airport.

In daily conversation, verbs like 전화하다 (to call), 연락하다 (to contact), 부탁하다 (to ask a favor), 질문하다 (to ask), and 요청하다 (to request) are formed by adding 하다 to a noun. However, when using object honorifics, the verb 드리다 is preferred instead of 하다 after these nouns.

• 어제 친구에게 연락했어요. 그리고 할머니께 연락드렸어요.

  I contacted my friend yesterday. And I contacted my grandmother.

• 친구에게 숙제를 부탁하고, 선생님께도 상담을 부탁드렸어요.

  I asked my friend for help with homework and also requested a consultation from the teacher.

In honorific expressions, 말하다 changes depending on who is being respected. For object honorifics, 말하다 becomes 말씀드리다, while for subject honorifics, it changes to 말씀하시다.

• 할아버지께 전부 말씀드렸어요. I told everything to my grandfather.　　Object honorific

• 할아버지께서 큰 목소리로 말씀하셨어요. Grandpa spoke in a loud voice.　　Subject honorific

4 Addressee honorifics

Addressee honorifics depend on the speech context (formal or informal) and the relationship with the listener. In modern Korean, sentence endings change based on whether the situation is formal or informal and whether respect is required.

	Informal	Formal
Honorific	-아/어요 A 다른 색 있어요? Do you have any other colors? B 네, 파란색 있어요. Yes, we have blue.	-(스)ㅂ니다 이제부터 이야기를 시작하겠습니다. Now, let me start talking.
Non-honorific	-아/어 A 주말에 뭐 해? What are you doing on the weekend? B 자전거를 타. Riding a bike.	-아/어라 시작해라! Get started!

Here are the three most commonly used sentence endings in everyday life:

▶ -ㅂ/습니다

-ㅂ/습니다 is used in formal situations, such as when speaking to colleagues at work or addressing an audience in an official setting.

- A 부장님, 말씀하신 서류 여기 있습니다.　　　　Speaking to a superior at work
  Manager, here is the document you mentioned.
  B 수고했습니다. Good job.

- 여러분, 지금부터 발표를 시작하겠습니다.　　　　Speaking officially in front of an audience
  Everyone, I will start the presentation now.

▶ **-아/어요**

-아/어요 is used in informal polite situations to show respect without being overly formal, such as when asking for directions or speaking to employees in a store.

- A 실례지만, 화장실이 어디에 있어요?　　　　　Speaking to a passerby
  Excuse me, where is the restroom?

  B 2층에 있어요. It's on the second floor.

- A 이 옷을 입어 봐도 돼요? Can I try on these clothes?　Speaking to a store clerk

  B 그럼요. 입어 보세요. Sure, go ahead.

▶ **-아/어**

The informal -아/어 ending is used in casual situations, such as when talking to younger family members or close friends, without the need to show special respect.

- A 지금 뭐 하고 있어? What are you doing now?　　　Speaking to a younger sibling

  B 영화 보고 있어. I'm watching a movie.

- A 잠깐 기다려 줘. Wait a moment.　　　　　Speaking to a friend

  B 알았어. Okay.

In real life, the choice of sentence ending depends on the context and the relationship with the listener. Within a family, parents may use informal speech when speaking to their children, while children may use informal polite speech when speaking to their parents.

- A 엄마, 우리 언제 집에 가요? Mom, when are we going home?　Child speaking to mother

  B 지금 집에 가. We are going home now.　　　　Mother speaking to child

In a store, a customer might use polite informal speech when speaking to the owner, while the owner might use formal polite speech when addressing the customer.

- A 생수 두 병 주세요. Please give me two bottles of water.　Customer speaking to store clerk

  B 알겠습니다. 여기 있습니다. Okay. Here you go.　　Store clerk speaking to customer

1 When talking to people you meet in everyday life

When speaking to people you meet in everyday situations, use honorifics based on the role of the other person in the sentence. The informal polite ending -아/어요 is typically used to show respect in daily conversations. Use the subject honorific -(으)시- if the other person is the subject, and the object honorific if they are the object. However, speakers do not use honorifics when referring to themselves, regardless of their role in the sentence.

- In a store setting   Customer   이게 얼마예요? How much is this?

                     Employee   20,000원이에요. It's 20,000 won.

- At a restaurant   Customer   죄송하지만 물 좀 주세요. Excuse me, may I have some water?

                     Employee   잠시만요. 물 갖다 드릴게요. Just a moment. I'll bring you some water.

2 When talking to someone you met through work

In formal work-related conversations, respect is shown using honorifics. If the other person is the subject of the sentence, use the subject honorific -(으)시-. If the other person is the object, apply the appropriate object honorific form.

- A 말씀하신 자료를 메일로 보내 드렸습니다. I have sent you the information you requested by email.

  B 감사합니다. Thank you.

- A 뭐 하나 여쭤 봐도 되겠습니까? May I ask you something?

  B 물론이죠. 무엇이든지 물어보십시오. Of course. Ask anything.

However, if you have a personal relationship with a colleague outside of work, such as meeting on weekends for leisure activities, you can use the polite informal ending -아/어요.

- A 요즘 아이들이 어떻게 지내요? How are the kids doing these days?

  B 덕분에 잘 지내요. They're doing well, thanks!

3 When speaking to the public

When addressing the public formally, use the proper honorific forms to show respect. Use the subject honorific -(으)시- when the public is the subject of the sentence, and use the object honorific when the public is the object.

- 이것으로 제 발표를 끝내겠습니다. 제 발표를 끝까지 들어 주셔서 감사합니다.
  This concludes my presentation. Thank you for listening to my presentation until the end.

- 손을 들어 주시면 마이크를 갖다 드리겠습니다.
  Raise your hand, and we'll bring you the microphone.

Quiz 64

INDEX